BEADS IN THE HEADLIGHT
A FLYING AGA TALE

Road Dog Publications was formed in 2010 as an imprint of Lost Classics Book Company and is dedicated to publishing the best in books on motorcycling, motorsports, and adventure travel. Visit us at www.roaddogpub.com.

Originally published as eBook in 2013.
This edition published October, 2015.

Copyright © Isabel Dyson, 2015
Cover photograph and design, Isabel Dyson

ISBN 978-1-890623-47-0
Library of Congress Control Number 2015952322

An Imprint of Lost Classics Book Company
This book also available in e-book format at online booksellers.

Beads in the Headlight
A Flying Aga Tale

by

Isabel Dyson

Publisher
Lake Wales, Florida

In loving memory of Edward and Garth

ABOUT THE AUTHOR

Isabel Dyson was born in Kent, England, in the 1980s and grew up in the richly historic, coastal town of Deal. The spirit of adventure was instilled in her from a young age, having grown up with two older brothers when it was still OK to play out in the street and swim in the icy waters of the English Channel.

Her taste for exploration was nourished by a television-free family home and fuelled by an early love of books, camping holidays, and relatives that were spread across the globe.

Isabel pursued her love of books and writing by later studying literature at university where she wrote for and edited the news for the student newspaper. After graduating, she moved to London without a job but soon found herself applying her skills in marketing.

While living in London, she met Byron, who matched her desire to travel with one for motorbikes. After a few years, they saved enough money to combine their passions and undertake a journey from Alaska to Argentina on an R100RS BMW, fondly named the Flying Aga. They documented their adventure in a blog before Isabel turned it into her first book on their return.

Isabel currently lives with Byron in Lincolnshire (a biker's paradise) where they are saving again for their next journey.

TABLE OF CONTENTS

Epiphanies and Stalemates

Minus Two Years

A young couple stood in the foreground of tea terraces that lined the contours of a mountain. They were smiling as sunshine blazed across the green landscape. It was a photograph that had been sent to me the night before by my cousin who was visiting Asia, and, as I made my way to work, the image wouldn't leave my mind. It chipped away as I weaved through a swarm of suits and polished shoes while an unusually glorious morning glistened off the nearby river. I passed the woman who sat on London Bridge every day, reading a book while she collected spare change, and, for the first time, something about her struck a nerve. The photograph had stirred a taste for adventure and her stillness at the edge of a passing storm sparked a desire to find the same peaceful detachment.

Byron and I had met by chance almost two years before that morning. Both of us had taken jobs straight after leaving school, before later attending university. We met in London two years after graduating and settled into a flat together where announcements blasted through the thin windows from Clapham Junction railway station across the road. The move prompted an end to reckless weekends and midweek hangovers, and, once we learnt to block out the din that flooded the little flat, it felt as if we had missed out on something that we couldn't quite place.

Work was exhausting, but, after leaving home early and returning late each day, we slowly cleared our debts and moved into the unfamiliar position of having money to spare. Just a small amount in the bank began to create options that, with time, released dormant dreams and epiphanies on London Bridge.

Long before my realisation, Byron had been convinced that some form of escapade was essential before we settled down for good. He had a passion for motorcycles that had been cultivated since birth and was resolute that the two-wheeled machines had a specific purpose in the world for adventures. I had nurtured a catalogue of countries that were ripe for exploring since the day I learnt my great-grandparents had escaped to a new life by crossing the Black Sea in a rowing boat. So, while we tended to our savings, adventure books and travel guides began to line the shelves and were scattered across the surfaces of our noisy flat.

As the prospect of a big change blossomed, we ramped up our efforts at stockpiling money. We reassessed all spending as a potential aeroplane ticket or dinner in an unknown land. Small sacrifices went a long way, and we stopped buying new clothes, turned off our heating, and ate dinner leftovers for lunch. We patched up torn jeans, dyed the colour back into faded clothes, and auctioned off half of our belongings online. Considering the long working hours that continued to sap each week, it wasn't the most exciting existence, but the thought of where it could lead perfected our capacity for thrifty living no end.

As the new lease on life took root, the question soon came about of where our savings would take us. With total conviction that he would return as a motorcycle in another life, there was little question in Byron's mind that, wherever we decided to go, we would get there with an engine set between two wheels. However, we had already concluded that we could only do the trip on our estimated budget if we camped, and, as a novice to the world of biking, it didn't seem possible to me that one motorcycle would have the capacity to carry the kit we would need for camping, as well as the necessary bike tools and personal luggage. We soon hit a stalemate and shifted our attention to destinations instead.

We wanted to roam free and witness landscapes and wildlife that we couldn't see in our own country. Byron aspired to ride the wide open highways of the United States, and I envisaged exploring the jungles, deserts, and mountains of South America, so it took very little time to agree that the American continent would be our destination.

The stalemate had lingered in the meantime, and we reflected on alternatives to motorcycling. Backpacking seemed too restricted to timetables and well-trodden routes, while hiring a car or camper van required saving at least double what we had calculated as an achievable budget. Hiking or cycling would have involved an altogether different trip and more years than we were prepared to give. None of the options offered much scope on my concerns about transporting kit, either, so, after some lengthy deliberations, I surrendered an inch and agreed to travel by motorcycle, on the condition that I learnt to ride one first.

I had no ambitions for us to take another bike as insuring, shipping, and fuelling just one would be costly enough. There was also no hunger to share the riding either, as Byron's dream to manage that part alone was unequivocal. I wanted to learn because the likelihood of getting stranded in the middle of nowhere would be greater on a bike, and it was a concern that I would otherwise be powerless to ride us to safety, should a necessity arise.

A sign of what to expect should have been obvious when I jumped on a train that didn't stop at the right station for the compulsory basic training. After backtracking and arriving late, it quickly became clear that the rest of the trainees already knew how to ride competently, whereas I had never even turned a key in an ignition.

The training was led by an instructor who began the day by demonstrating how to start the engine, before each of us had to follow suit. He showed us how to control the clutch to bite, before we then had to control the clutch to bite. How to ride in a straight line soon followed, and all was going well until a couple of steps later we were instructed to ride in the shape of an eight and change gears. The task was a piece of cake for the nine men who hadn't needed the demonstration in the first place, but, after less than an hour, it was way beyond my capability. I had soon been allotted a corner of the inner city school playground to ride alone in straight lines where I found myself frequently accelerating instead of braking, before dropping the bike to save it from colliding with a wall.

We were supposed to embark on the open road during the afternoon, but, to my relief, the instructor tactfully suggested that I might like to return for another playground session instead. It wasn't until he had disappeared that his colleague explained that, for all the money the day had cost, I would have to fork out for another full day to do it again. Since I was only learning for potential emergencies, I left the money in our savings pot and entrusted the task to Byron, who had a vested interest in eliminating my confusion between the clutch and the brake.

Some weeks later, while dodging three excited family dogs along the muddy lanes of Lincolnshire, Byron successfully taught me how to ride, and I finally agreed to do the trip by motorcycle.

While the certainty of the adventure continued to grow, it took all of our willpower to resist taking out a loan. It would have meant leaving much sooner than our saving strategy would permit, but it was important to us that we earned every penny before we hit the road. As the seasons came and went, we resorted to small rituals to help contain our growing impatience. We counted the top row of tiles that wrapped the bathroom walls in our flat and worked out that once a small, rubber-sucker-tea-towel-holder had made two circuits of the room, sitting on each of the top row tiles for a week at a time, we would have saved enough money to leave.

Without fail, every Sunday evening we would ceremoniously move the sucker onto its next bathroom tile and mark one week closer to our departure. The significance was yet to emerge, but, on our eventual journey, Sundays would become the one day of each week that stood out from the other six. To complete the ritual, we lit a giant candle for two hours and let it burn closer to a pin we had stuck halfway down its body. The two indicators were priceless in reminding us what the future held, before another tussle with the working week began.

The budget we were building during the long wait had not been based on anything specific. We had arrived at the sum by multiplying the amount of money we could afford to save each month by the number of months we expected our staying power in London to last. We had no idea how much petrol would cost in each of the US states or what the price of food would be in Canada. We didn't know if it was possible to purchase road insurance for Central America or if campgrounds even existed in South America. We had no idea how many miles we would actually cover or the number of months it would take. We hadn't even factored in the purchase of the motorcycle itself, let alone the minor task of getting it and ourselves across the Atlantic Ocean and back again. In our eagerness for adventure, we had simply hoped that the final amount we had agreed to save would be enough to live for a year on the road.

The middle of May was the month we had chosen to begin the trip, and we planned a very loose route solely on that time of year. The month would lead the Northern Hemisphere into summer and the Southern Hemisphere into winter, and the seasons alone concluded our decision to begin as far north as possible and to end as far south as our money, or the road would take us. The space in between was to be a case of pure exploration.

Our slack planning was a deliberate choice. We had met on the high street in Clapham on a night when neither of us had a plan. Byron was supposed to be resting for a triathlon the next morning, and I had just returned from a holiday. We only met for ten minutes and didn't see each other again for two weeks. We didn't have a plan on our first date or our second date. We didn't even plan our move into the noisy flat together. It was a lack of planning that had worked for us, and we hoped that travelling by motorcycle would ensure it continued that way.

There was only so much that adventure books and travel guides could have done to help our expectations, anyway. There was nothing that we read which could have prepared us for the experience of riding past wild bears at the side of a road. No travel guide explained about lone moose or bison herds visiting campgrounds. No words could have conveyed the true heat of a US-American summer or the power of a Peruvian desert wind. The dread of an approaching truckload of Mexicans during a puncture repair had never been described in any adventure book we had bought, and the devastation that the roads of Honduras could inflict on a motorcycle remained unknown until six months into the eventual journey.

We had read accounts about winching motorcycles from dinghies onto yachts, but nothing could have primed us for the quiet panic that set in while it was happening. Routes through passages known as the Devil's Backbone and the Mountain of Death were more likely to have been theme park rides than the backdrop of future wonder and despair. The mix of torrential rain and wild camping had never been associated with the notion of catastrophe in anything we had researched, and, most significant of all, the kindness of complete strangers was still, for the most part, a Sunday-school story.

When occasional interludes of panic about the inadequacy of our savings and plans weren't getting in the way, other emotions almost got the better of our hopes for adventure, as we became increasingly aware of natural disasters, terrorism, and kidnappings that were occurring across the American continents.

My eldest brother, Edward, had died only two years previously, leaving behind his wife and toddling son, and I agonised over the impact this trip might have on my grieving family. My other brother, Henry, had served with the British military before working for a long period in South America, and I knew all too well the ordeal of waiting for information after a distressing news report.

Fears of being vulnerable abroad and anxious about the stress that the trip might have on our relatives would bear down on us every few months and eat away at our resolve. Somehow, though, we always salvaged a rationale that tipped the balance.

Edward had shared the same aspiration for adventure, but he never got to witness the jungles and deserts that had fascinated us both before he died of a brain tumour at the age of thirty. Byron's mother, Paula, had suffered with multiple sclerosis for decades, and it was cruelly preventing what should have been a retirement spent roaming the world. Both our grandfathers had endured dementia and Alzheimer's just when their pensions should have freed them from a life of hard work. Each time our resolve wavered, a powerful sense of loyalty to all of them reminded us to stick with our initial instincts and follow our dream while we were still capable of doing so. If we had learnt anything at all from the heartache that had struck our families, it was that time was of the essence.

Edward's wife, Victoria, had organised a charity event the summer after we agreed to do the trip, and it was there that we met her uncle, John. As a fellow motorcycle enthusiast, he and Byron were soon lost in a conversation that lasted the entire evening, and, by the end of it, John had offered to sell us a bike for our trip. The two of them had already agreed that the BMW R100RS would be ideal for the journey, and, judging by a few photos, we could see it had been kept in pristine condition, despite its thirty-one years.

Byron was a handy mechanic and had already convinced me that we would be better off with an older bike. He would be able to work on one himself, whereas modern engines tended to rely more on digital input for diagnostics and repairs, not to mention that they cost more than we could afford. The combination of the event in Edward's memory and Byron's vision of the ideal motorcycle left us convinced that John's BMW was destined to carry us on our adventure.

John lived in Scotland, so we took a couple of days off work the following year to go and collect the bike. It was a freezing cold March, and we had managed to find a cheap ticket to fly north, but the prospect of riding back to London was bittersweet. Although we would finally be in possession of the key component for our trip, we were also yet to invest in robust, cold weather kit. As a substitute, we brought a huge bag that was rammed with as many clothes that we could physically wear at once in the hope that they would ward off hypothermia on the way home.

Byron's eyes lit up as soon as we walked into John's immaculate workshop. At the sight of the 1979 BMW R100RS, every confidence in the trip was confirmed. The original fairing had been removed, and the bodywork had been repainted with the same enamel shade used on cast iron Aga stoves, while the wheels had been sprayed black. From an aesthetic point of view, it looked the part and suited our hopes for a slightly retro, self-sufficient adventure.

Once the details of its mechanical particulars had been passed on, we set off into the Highlands of Scotland alongside John on his Norton. Unseasonal sunshine christened our first ride as a complete team, although our fears for the long trek south were later realised. Terrific winds blew from the east, while miserable grey clouds tailed us for the entire four hundred miles. It took over an hour to regain full movement in our numb fingers and toes during a break at a service station, prompting us to later invest heavily in decent kit.

We stopped again further south at Byron's Lincolnshire family home, where he and his brother, Leo, christened the bike. With a playful jibe at its capacity to do anything but fly, as well as its shared colour with the cast iron stove, our thirty-one year old BMW R100RS was given the enduring moniker, the Flying Aga.

AMERICAN CONTINENT

ALASKA
CANADA
USA
MEXICO
BELIZE
HONDURAS
GUATEMALA
PANAMA
COLOMBIA
EL SALVADOR
VENEZUELA
NICARAGUA
GUYANA
COSTA RICA
SURINAME
ECUADOR
FRENCH GUYANA
PERU
BRAZIL
BOLIVIA
PARAGUAY
CHILE
URUGUAY
ARGENTINA

KITTING UP AND
SHIPPING OUT

MINUS ONE YEAR

During the weeks and months following the purchase of the Flying Aga, Byron regularly returned home from work with newly acquired travelling paraphernalia. Titanium cutlery, a stove that ran on petrol, and a waterproof first aid kit appeared with a stowaway saucepan set and plastic meal-kits. We had already bought a tent, some decent mattresses, and waterproof roll bags for a previous, much shorter trip, and, as the pile grew, we faced the dilemma of transporting it all on one bike.

We only had two soft pannier bags that had seen much better days, a tank bag with broken zips, and a top-box that could carry just one helmet. So, as the rubber-sucker-tea-towel-holder chased the tiles in the bathroom, we turned our attention from camping gear to kitbags, and Byron had soon sourced a craftsman in Chester who made aluminium panniers.

The prospect of secure, waterproof, and lightweight boxes was more than enough reason to arrange a trip to Chester, and it wasn't long before we were standing in Vern's workshop, accompanied by his dog and a mug of strong coffee. A customary bike-chat-challenge which, as an outsider had taken me a while to decipher, was soon in full swing. Deployed when bikers first meet, the stealth face-off is a means of determining how authentic the other biker is by using the disguise of casual conversation to gauge the quality of their motorcycle knowledge. I sensed the showdown concluded in mutual respect, as it wasn't long before Vern agreed to make the panniers for us.

While measurements were taken and frames were drawn up, I proposed that the boxes should probably be as big as Vern could make them. The suggestion prompted a few sympathetic glances in Byron's direction, as if it hadn't been him accumulating enough apparatus to equip a small army.

After inviting us to join his annual barbecue campout, being held a few weeks later, we waved goodbye to Vern and his dog with excitement knowing that the Flying Aga would soon be sporting some rare and robust panniers for the fast approaching adventure.

Later that year, however, Byron's father, Garth, died in a car crash. The shock and devastation completely threw us, and for a long time all thoughts of the trip were forgotten. Our priorities changed entirely, and the idea of leaving our families behind became unthinkable.

Life had so cruelly shifted again. As the weeks and months passed by, we tried to adjust. Another winter set in, and the Flying Aga was taken to a garage for hibernation, while our camping gear and stockpile of supplies were relegated to gathering dust under our bed. The maps and travel guides, which had scattered the flat, were replaced by photographs and other precious memories as we lost all desire to explore a world that, not for the first time, seemed so merciless.

Garth had been the earliest influence on Byron's enthusiasm for motorcycles, and he had even talked of meeting us to ride a chunk of the US together. Memories of his support for our trip began to flood back the following year, and, as the weeks ticked by, a semblance of our old routine returned. We plucked the maps from the back of the shelves and checked on the Flying Aga in its winter nest. Gradually Garth's influence, and the rationale that had tipped the balance for us in the past, reignited our former resolve. A greater belief than ever before emerged, and we realised that we had to seize the opportunity before it became little more than a perpetual dream that we wilfully let slip away.

So, on one cold evening in the middle of winter, we huddled together on the well-worn sofa in our flat and, with the blessing of both our families, we booked two one-way flights to Alaska.

The flights were the final step in closing the deal on our dream and spurred us into a flurry of final preparations. Our already substantial stash of equipment was complemented with spare inner-tubes (the lack of which had us stuck for two hours on the A2 the previous summer while we missed my friend's wedding), and an intercom system (the necessity of which became clear during a storm in the same previous summer, following a plunge into a French ditch without means to communicate).

We became regulars in the local GP surgery where we were pumped repeatedly with all manner of tropical diseases. We exhausted the scanners at our respective offices by making copies of passports, visas, vaccination certificates, driving permits, and vehicle ownership forms.

After calculating that it was likely we would need to stay for more than ninety days in the US, we spent hours on the application process for tourist visas. Once the paperwork was complete, we then spent half a day in the queue at the

US-American embassy where, despite a grilling on the misdemeanours clocked up during misspent teenage years, we were granted extended leave to tour the country.

We moved out of our flat the weekend before we left our jobs. The enormity of the events we had set in motion finally sank in at a nearby scrap yard when our well-worn sofa disappeared from sight in the rear-view mirror of a hired removal van. A miserably long day of packing in the rain followed before we drove the van north and transferred our worldly belongings into a spare room at Paula's house. After driving back to Clapham Junction the next day, a final cleanup operation lasted the entire night.

We locked up our first shared home together for the last time the next morning. All of our kit was packed into the newly crafted panniers, the small top-box and an army surplus, soft pannier bag that Byron had screwed onto the windscreen in an attempt to balance the rear weight. Fully loaded, we rode to the West London warehouse of James Cargo, an agent that was arranging the passage to Alaska of the bike and our gear.

We were spending our final week in London at my brother's flat, and, as we boarded a train with just one small bag of belongings each, our new position in the world hit us.

We had willingly made ourselves homeless, and at no more than thirty years old, we would match the recklessness a week later by voluntarily becoming unemployed in the midst of a recession.

We spent the final few days on home turf with our respective families. Just two days before we left, Byron's brother, Dom, and his fiancée, Kate, brought their first child, Jude, into the world. Byron was thrilled to get to meet the little man, while two-hundred miles away in Kent, I was busy throwing pebbles into the sea from the beach at Deal with Edward's son, Harry.

After regrouping later that week, one last night was spent in London. Everything we had done over the past two years had been building up towards leaving Heathrow airport the following morning, and, although we had invested a great deal to ensure the onward journey became a reality, it felt like a dream as we boarded the aeroplane to Alaska.

The flight stopped over in Iceland where we began chatting to a US-American couple who seemed unconvinced by our plans, and we couldn't blame them. Based on a long standing love of motorcycles, one solitary photograph, and a stranger on London Bridge, we were on our way to Alaska with a carry-on bag each, no return ticket, and not much of a plan to speak of.

Roaming Moose and Pickup Trucks

We landed in Anchorage in the dusky twilight of late evening and hailed a yellow taxi. We had booked a hotel in the city to tide us over until we could collect the bike and our camping equipment. The room had been a cheap find, and we soon discovered why. It was positioned above the hotel boilers, and, although we were closer than we had ever been to the Arctic Circle, it felt like we were sleeping in the tropics. By the time we settled into the little furnace, our body clocks were nine hours ahead of local time, and we couldn't work out if we should turn in for the night or go and celebrate our arrival. Complete fatigue resolved the quandary, and, after a restless few hours of sleep, we took the hotel shuttle bus to the airport the next morning to track down the Flying Aga.

The driver was a particularly unforthcoming lad who had just arrived from a remote village to work a season in the city. Our eager efforts at small talk went straight over his head as he tried to navigate the multi-lane highway and missed the airport turnoff. When he eventually dropped us at the departure gates,

17

we wandered aimlessly through a succession of nearly deserted terminals before we found the office where we could process the bike's temporary importation into the country.

Conscious of our every move in the presence of gun wielding office clerks, we waited in silence, and, just as the reality that we were so far from home began to sink in, a British accent completely threw us.

The guy ahead of us in the queue was from my home county of Kent and was soon explaining that he had lived in Anchorage for the past five years. As he went off to collect his cleared parcel, he invited us to a barbecue that weekend. Unfortunately, we weren't staying in the city that long, but his offer was the first of a multitude of invitations that came from complete strangers across the continent.

Following some grave expressions and extensive computer checks, our paperwork eventually passed the scrutiny of the gun toting clerks. The Flying Aga was approved for temporary importation, and the officer pointed us in the direction of a few enormous warehouses and aircraft hangers. They lay on wasteland about a mile from her window, and she explained that we would find the bike somewhere in their vicinity.

There was no pavement beside the highway, so we ambled along the grass verge and soon spotted a moose at the corner of a junction ahead. Unwilling to let such a rare photo opportunity pass by, Byron ran across the open road towards the enormous beast. Visions raced through my mind of our adventure ending right there and then, cut short as the huge creature charged at an overexcited tourist. Luckily, the moose didn't react to either Byron or an enormous pickup truck that screeched to a halt when the animal casually strolled across its path.

Byron returned to the grass verge in one piece, and we continued to the air cargo depot, where we encountered more armed people. A stout lady took our paperwork and instructed us to wait for her back in the car park, and, with no experience in retrieving imported bikes from foreign warehouses where moose lingered nearby, we did as she said and sat on a curb watching the most enormous pickup trucks going about their business.

It was the tail end of a winter that would have encased the state in thick snow and limited daylight. On that sunny May morning, though, it was difficult to comprehend the necessity of vehicles that towered above a six-foot Byron. As we sat watching them in awe, a forklift truck carrying a huge wooden crate made its way out of the security gates and towards us. The same lady who told us to wait for her, carefully inched the load to the ground beside us and disappeared back through the security gates, leaving cheerful instructions to find her when we were done.

We sat in silence for a few seconds, staring at the crate. Although we hadn't given the retrieval of the bike too much thought, breaking into a nailed and industrially stapled wooden box in the middle of a busy car park wasn't a scenario that had occurred to us. All of our own tools were secured inside the crate, so Byron set off towards the warehouse in search of alternative means, while I guarded our trusty steed that had flown over four thousand miles to join us.

Before long, Byron was bounding back across the car park with a claw hammer in one hand and a crow bar in the other.

Although the box was securely fastened, the tools made light work of sending planks of splintered wood and long nails flying across the tarmac to unveil the Flying Aga beneath a richly blue, Alaskan sky.

Three hours after entering the car park by foot, we rode out of it by motorcycle, on high alert for wandering moose. After navigating the city's one-way grid of numbered avenues and lettered streets, we unloaded all of our kit into the sweltering hotel room.

Despite the time we had spent packing and unpacking before we left, it was immediately clear that we had brought too much luggage. Our clothing was minimal, with one set of cold weather clothes, one set of hot weather clothes, one running and hiking kit, and a few surplus T-shirts. I had managed to squeeze in the smallest set of hair straighteners I could find, and Byron had snuck in some excess tools, but we had still been under the impression that, for the most part, we had packed a bare minimum.

It was only when the entirety of our kit was strewn across the humid room that we realised our miniature foldaway camping table and small wooden chess set weren't really crucial to the journey. From that moment on, we compiled daily lists of the items that could be given away or sent home.

Eventually the heat of the room drove us out into the cooler air of the city. Hunger had set in, and we made our way into a bar where the first of many unforeseen cultural disparities reminded us that we were a long way from home. With our identification hidden back in the hotel room, we were refused the sale of alcohol but were still expected to tip the barman when he served us soft drinks. Undeterred, we settled in for the afternoon and tucked into a feast of caribou burgers. A stunning view of distant snowy peaks was lit by the strong sun, and, with occasional free refills of fizzy pop, we soaked it up from a balcony for the rest of the afternoon.

Following another night in the sweatbox, we made the most of the hotel's multicoloured cereal and instant coffee breakfast before checking out. We had planned to spend one more night in the city, so made our way to a nearby campground that lay precariously close to a freight railway line.

With very little grass to peg down a tent, it wasn't long before we learnt that camping and tenting were two different activities in North America. Most of the sites that we later encountered on the road catered for the camping that was undertaken by huge recreational vehicles which were bigger than coaches and seemed to dominate the campgrounds of the nation. They were obviously good for business, as very few sites ever left much space or grass for tents. The natural territory for pitching tents, or the activity of tenting, turned out to be in national or state parks, rather than at just any campground.

Once we had pegged down our suddenly modest, three-man tent in the shadow of a few enormous RVs, a half-mile freight train lumbered down the neighbouring line. When it blasted its whistle, we felt a flutter of anticipation, as if it had just officially marked the start of our all-American road trip.

Despite our initial aspirations to travel free of technology, in the greater interest of saving space, we had packed an iPad, an iPod Nano, and a Kindle, which had all generously been given to us as parting gifts. Although we had relocated to the great outdoors with illusions of roughing it, it was a revelation to discover that we could pick up an Internet signal inside our tent. We used it to arrange a meeting with the Northern Riders BMW Club, which Byron had already contacted before we left the UK.

We assumed we would be joining a scheduled gathering that evening, but soon found out that the other riders had travelled from across the region especially to meet us. Over burgers and chips in a local diner, they spent the evening giving us tips and advice about riding in the state. They even presented us each with honorary club T-shirts, as well as map clippings and contact details, before seeing us on our way. Although the evening had been punctuated with a few unsettling tales of hazardous moose and treacherous weather conditions, we were flattered to have received such a welcome from the club.

We arrived back at the tent late that evening, just as the last glimmer of daylight faded. The warm sunshine of the previous two days and the heat of the hotel room had fooled us into the belief that summer had already arrived. By the time we climbed into the tent, though, the cold Northern air was biting hard. We layered up in vests, pyjamas, new club T-shirts, thermal tops, scarves, hats, gloves, and waterproof socks, before crawling into conjoined sleeping bags. The improvised nest was topped off with an oversized, polythene-backed, red tartan picnic blanket for insulation, and we huddled beneath it for the rest of the night, concentrating on keeping every inch of exposed flesh concealed from the icy air.

We woke up with a five o'clock sunrise and were preparing an early breakfast when the sound of rustling caught our attention. There had been no sign of life from the other campers, and we edged around the side of one of the huge RVs to investigate what it could be, when a moose suddenly appeared. A series of anecdotes the evening before had illustrated how dangerous the short-sighted, slow-witted beasts could be, and we froze to the spot as it lumbered within inches of our tent. It was much bulkier than a horse and had some nasty scars running up its legs and across its back, which went a long way to clarify the ominous warnings from the Northern Riders Club.

Inspired by the sighting, we wasted no time in setting off on a cold, northerly ride towards Denali National Park, where we hoped to encounter a much greater abundance of wildlife.

Our route took us close to the hometown of Brandon, who had attended the gathering the night before. He had recently bought a similar bike to ours and was planning to take it on a trip with his wife, Stephanie, once their kids were older.

The whole family welcomed us to their home like old friends, and, after exhausting the introductions to their collection of pets, the children resorted to familiarising two scruffy, foreign motorcyclists with what they believed would be an anomaly of household appliances, most notably a TV remote.

We came from a small island that would fit seven times into the vast wilderness of Alaska. Before the trip began, we had contemplated its size with some trepidation and had also struggled to form any idea of what to expect from its renowned Republicanism. However, the kindness and hospitality of total strangers had made us feel at home after only three days there, and it was with some reluctance that we left the warmth of Brandon and Stephanie's family later that afternoon.

Although the air had been warm when we were stationary, the drag caused by the moving bike soon left us shivering uncontrollably. When we reached the highway, ominous grey clouds concealed the afternoon sun, and a painful chill sapped at our body temperature. The prospect of an imminent rain or snow shower filled us with dread, and we turned up the music on our intercom, hoping for a distraction from the discomfort.

All signs of civilisation fell away as the highway opened up. The route led us through dense woodland, where a sense of foreboding took root in my mind, and, although the threat from the clouds was yet to materialise, the music did little to subdue an emerging anxiety.

The rapid passage from leaving home to riding through one of the most remote locations in the world had caught up with me. Other than a British prepay mobile telephone and an iPad, we were travelling without any other means of communication, and, having passed very few other vehicles on the road, unease settled into my cold bones. I scoured the thick forest ahead, searching for the deer or moose that I felt sure would be the cause of our imminent demise and I wondered how long we might have to wait until somebody discovered the resulting wreckage. Byron had instantly relished the open road, and, by the time we pulled into the first petrol station, I knew I had to sort myself out or risk ruining our trip before it had even begun.

We were navigating our way around the flip pumps and the prepay system to fill up the tank when a giant of a man approached us. With a drawl that we were yet to recognise, he bombarded us with questions about the Flying Aga. He had a dominance that was difficult to ignore and soon launched into an explanation of his own plans, while his wife tried to steer him back to their pickup truck. Just when we thought she had succeeded, he outmanoeuvred her and returned to ask if he could bless our bike.

We were taken aback by the request, and, while we struggled to envisage what he meant, he took our silence for consent and, with his wife, grasped our hands to form a semicircle around the Flying Aga. We were unaccustomed to the role of preachers, and all manner of assumptions about holy water and hymn singing raced through our minds as we attempted to predict their next move.

The process turned out to be a simple one in which he spoke to Jesus and requested the safe passage of our bike and the protection of everyone that it carried. As he entreated Jesus to prevent any mechanical issues from defeating our venture, his wife chanted softly towards the petrol-stained ground.

With the swiftness of its beginning, the rite came to a close, and, before we knew it, they were waving goodbye. Our restraint crumbled the second that we dared look one another in the eye and tried to picture the same scenario happening in a petrol station back home. In spite of our scepticism at their forthrightness, though, my fears that had been escalating in the hours since leaving Anchorage began to subside when we resumed the ride.

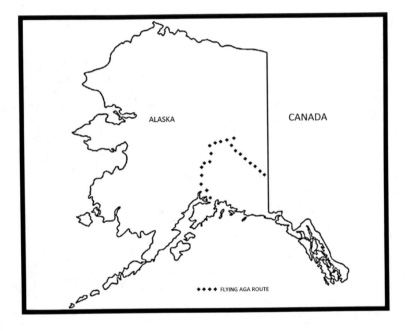

ALASKA

CANADA

◆ ◆ ◆ ◆ FLYING AGA ROUTE

INTO THE WILD

The wilderness that we had been anticipating in Denali National Park turned out to be well landscaped in a campground where each pitch had been equipped with a picnic table and a fire pit. Any initial disappointment at the orderly setup quickly waned though when daylight failed to recede late that evening and a moose wandered past us with its calf. Nothing else stirred on the site, and we watched from the edge of a roaring campfire as they sought shelter in a small wooded area opposite our tent.

After another frosty night of sleep, the moose and its calf were still in the trees the following morning when a campground attendant approached us and casually asked if we had spotted a black bear in the vicinity. It took a minute to register what he had said and, after asking him to elaborate, he explained that another camper had reported a sighting less than fifty meters away from our tent. The attendant had no doubts as to what the camper had seen and believed the bear was tracking the moose calf.

While the attendant continued to explain about bears and moose, Byron recalled being woken in the night by a low grumble and some movement outside our tent. He had assumed it was the moose foraging for berries but suddenly realised that we may have narrowly missed an encounter with a bear. The revelation had us firmly backtracking on our presumption that the campground did not seem particularly wild.

Although the potential close call was a terrifying prospect, the fact that the bear was still somewhere nearby stoked our curiosity to catch a glimpse of the beast. We roamed the campground all morning, and, although the moose and its calf were still in the trees a couple of hours later, the bear remained well concealed.

We eventually gave up on the search in favour of exploring the nearby park and, when we returned that evening, all signs of the moose had disappeared. We realised its departure meant we had missed the chance to see the bear but with some relief, we knew we would at least be able to sleep soundly.

Later that evening, we huddled in the campground laundrette and soaked up the warmth from the tumble dryers. We had found another unexpected Internet signal and used it to launch an online blog of our journey. There had been a closely fought dispute between us as to whether or not we should burden ourselves with an obligation to frequently document the trip, and the inclination not to bother had been beaten by the likelihood that we would eventually forget the finer details if we didn't keep some kind of account. We were also still conscious that our families would be anxious about us, and a blog could show them where we were in the world, so a narrative of our adventure commenced in the heart of Alaska.

While we launched the online journal, we took it in turns to sneak a hot shower in the adjoining bathroom. On top of the entry fee into the park and the nightly campground fee, there was an additional charge to use the showers. Having just spent a fortune on the smallest amount of food at a nearby convenience shop, we had serious concerns about how long our budget was going to last, so after spotting that one of the shower doors had been left unlocked, we decided to save a few dollars and risk the wrath of the campground attendants in order to smell less like the travellers we were fast becoming.

After another freezing cold night huddled in our makeshift nest, we decided to venture further into the colossal park. However, having packed the bike with a substantial stash of tools and camping equipment, there had been no space for many personal possessions, let alone hiking gear to equip an exploration on foot. The road into the park was restricted to designated buses, and the only other way to delve deeper into the wilderness was to board one of them.

It took six hours for the driver to skim the periphery of Denali National Park. Very distant grizzly bears and striking herds of caribou sent his busload of tourists rushing to poke long lens cameras out of the windows on a drive that was full of constant wildlife-spotting stops and starts. Grazing Dall sheep, scampering snowshoe hares, one porcupine, and an indefinite glimpse of a lynx sent the small army of cameras into overdrive.

The unpaved, bumpy road led us alongside a magnificent, snow-draped chain of mountains where Mount McKinley, the highest peak in North America, towered 6,000 meters [20,321 feet] above sea level in the distance. Meltwater cut ribbons through dry beds of rock, and, as we wound our way higher, a spectacular view of thawing lakes unravelled across the land below. We were too early to see the park blossom out of its grey winter coat, but the driver reasoned that its stunning summer colours came hand-in-hand with the infamous Alaskan mega-mosquitoes, a swarm of which, he cheerfully informed us, could quickly suck a naked body entirely dry of blood.

We packed up early the next morning and made our way north out of the park. The ride was as spectacular as the bus tour the day before and flanked the same mountain range and wild landscape most of the way to Fairbanks, where we refuelled and stocked up on groceries. Despite local grumbles that the petrol was the most expensive in the country, it still only cost half the price of the fuel back home, and the prospect that it would get even cheaper counterbalanced our growing fears for the budget. We stuffed the groceries into a rucksack that became a permanent attachment to my back over the following couple of months and rode out of the city into another dense forest.

Occasional roaring rivers and eerily still lakes peppered the route to Chena Hot Springs. The thermal pools literally lay at the end of the road and had been developed into a tourist resort some fifteen years earlier. Geothermal research and other alternative energy experiments were being carried out at the site, so we pitched the tent somewhere in the muddy residue of a wooded area, away from the science labs.

Although showers ran from the naturally hot water in the resort, the only facilities near the camping quarter were pit toilets. The national park eco toilets hadn't been too different to regular, plumbed-in facilities because their high chimneys worked well to ventilate deep pits, but these toilets added a few points to our roughing-it scoreboard. With crude bear warnings nailed to the doors, they were simple wooden sheds with shallow, composting trenches where nothing was out of sight or out of smell.

We soaked away hours in the largest hot spring pool, enjoying what was essentially a huge, outdoor bath with an overpowering scent of egg. Eventually, our capacity to handle the heat was defeated, and, with wrinkled skin and light heads, we stumbled to the laundrette to do our first batch of living-on-the-road laundry. That evening we built another campfire, while the phenomenon of almost perpetual daylight continued to assist our constant lookout for bears.

A chill had reinstated itself in our bones the next morning, and, after a lengthy pack up, we rode back through the dense forest to Fairbanks, from where we joined the Alcan Highway. The highway was over 1,300 miles long and had been constructed in just eight months during World War II. It cut into the wilds of Alaska from British Columbia and the Yukon Territory in Canada, and was infamous for its remoteness and often weatherworn surface.

A few miles along the road, we passed through a town that had registered its name as North Pole in the 1950s. The change had been an enterprising bid to attract year-round festive tourism, but, with candy cane street lights and a giant Santa Claus statue, it was a peculiar place to happen upon in June. We didn't hang around long and, after stopping in a giant Christmas gift shop to pick up the first of a collection of state stickers that would eventually adorn our panniers, we resumed our route towards Canada.

Although the sun had reappeared, the air remained bitingly cold, and the hours spent riding through the feral landscape gradually drained all feeling from our hands and feet. Any attempt to hold the camera and capture the spectacular backdrop was rendered futile, and, although Byron kept us on a level course, his hands were always white and drained of blood whenever we stopped to refuel.

Our necks and shoulders would ache from sitting without support for so long, and our knees didn't escape the strain either. Long breaks at petrol stations were largely spent stretching out muscles and joints while gulping down instant coffee and willing our blood circulation to recover so we could make progress on the road. We had invested in decent riding gear after collecting the Flying Aga from Scotland, but the air so very far north was inescapably cold, and, short of electric vests and heated gloves, nothing could help to fight it.

High winds and heavy rain set in some hours later, transforming the already scarcely bearable and isolated ride into an insufferable struggle. Pitching a tent was the last thing we could face, so we checked into the first roadside motel that we came across. It was in one of the many tiny interior Alaskan towns that had initially been military outposts during the construction of the Alcan Highway and didn't seem to have grown since.

The motel fitted well into our unfolding All-American road trip, and, in the spirit of every decent fugitive tale, we slid our dollars under the glass window to an overweight, chain smoking receptionist, who exchanged them for a room key and just one instruction; to be gone by ten o'clock the next morning.

The establishment was a wooden construction with room doors that opened onto the gravel, where we parked the bike. Unlike the portrayal of motels in films, though, the walls were without cracks, the sheets were clean, and there were two separate rooms to sleep in, even though we had only paid for one.

As we unloaded our bags, the owner of a parked chopper appeared at one of the doors. He staggered out to introduce himself with a name that we heard as "Dagger," and we didn't like to ask twice. He gave the Flying Aga an indifferent onceover before slurring an explanation that we hadn't asked for, about a nineteen-year-old daughter's birthday and taking her on a celebratory road trip. He was in his mid-fifties so it could have been true, however, our cinematic perception of the dubious motel guest had preceded him, and his explanation never stood a chance. It was difficult to imagine any teenage girl choosing to celebrate a birthday by going on a bitter cold, motorcycle trip with her drunken dad.

Dagger swayed vacantly while his one-sided dialogue continued. The supposed daughter stayed hidden inside his room, and we eventually made our excuses to follow her example. On the way back to our room, a man with a thriving white beard pulled alongside us in a dilapidated truck. Being a frustrated eccentric, Byron was instantly drawn to him, and, with considerably more coherence than the other guest, he told us about a tiny town not too far away, where he had retired to. It had no plumbing or electricity and boasted a population that ranged from fifteen to one hundred over the course of each year. Byron listened intently and made a mental note of where he would spend his old age before we bid goodbye to the old man and took shelter from the elements.

We missed the departure of Dagger and his young pillion the next morning and decided to head in the opposite direction of their planned northerly bearing. The white bearded man from the day before had warned us that the winter conditions had played havoc with the route to Inuvik, which lay seven hundred miles north along nothing but unpaved, thick gravel and mud. With few provisions and no means to contact anybody, we had decided to stay on the Alcan Highway and continue south.

Although the prospect of ploughing up to the northern coastline had been a mere challenge in Byron's eyes, we were riding a vintage road bike. Just as our lack of hiking kit had limited our exploration of Denali, our choice of bike also posed a few restrictions.

The road cut through thick forests of coniferous trees before tracing its way alongside rivers and striking mountains. A grey sky prevented the sun from warming the air, but the dramatic landscape kept us captivated, and we soon reached the border crossing to Canada.

We spotted a woman filming her partner playing the harmonica beneath a territorial welcome sign, and Byron pulled to an abrupt stop. He had been teaching himself to play the harmonica before we left home and soon had the Canadian musician showing him a few techniques before they embarked on an impromptu jam together.

Once the spontaneous musical union came to an end, the Canadians ventured into Alaska, while we rode towards the Yukon Territory of Canada. One visible officer was on duty at the modest border post, and, after inspecting our passports, he asked if we had any money or bear spray to declare. His cheerfulness crumbled into genuine concern when we assured him that we didn't have either. He couldn't believe that we had been camping in what he called "grizzly country" without bear spray.

The spray was intended as a final line of defence in a bear encounter but it had been expensive whenever we had seen it for sale, and we always talked ourselves out of buying any. Perhaps naively, we had taken selective faith, instead, in the assurances of park rangers and camping attendants who told us that bears were not dangerous unless provoked. The guard reluctantly stamped our passports, after we assured him that we would buy some at the first opportunity, and, just as we got ready to ride across the first land border of the trip, Dagger pulled up.

The road conditions on the route north had sent his

chopper sliding out of control and had forced him and his pillion to backtrack south. It was good to hear that we had made the right decision without the hassle of finding out first hand, but we were less than keen to gain the new riding companions.

CANADA

YUKON TERRITORY

NORTHWEST TERRITORIES

NUNAVUT

BRITISH COLUMBIA

ALBERTA

SASKATCHEWAN

MANITOBA

ONTARIO

QUEBEC

NEWFOUNDLAND AND LABRADOR

PRINCE EDWARD ISLAND

NOVA SCOTIA

NEW BRUNSWICK

● ● ● ● FLYING AGA ROUTE

BEAR SPRAY AND BISON

10 Days on the Road | 856 Miles on the Clock

We left Dagger to face the bear spray scrutiny and made a head start into Canada. Ice damage had scarred the surface of the road with cracks and potholes for a hundred miles, and, after zigzagging around the worst of it, we came to a petrol station where a young lad sat on a stool in front of its only pump. He stopped playing his guitar to flip us a peace sign as we pulled in.

There were few other signs of life in the area, apart from a couple of token houses and cabins that were scattered across the seemingly endless terrain. How their inhabitants endured the brutal winters or sourced produce to survive remained a complete mystery. We pumped our fuel, and the boy sent us on our way with another peace sign before he returned to his stool and his guitar.

Before we tackled the long distance to the next town, we pulled into a clearing to eat beside one of many beautiful roadside lakes. The cost of food and the infrequency of places to buy it had quickly taught us not to leave civilisation without ingredients for a picnic. As well as the coffee breaks at petrol stations, roadside sandwiches fashioned with a pocket knife became the most anticipated half-hour of every long and fantastically remote ride.

Although the icy drag caused by the moving bike banished all feeling from our limbs, the standing temperature was still tolerable. The breaks gave us the chance to shake the feeling back into our frozen bones and numb bums while we restocked on energy and absorbed the phenomenal surroundings. The solitude of the lakeside picnic was broken only once by the roar of an engine and the flash of chrome on the road above. Dagger had overtaken us on his faster bike, and, with some relief, we acknowledged that there was a slim chance of us ever catching him up.

With a land mass close to twice the size of Britain, but a population of just under 35,000 people, it came as little surprise that the vehicles on the road in the Yukon Territory were far outnumbered by the wild animals teeming in its grass verges.

While I fumbled for the camera, Byron would slow down as we drew near the magnificent wild bears, elk, and moose that foraged for food beside the road. My cold-deadened hands didn't always focus an image first time, though, and we would risk backtracking for another attempt. Having watched us closely as we passed by seconds earlier, it was always the bears that noticed the revisit. Although we never dared risk coming to a standstill, they would ominously lock eyes with us and follow our course down the road until we returned back to a safe distance.

Later that afternoon, we rode into Whitehorse where over two thirds of the Yukon Territory population lived. After passing through hundreds of uninhabited miles, the small city abruptly flung us back into the modern world of shops, restaurants, and streets. We found a campground on its outskirts and pitched the tent on the banks of the Yukon River, in the shadows of impossibly tall pine trees. After surviving our first week in the wilderness, we decided to hang around and spend a couple days catching up on chores.

We fulfilled our promise to the border official and forked out for bear spray, which was sold to us with very specific instructions of it being an implement of defence and not prevention. The product was essentially a canister of tear gas, which, supposedly, had left one couple with severe burns after they had mistakenly used it like mosquito repellent.

Before we returned into the unknown, we had a final task to send my brother a suitably North American, thirtieth birthday present. The search led us into a local sport shop where it was immediately apparent that football shirts or baseballs would not be found. It was a North American sport shop where, outside the realm of motorbikes, all of Byron's dreams came true.

Rifles were stacked in racks, boxes of ammunition were piled across the shelves, and hand guns were hanging in abundance from the walls. The entire shop was a novelty to our no-right-to-bear-arms culture, and the shop assistant was soon explaining the local laws to us. No matter how Byron phrased his questions, though, it was very clear that we wouldn't be leaving with any of the firearms on display. Eventually, we picked out a hand-crafted hunting knife to send home as the gift and left the assistant in peace.

The next morning we woke up absurdly early and extremely cold in our poorly insulated nest and, unable to get back to sleep, we decided to layer up and ship out. It was so early that we had to break open the campground gates before hitting the deserted, dawn highway. Although we had soon clocked up some good mileage, we had also underestimated just how cold the early hours would be on a bike. On an already exceptionally frosty morning, the drag of the bike increased the speed with which we lost all sensation in our limbs, and we were forced to pull over a lot sooner than we would have liked.

It was our first defrosting break of the day in a petrol station that doubled up as a grocery store, and a few residents had congregated to enjoy a chinwag over an early morning brew. It took longer than usual to regain movement in our fingers and toes, and, although we were up to speed on the local gossip by the time we left, the benefit of our head start was rendered redundant.

During construction of the Alcan Highway, an injured soldier had been taken to an accommodation and supply camp to recuperate. While repairing a signpost there, he added a sign from his hometown to the marker and sparked a craze that saw a further 72,000 signs added to his lonely placard over the subsequent seventy years. Later that day, we stopped by for our daily picnic break to see what the oddity of a signpost forest looked like.

Hundreds of towering stakes were spread across a couple of acres, displaying all manner of national and international signs from roads, towns, streets, schools, state parks, and even vehicle registration plates. Handmade signs fashioned from dinner plates, wooden spoons, and saucepan lids had also been fixed to the stakes, and, as we wandered through the forest, we were inspired to leave our own mark. With few suitable resources to choose from, we elected to sacrifice one of our two cheese-graters-cum-colanders-cum-chopping-boards from the camping dinner kits. After etching the credentials of our trip into the plastic surface, we found space on a stake and screwed in our contribution, just below a wooden sign from Dietwil, Switzerland that had been left ten years earlier.

We entered British Columbia a short time later where we eventually stopped slowing down and frantically reaching for the camera, as a wealth of bear, elk, and bison became commonplace at every turn in the road.

The bison were huge prehistoric beasts, and no amount of diagrams or photos could have prepared us for being in such close proximity to them. Like the bears, they appeared to be built from little else but muscle and fur. They grazed in huge herds at the edge of the road but rarely raised their low hanging heads when we passed within touching distance, unlike the elk that would flee into the woods on our approach. In contrast to both the bison and elk, the bears continued to stand their ground and, with forbidding stares, made it very clear that they were alert to our presence.

A herd of bison had congregated around the entrance to the campground where we ended the day. We unintentionally spooked them as we drew close, and they stampeded in a formidable charge that would have crushed anything unfortunate enough to have been in its way. Excluding the herd, which quickly settled down to graze in the site, we were totally alone on the campground.

The manager was a rugged guy with leathery skin and piercing blue eyes that spoke only of mischief. His straight talking indicated that he would have been more at home hustling on the streets of a city than hauling wood in the wilderness, and he quickly became our favourite attendant. We later heard of a scheme that offered a remote existence to repeat offenders and informants as an alternative to jail time or retaliation. Apparently, the northwest was one such out-of-the-way environment, and we were convinced that he was channelling too much rogue not to have been a candidate.

After buying firewood from him, we built another campfire. The long daylight hours were proving to be an invaluable factor in our fast progress through the immense northwest corner of the continent. We had set off before six o'clock that morning and, despite numerous stops along the way, we had still managed to cover four hundred miles of single-lane highway before pitching a tent and eating dinner in daylight beside the campfire that evening.

Byron stayed by the fire to play his harmonica, while I went to a neighbouring lodge to make use of what we now realised was widely accessible wireless Internet. The herd of bison grazed nearby, and, after a while, Byron edged towards them, hoping to get a better look in the waning daylight. As he inched closer, the unexpected roar of four Harley-Davidson motorcycles sent the whole herd into another bolt.

The noisy bikes turned out to have been hired by a group of Mexicans who were on a touring holiday. When they caught sight of the Flying Aga, their enthusiasm soon quashed any hostility Byron had held against them for scaring off the bison. After a customary motorcycle chat, the group eventually retired to their rooms inside the lodge, but not before asking how much we would accept for the bike when we had finished our journey. Although any amount of money would have been a great help in getting us home at the end of the trip, Byron told them proudly that the Flying Aga would never be for sale.

While the second bison stampede and the Mexican alliance was going on outside, I had been minding my own business inside the lodge when a guy took a seat next to me and launched into a story about a bear attack.

Back in 1996, he had gone to the house of a friend who turned out not to be home, and a grizzly bear was taking advantage of his absence. Having been caught off guard, it unleashed a horrifying attack on the storyteller, who at some point resorted to playing dead. The bear fell for it. However, instead of leaving him alone, it partially buried him for a few hours until it had finished its business at the house and finally left the vicinity. It was before the age of mobile telephones, and the unfortunate victim found himself literally holding his guts in place while he stumbled along the road to flag down help.

Having relished telling the tale to someone who was about to spend the night sleeping in a deserted, heavily bear populated, Northern Canadian campground, the man mistook my silent fear for a lacklustre response. In a bid to extract a more satisfying reaction, he promptly lifted his top to show me the scars and his still-broken ribs, which protruded from his back. It was at this point that the Mexicans entered the lodge, and I seized the opportunity to escape and leave them at his mercy.

After regrouping with Byron outside, I relayed the gruesome tale and we climbed into the tent for a night of broken sleep with the bear spray, a knife, and a hand axe close by.

We were near another thermal spring and took a break from the road the following day to thaw out. A lengthy boardwalk led across swampy terrain into a nearby forest, and we traced its twists and turns through dense woodland to reach the hot pool. A bed of white gravel lay beneath crystal clear water, which was framed by striking, electric-green foliage. The outlet that heated the natural pool bubbled in a far corner, where piles of pebbles were placed as symbolic offerings on top of smouldering white rock by bathers who had braved its searing heat.

A long bearded, leather skinned trucker told us he had been a regular user of the springs for decades and took no time to adopt the seemingly favourite local pastime of scaring tourists with anecdotes of bear attacks. He recounted a particularly horrifying ordeal of a woman and her two children who had inadvertently surprised a bear that was grazing close to the boardwalk. The bear left her young son terribly injured after killing her, along with a man who had tried to fend off the attack.

Fortunately, the only incident we encountered was a man who got too close to the source of the spring and fainted in the water. He had been thrashing about in the pool when Byron waded out with another bather to rescue him. They slapped him back to consciousness before putting him in the recovery position, while he proceeded to vomit continuously until a park buggy arrived to cart him away.

That evening, a fellow camper joined us in the lonely campground. Mike was cycling over 3,700 miles across the country to raise money for his local hospital. He was the first of many cyclists we met that were undertaking heroically long rides through the vast continent. We sat by a campfire with him, swatting at a plague of blood sucking black flies that swarmed towards the smoke, while the three of us recounted numerous bear attack stories that had been told to us. We unanimously agreed, or possibly hoped, that most were embellished entries in a local contest to see who could torment the most tourists.

Two days later, we reached the end of the Alcan Highway. We had ridden over 2,000 miles through the vast Northwest where uninterrupted, natural splendour had distracted any urge to clock-watch, and the prolonged daylight hours had tricked us into extreme endurance.

Despite my intermittent battles against urges to doze off, we had relished the solitude. Our minds had been free to wander for days on end, and, after turning off the intercom, we would shout and sing and cry and laugh with the complete abandon of knowing that nobody could hear us, not even one another on the moving bike.

Apart from the first ride out of Anchorage, we had almost immediately acclimatised to outdoor living and long, daily journeys. If ever one of us faltered, the other soon brought them up again, and, together with the faithful Flying Aga, it slowly began to feel like anything was possible. We had waited so patiently for the journey to begin that once it had finally started, we were determined to savour every second.

Most of the days had come to an end at campgrounds,

where we would realise that up to twelve straight hours had passed by in a flash. Magnificent rolling taiga and daunting peaks had paved the way each day, while frozen lakes and raging rivers intermittently cropped up at the edge of the road. Roaming wildlife perfected the route, and, despite one close call with an indecisive mountain goat, we had remained upright throughout.

Every evening was spent pitching the tent and finding food while fighting a sudden rush of fatigue, but we always woke each morning and thought nothing of doing it all over again.

Our time on the Alcan Highway ended in Dawson Creek, where wild forests had gradually been replaced by arable land and small towns that proudly exhibited commemorations to their pioneering origins.

Small museums featured entirely dismantled and reconstructed homes and churches from across the region. A giant generator that had once run an entire town was on display, and cars older than a hundred years were still fired up to undertake an annual drive along the historic highway. Amateur cine-films documented the brutal conditions in which, in just eight months, the comparatively tiny scar of the Alcan Highway had been cut into the wilderness.

We continued our southern course with great affection for the region, which had so magnificently marked the beginning of our journey.

GLACIAL LAKES AND RAGING RIVERS

20 DAYS ON THE ROAD | 2,387 MILES ON THE CLOCK

The Flying Aga had persisted triumphantly through the icy temperatures and along the bumpy roads further north. One minor issue of tank slapping, where the handlebars would oscillate like a pendulum due to the imbalance of front and rear weight, had occurred at low speeds, but there was little we could do about it, other than continue to compile lists of the luggage that we planned to offload.

The harsh cold of the North finally began to ease when we cut into Alberta. Our red tartan picnic blanket. with its polythene backing. was no longer required for insulation at night, and, although the lengthy daylight hours continued, longer periods of darkness gradually crept in.

On the road to Jasper National Park, dazzling glaciers and enticing lakes glistened in the sunlight, while ribbons of meltwater fell vertically from the great height of surrounding rocky peaks. The abundance of natural beauty was too much for our modest lens to capture, so we packed it away and simply enjoyed the brilliance.

Evidence of a booming tourist trade soon emerged when the park road widened, and we passed more vehicles in two hours than we had done in the previous two weeks.

We set up camp a few miles outside Jasper town, at a site that had over seven hundred pitches. The tent proved its reliability through a night of heavy rain, which eventually woke us up early the next morning. Although we were short on hiking gear, we were determined to witness the interior of at least one national park away from the road, so, when the morning sun burnt away the remaining rain clouds, we set off on one of many trails.

We followed the twists and turns of the Athabasca River, where a plastic bottle bobbing in the water caught our eye. A message inside had been written five months previously and offered a prophetic outlook on our journey, reading: "Life is like a message in a bottle, to be carried with the winds and the tides."

We were equipped with an improvised hiking kit made up of running shoes, motorcycle waterproofs, and emergency layers of T-shirts, as well as a flask of tea, a small picnic, and the canister of bear spray. After joining a trail that veered away from the river, up a mountain ridge, and deep into the forest, we didn't see another person for the rest of the day.

We reached the Valley of Five Lakes after a few hours and settled down for a picnic beside the edge of the first lake. The sun had streamed through the tall forest canopy all day, keeping us warm for the first time without the need for hot springs, instant coffee, or tartan blanket insulation.

Mesmerising shades of blue glimmered in the secluded lake, which quickly became an irresistible temptation. Byron succumbed first and stripped off before wading into the water. His reaction left me with no doubt that its tropical appearance was simply a glacial ruse, and I stuck firmly to the wooded shore as he grimaced against the icy chill.

Ominous grey clouds eventually closed in on the exquisite spot, and we tore ourselves away to resume the trek. We followed the trail through more dense forest and over high ridges, before crossing wetlands to reach the highway. The heavens soon opened once again, and, despite our oversized waterproofs, resistance was futile against the torrential downpour as we traipsed along the edge of the road, back to the campground.

On our return, a hut with a wood burning stove quickly became our sanctuary against the miserable deluge. Although the temperature had not dropped, we were soaked and freezing. By a stroke of luck, someone had left a stash of dry wood in the refuge, and we quickly got the stove blasting out enough heat to warm us up and cook a feast of spaghetti for dinner.

Thankfully, the tent continued its resistance against the weather that night and offered us heroic protection from an almighty thunderstorm. The tempest continued to rage above us throughout the next day, so we returned to the wood burning stove to wait it out.

Relief came the following morning when sunlight broke through, and we woke to the picturesque sight of a herd of white-tailed deer grazing among the tents. The forecast had shown that the respite would be brief, so we joined the other campers in a frantic rush to sponge down our sodden tent and pack up before the opportunity passed to ship out while it was still dry.

When we joined the highway later that morning, the water of the Athabasca River churned in fury against its banks, ripping out whole trees from their roots and carrying them away on violent rapids. Just two days earlier, we had fished out a plastic bottle that had bobbed calmly in waters that were now thrashing in turmoil, and we realised that our hurried departure was a wise move.

We were optimistic that the storm would take a while to reach Banff National Park, further south, and so headed there, hoping that we might get one clear day to explore another park. Due to countless stops at breathtaking canyons, waterfalls, and lakes, it took us ten hours to cover 180 miles on the Icefields Parkway.

When we finally arrived in Banff, the attendant at a campground broke the bad news to us. Not only was the terrible weather less than a day behind, it was also forecast to last the rest of the week.

The thought of spending any more time than necessary in drenched and inadequate off-bike clothes with only a small tent for shelter was less than appealing. The prospect of riding hundreds of miles while water pounded across our helmet visors and seeped through the gaps in our kit was even more unattractive. Pitching a tent in the rain and waking up the next morning to pull on soggy kit in a damp interior topped off every disagreeable aspect of touring in bad weather. Consequently, we were shamelessly committed to chasing the sun whenever possible and resigned ourselves to moving on early the next morning.

The night had remained mercifully dry, and we set off back into British Columbia under clear skies. The fortuitous start was short-lived though, and, after the first hour, it rained heavily for most of the day. It wasn't until dusk began to fall that the clouds finally cleared and made way for a photographic magic hour that spread a warm glow across an arid landscape.

Our weeks spent riding through the sparsely populated wilderness came to a complete end when we arrived in Kamloops, the desert of Canada, where a sweet smell in the balmy air heralded the change.

ELECTRICAL FAULTS AND CONSPIRACY THEORIES

25 DAYS ON THE ROAD | 2,875 MILES ON THE CLOCK

It was quickly apparent that we had left the tent-friendly campgrounds of the national parks behind when we were once again relegated to the grass borders of a site on the outskirts of town. Happily, though, hot showers were inclusive, and the air was decisively warmer.

After spending a day doing chores and stocking up on food, we climbed to the top of a hill that overlooked the whole valley. Accompanied by a flask of tea and a flapjack, we watched a remarkable sunset illuminate the underside of an enormous cloud bank. It transformed the soft lining with every shade between orange and red, before sinking below the horizon in a scene that, in one fell swoop, erased any remaining trace of uncertainty about quitting the life we had left behind.

During another storm that night, the Flying Aga fell off its centre stand. We heard a crash and raced from the tent into the rain to heave it upright on the soft, wet turf of the tent relegation zone. The incident kept us half awake for the rest of the night as we listened out for the sound of it taking another tumble, although luckily it stayed put until morning.

It was Sunday and the one day of the week that had begun to stand out against the others. Although we had kept track of dates, we no longer had reason to take notice of weekdays, and they had slowly become indistinguishable one from another. Only when the roads were light on freight traffic and heavy on motorcycles did we realise that another week had drawn to a close. Towns were calmer, and families were always out in force. Shops were either shut or they closed early, and, very often, campgrounds were emptier as Mondays beckoned vacationers back to work.

Our next stop in Vancouver was a short distance away, so we packed leisurely before eventually leaving the site at lunchtime. Although the Flying Aga had been running like a dream, it began stalling mid-highway. We were eventually forced to coast onto the hard shoulder, where it failed to restart.

Mindful that we could be there for a while, we rolled it down a verge where Byron tinkered with the ignition cables. The power soon returned, and we wrestled the bike back up the steep bank where it proceeded to cut out again. Another inspection revealed the wires leading from the ignition switch were loose, and, after patching them up, we limped to the nearest parking lot.

It soon became clear that the actual ignition barrel was slack and had most likely shaken free following weeks of riding along rough, ice-damaged roads. Unable to do anything about it in the car park, we set off on a nerve-racking ride where the bike continued to cut out in the middle of unusually heavy Sunday traffic. The only thing that kept us on the road was Byron's ability to reach around and press the barrel back into place each time it came loose, all the while continuing to navigate the busy road.

Not long after setting off from the car park, something brushed against the inside of my calf, and I turned around just in time to catch a glimpse of something paper-like flying across the road behind us. It disappeared into the central reservation [median], and we pulled off at the next junction to check what it could have been.

A quick scan confirmed that we had lost one of the triangular side panels that covered the wiring just below the seat. We rode back down the highway, scanning the reservation while holding in the ignition barrel, but most of the overgrown, dividing ditch was concealed from sight. We still rode up and down the highway a further three times until we eventually accepted the first loss of our trip.

Half-an-hour east of Vancouver, we pitched the tent on the thick, mossy surface of a campground where enormously broad trees blocked out any hint of daylight.

We rode into the city the next day and met up with Alan, Byron's friend from university, and his friend, Neal. They had just spent a ski season in Whistler and were moving to Australia the next day. It didn't take much convincing to park the Flying Aga and climb into the back of their car to enjoy the long forgotten experience of travel without heavy kit and helmets. Summer sunshine lit up the vibrant city as they took us for a welcome day out of salmon burgers in the harbour and ice creams on the beach.

Later that evening, we returned to our tent in the rain. The miserable weather continued throughout the next day and wiped out our plans to visit Vancouver Island. Instead, we waited it out under a gazebo on the campground and used the time to take a closer look at the ignition problem.

Epoxy resin was needed to reseal the component, and, on a mission to find some, Byron befriended the campground maintenance man. He lived in a converted school bus next to an enormous corrugated iron bunker that doubled up as his workshop. It soon transpired that, as well as a handy man, he was also a budding conspiracy theorist and, after donating some glue to our cause, he went on to offload a lifetime of suspicions onto a not entirely unwilling Byron.

At some point, I returned to the tent to discover that two apples had disappeared from its interior and the zip on my toiletry bag had been freshly gnawed. I put the fruit theft and bag damage down to sneaky birds or squirrels, until Byron returned from the bunker with tales of aliens and conspiring governments. Added to the combination of wretched weather and daylight deprivation, the theories made the site progressively creepier, and a desire to get away from it sent us packing first thing the next day.

Before embarking on the trip, we had joined a website where people from across the world offered free board and lodging in exchange for labour. A farm south of Vancouver had invited us to stay on the basis that they could exploit Byron's mechanical skills to fix some of their broken machinery. It had been described as a racehorse stud farm, but we were soon introduced to an assortment of farmyard animals, plus one dog and one llama.

Doug and Elaine showed us the ropes. They were from Scotland and had been staying at the farm for a couple of weeks while they waited for Russian visas to arrive in order to continue their travels. The farm was a beautiful little place where geese and chickens meandered through the flower beds, and the llama watched over roaming sheep. Mares and their foals grazed in a meadow while peacocks vied for the attention of anyone who was watching.

Byron fixed a broken lawnmower, a busted milking machine, and a few damaged barn lamps. He also sorted out a crippled quad bike, a vintage Corvette, and a bright yellow Mustang. I joined Elaine in the smelly job of moving an abundance of turkey chicks to an outdoor enclosure before we were tasked with coaxing a psychotic sheep into the back of a wagon.

Unfortunately, there was little else to do in the area once the work was complete, and there was only so much distraction that a resident performing parrot could provide. So, after all the machinery was fixed and Byron had serviced the Flying Aga for the first time on the trip, we bid farewell to Doug and Elaine, our first firm friends of the journey, and we rode back towards the US, just one mile away.

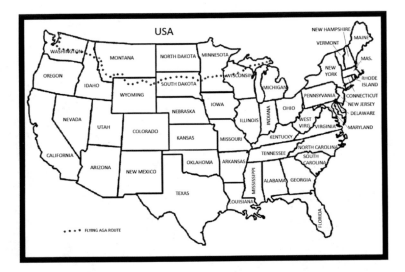

USA

FLYING AGA ROUTE

Native Indians and Rodeo Cowboys

34 Days on the Road | 3,240 Miles on the Clock

A look of indifference was quickly replaced by one of concern when we declared to the border official that we would be leaving the US via Mexico. The sudden change soon became the standard reaction whenever we revealed our plans to visit the country's southern neighbour. Undeterred by his counsel that it would be irresponsible not to change our plans immediately, we rode south into Washington State and took a left turn towards the east coast.

As we navigated the busy state highways, a few waves and thumbs up from car windows hinted at the country's great enthusiasm for motorcycles and road trips.

Another storm dampened our spirits in the Cascade Mountains, and we began to wonder if the same disappointing weather that hit every summer back home was going to accompany the entire trip. Happily, the downpour stayed in the mountains as we descended into the tropical climate of a town that was not too dissimilar to North Pole in Alaska.

Where North Pole had been transformed into Santa's Grotto to attract tourism, this town had been redesigned as a Bavarian village. It was an eerie place where tourist office staff wore lederhosen and every sign had been painted in gothic script. It did, however, offer the first of many insights as to the high regard afforded to ancestral roots in the country. Although we later discovered that this regard occasionally got lost in translation after witnessing one man proudly declare his Scotch-American lineage to a Scottish national. The hopeful brotherly bond grew awkward when attempts to explain the difference between a whisky and a person fell on deaf ears.

In complete contrast to the previous month, we left the Bavarians behind and rode for seemingly endless miles through rolling farmland where small white clouds hung like nursery mobiles from an infinite, blue sky. We failed to find a campground off the highway that evening and eventually pulled into a small town where a group of kids directed us to the nearby village green. A small sign that hung from a lamp post generously offered the spot for free camping.

Although we had been prepared to wild camp on the trip, our vulnerability still got the better of me that first night. Dreams littered a restless sleep, in which our tent was dismantled by locals with pitchforks while we slept, before they made off with the Flying Aga.

With the tent fully intact the next morning and not a soul in sight, we packed up and set off across more vast, agricultural land into Idaho. We were short on our usual sandwich supplies, so stopped for lunch at a roadside diner.

Byron quickly deduced a way to counteract our recent shortfall in calorie intake by choosing the one dish on the menu that came with its own health warning. The Gut Buster arrived with enough fried sausages, fried bacon, fried eggs, fried black pudding, and biscuits covered in gravy to feed both of us for at least two days. With biscuits that were solid, doughy dumplings, and gravy that was made of sausage drippings and batter mix, the health warning was no joke.

A bead of sweat trickled across Byron's brow as it was placed in front of him, but it was too late to turn back. The waitress had clocked our accents when she took our order, and, after she had given Byron an uncertain glance about his choice, he now had something to prove. As well as demonstrating his personal capacity, he was also eating for our country's reputation in the realm of gluttonous dining. The ordeal that followed was painful to watch, but he eventually prevailed and cleared the plate, all the while upping the odds of coronary failure.

With the point proven, he walked proudly from the diner and out of sight from its staff before collapsing to the curb where he solemnly swore to never underestimate a US food warning again.

We crossed into Montana later that day and rode long into the evening until we eventually pulled into a state park where tepees had been set up for hire. We were hung over from the gargantuan lunch and quickly elected to leave the tent packed away that night.

Our sleeping kit was soon spread out across the spacious, carpeted floor of one of the huge, conical tents, and we settled down for the evening beside a crackling campfire outside. The sound of scratching woke us up the next morning, and we discovered that we had been shacked up all night with a chipmunk that was visibly eager for us to vacate his sizeable den.

After obliging the little rodent, we realised that we had crossed from Pacific into Mountain Time the day before and, as a result, had lost a second hour from the nine we had gained on arrival in Alaska. We had hoped to reach Yellowstone National Park early that afternoon, but the lost hour meant that we set off later than expected and would probably arrive at the park too late to get a pitch in one of its popular campgrounds.

The temperature was in the low twenties, and, although the heavy bike kit was tolerable when we were moving, in contrast to the cold northwest, it had become increasingly uncomfortable when we were stationary. The minute we came to a stop, beads of sweat would rise on our foreheads and begin an uncomfortable trickle down our spines.

Aside from saving our skin in a crash, the kit had been essential for warmth further north in the Rocky Mountains and would serve the same purpose again when we reached the Andes in South America. Unfortunately, though, we had no free space to pack it away, so continuing to wear it was our only option during the miles in between. As a result, the petrol stations that had provided much anticipated shelters less than two weeks earlier were now approached with haste and the aim of hightailing it away as quickly as possible.

Ironically, just when we wanted to spend as little time as possible off the bike, the Flying Aga began to attract more and more attention whenever we stopped. Enthusiasts would approach us who had once owned the same model or, with enough time, could recall the name of a friend who had once ridden one. Although usually welcome, prolonged conversations about motorcycles and riding would leave us intolerably hot and desperate to get back on the road. On the plus side, though, the chats would usually end with a divulgence of an off-the-beaten-track route to ride.

We met Cole Boehler, the author of *Motorcycling Montana*, in a petrol station on our way to Yellowstone. He directed us away from the main highway and through some unadulterated cowboy country where the sky went on for miles, and we could almost hear hoof beats reverberating off the barren landscape. To top off the detour, it ended in a couple of tiny towns where original, clapboard-fronted saloons and tiny wooden dwellings were still inhabited as working towns.

Together with the lost hour, the diversion meant we missed getting a spot in one of the Yellowstone National Park campgrounds, so, instead, we checked into our second motel of the trip. After winning over a cheerless, elderly receptionist, we managed to barter the cheapest price for a room that came with a fridge and air conditioning. It was an unexpected luxury, and we didn't leave the cool haven for the rest of the evening, savouring a hot shower and cable TV before enjoying an unbroken night of sleep with a solid roof over our heads.

The next morning, we cooked a breakfast of oats in the gravel car park before racing fifty miles through the national park to get choice pick at a campground that had opened that day for the season.

The sun beat down, and it was sweltering as we assembled the tent. However, at over 2,000 meters [6,561 feet] above sea level, a chill still lingered in the shade of the surrounding lodgepole pine forest where, shortly after we set up camp, Byron disappeared. He returned some time later dragging a dead, nine-meter, lodgepole pine tree behind him before disappearing again and returning minutes later with another one.

He set about chopping up the trees with the hand axe that we were using as a tent peg mallet. Woodchips flew everywhere as he hacked away while occasionally throwing the odd dirty look at fellow campers who unloaded what he deemed to be inferior, neatly packed boxes of purchased firewood from super-size pickup trucks.

Our limited plans meant we rarely had much knowledge of the sites that we visited along the way, and we only knew Yellowstone as the home of the Old Faithful geyser and Yogi Bear. It quickly became apparent that these attractions were two small drops in a vast ocean. As the largest volcanic system in North America, lava flow and volcanic rock are commonplace in Yellowstone. No less than 290 waterfalls exist in the park, as well as one 130-square-mile lake that plummets to depths of 120 meters [656 feet].

Under bright, sunny skies we decided to test the inviting water of the enormous lake, but, within seconds of braving a paddle, we were gripped by the physical pain of freshly defrosted icy water. However, the exhilaration of being in such a fascinating place, perhaps for the only time in our lives, brought out the bravado in us. Despite the painful after-ache of the brief dip, we challenged one another to dive in. Not wanting to be outdone, we both ran and dived at the speed of lightning and were instantly seized by the agony of contracting muscles and freezing blood. With adrenalin pumping through our veins, we sprinted back to the deserted beach where we dried out and a breed of stealth mosquitoes enjoyed more than their fair share of us.

Over the next couple of days, we toured the park in the company of holidaymakers who were all sporting oversized cameras and bum-bags. Vibrant-coloured pools burrowed deep into the earth's crust, and all manner of erupting geysers and steaming pots vented on the horizon. Vivid red and orange mineral deposits stained rocks and cliffs that loomed beyond pure white, dead tree stumps. Deep pools of boiling mud lay ominously beside wooden boardwalks while rural trails led alongside the banks of unbridled rivers that tumbled into huge ravines.

At the overlook of one breathtaking canyon, a few other tourists asked us where we were going on the Flying Aga. They were all from the US, and we should have known to judge our audience better, but the damage was done when we revealed our intentions to ride through Mexico. Courtesy of most national media outlets, predictions poured out of the terrible things that would happen to us there.

Although we had grown used to the response, it reached a new level when one of the women pointed at me and asked if I was chipped. We were eager to move away from the scaremongering, but curiosity got the better of us, and we asked her what she meant. With absolute conviction she explained that I would be foolish not to have a microchip inserted under my skin, so that, after I was inevitably kidnapped and sold into the white sex slave industry, somebody might still be able to identify me. We could only think to ask if she was speaking from experience, but she proudly replied that she had never visited Mexico in her life.

After spending a final night warding off mosquitoes with another campfire, we set off on the park loop road early the next morning and missed the turnoff that we had been aiming for. By the time we realised our error, we were halfway to the other end of the loop so continued along the wrong course in what became an eighty-mile detour.

The landscape changed almost immediately when we finally found our exit, and we rode deeper into Wyoming where craggy red rocks and dry hills framed the entrance to countless cattle ranches.

Oppressive heat had us breaking early in the day, just beyond the Buffalo Bill Reservation in Cody. We found a campground where tent sites were laid out in a quarry at the bottom of a steep, winding hill and we pitched in an olive grove that was nestled beside a beautiful creek. It was idyllic, and we cooled off in the shallow water, close to the rusty frame of an old mangled car that looked like it had crashed many years before and no-one had ever thought to move it.

Two nights later, we were feasting on a chuck-wagon supper of meat and beans in a nearby barn where a group of cowboys entertained a crowd with some honky-tonk music. Without Stetsons or chewing tobacco, we felt slightly out of place but. when the cowboys made a game of spotting the outsiders in the audience, somehow we avoided their scrutiny with more success than the folk from Michigan and Ohio.

Following the feast and the gig, we climbed the bleachers in the rodeo arena next door. As we searched for a seat, the national anthem struck up, and the whole stadium paused to hold hands over hearts and sing. When it finished and we resumed our search, the arena stopped again to bow its head in prayer.

As we had made our way inland, billboards quoting the Bible or denouncing abortion had lined the roads. A minimum of four different Christian denominations also had a strong presence in even the smallest of towns, so the public display of faith came as little surprise.

Following the final call for God to bless America, an evening of extraordinary skill and true grit unravelled. The night ended with the chaotic scene of hundreds of kids from the audience chasing a small calf around the showground to retrieve a red ribbon tied to its tail.

We met Mike and Steve the night before we left the spot beside the creek. They were teachers using their summer holiday to ride from Florida to Alaska and, after spotting the Flying Aga, they wanted to know more about our trip, so we spent the evening chatting to them over tequila and cold beers. After imparting a list of choice places to visit on our route through the US, they went on to enlighten us about a few cultural disparities we had picked up on along the way. For instance, they confirmed that, contrary to what we were used to in the UK, many of their fellow citizens would think nothing of disclosing a political allegiance or the finer details of their incomes, but they would frown at an unconcealed bottle of liquor or a reference to sex before marriage.

Five days after intending to stop for just one night, our plan to leave the site at the crack of dawn was scuppered by the tequila. We eventually pulled out of the campground on the brink of fast rising heat and rode towards the one hundred-mile plateau of the Bighorn Basin.

Stopping was unbearable in the smouldering climate, and we rode for miles without a break, crossing the immense bowl of land before eventually reaching its eastern mountains where we climbed into the relief of cooler air. The combination of low octane fuel and thin air didn't mix well with the Flying Aga and it began to lose power as we gained altitude. It choked and sputtered its way into the Bighorn Mountains, and we pulled in at an overlook to give it a break.

The expanse of dry land below was scarred by twisting rivers and small canyons, but a thick heat haze concealed a complete view of the basin. We had begun to strip off the worst of our heavy riding gear when a car pulled up behind us and two couples scrambled out to light up cigarettes. They had noticed our registration plate and, with strong Liverpool accents, came over to say hello.

Of all the remote places we would visit on the journey, we never again came across four, chain-smoking, fellow English tourists 2,000 meters up a sacred Native American mountain while we were mid-strip.

If it hadn't been for the list Mike and Steve had given us the night before, we would have ridden straight past the small sign that directed us off the highway and along an unpaved track. We pulled into a clearing where a couple of park rangers manned a small shed. They topped up our water bottles and offered to watch our jackets and helmets while we ventured onto the trail that led to a Native American Medicine Wheel.

The site sat a mile and a half up the mountain, and our exposed skin soon turned a shade of berry-red in the high altitude sun. The walk was stunning, though, and led us past summer meadows on one side and banks that were thickly packed with snow on the other. An occasional cool breeze blew across the mountain and offered brief relief as we melted in our heavy boots and thick trousers.

The Medicine Wheel was set close to the edge of the mountain peak, almost 3,000 meters [9,842 feet] above sea level. It looked like a giant bicycle wheel lying on the grass with radial spokes made of white rock. The configuration was laid on a sacred ceremonial site that had been used by Native American tribes for at least 7,000 years. We met a Crow Indian on the climb up who explained that it was still used for ceremonies and rituals by many tribes, evidenced by the offerings hanging from its surrounding fence. We spent some time sitting near the spot, listening to the winds that whipped across the summit while attempting to catch a morsel of its spiritual energy before clambering back down the trail to nurse our sunburns.

Full power returned to the Flying Aga as we descended the mountains and rode into our first encounter with prairie land. An endless horizon of scorched terrain was occasionally punctuated by crops or herds of cattle, and, every so often, we would ride through a tiny farming town, but just as soon as one appeared, it would vanish again.

We rode for hours and hours, becoming unbearably parched until we eventually came upon the Spotted Horse. Despite its official population of just two people, the saloon bar was marked as a town on our roadmap of the entire North American continent. Its handful of clientele turned simultaneously to weigh us up when we opened the door onto a blissfully chilled wall of air. They soon got back to nursing their beers and playing pool while the barmaid served us a couple drinks and ice-cream sandwiches. It turned out that the saloon bar was a popular pit stop for bikers who were making their way to the legendary annual Sturgis rally, and we were, by no means, unusual customers. We chatted to the owner, and he soon revealed that the other half of the population had since moved away, taking the total number of inhabitants in the town down to just one.

That night, we camped in the nearby city of Gillette and made the most of a grocery store and the now vitally essential campground showers. It turned out that the suffocating temperature which had plagued us since we left Yellowstone was, in fact, a heat wave that had been roasting the entire Midwest. The conditions had even made the news back home where equivalent reports would have sent the national population out to spark up its barbecues.

We weren't at home, though, and the heat was more intense than we would ever have experienced in the UK. Temperatures of up to 45-degrees [113° F] had been the cause of multiple deaths. They had also spoiled crops, buckled roads and railway lines, and initiated an ongoing wildfire alert.

Despite the abundance of air conditioning in the country, it didn't extend to our motorcycle and camping existence, and we could find no escape from the heat. We weighed up the merits of continuing to wear our bike kit but risking the likelihood of passing out mid-ride or of taking it off completely and risking painful gravel burns, or worse, if we came off. We compromised by removing one item of kit each and strapped my trousers and Byron's jacket to each of our roll bags. If there was a crash in the cards, then, between us, we might still be able to form one fully functioning body. Unfortunately, the helmets were non-negotiable and continued to generate the worst imaginable rivers of perspiration.

To conclude the torment, the temperature only dropped slightly during the night while the humidity loitered insufferably. Were it not for the army of mosquitoes that descended each evening, we would have opted to sleep under the stars instead of inside the airless tent.

Unbearable Heat and Deafening Thunder

46 Days on the Road | 5,064 Miles on the Clock

A storm to humble all storms had been forecast to follow the heat wave, and, when we passed into South Dakota, an ominous cloud stretched across the horizon. As we drew closer, its proximity to the ground suggested that it might not be the storm we had been nervous of, and an orange tinge and smoky odour soon confirmed that it was coming from a wildfire. Since leaving Anchorage, we had passed thousands of fire-scarred acres but were yet to witness the source of their destruction.

Dense smoke hung in the sky above, as we passed through the immediate aftermath. An eerie red glow fell across the already rust coloured landscape, as the smoke reduced the formidable sun to a small, pink circle. We dismounted the bike at a railroad crossing to watch as a half-mile freight train loomed through the smog and coasted by. After the last carriage disappeared from sight, it was obvious that visibility was impeded on all sides, so we rode away from the scene and passed back into glaring sunshine where breathing became less laboured once again.

The Crazy Horse memorial came into view some miles later when we rode into the Black Hills. In 1948, a sculptor who had worked as an assistant on the Mount Rushmore memorial accepted an invitation from a North American Indian chief to carve a monument that would depict a warrior pointing from his horse to the surrounding land. It was to be the largest mountain carving in the world and would honour their heritage in the region.

Korczak Ziolkowski spent the first five years of the project using just a sledge hammer and a hand steel to drill holes for dynamite that blasted out the rock while he worked and lived alone in the mountains. He dedicated the rest of his life to the venture, and, although he had since died, his wife and children were keeping the commission going. It had taken sixty-four years just to complete the warrior's face and to begin blasting the outline of his horse. The ongoing feat was mind blowing and had us captivated for a couple of hours before we set off in the searing midday heat to visit nearby Mount Rushmore.

Four sculpted presidential heads sat high in the face of a towering granite mountain that was visible long before we reached its base. The symbolic monument had been designed with an initial aim of encouraging tourism in the region and, on that particular day, it was clearly succeeding. In order to avoid the crowds we agreed that a drive-by photo would suffice, but as I leaned from the bike to take a couple of snaps, a gatekeeper came running out and waved at us to stop. Byron quickly twisted the throttle and we burnt rubber to escape the wrath of the attendant before continuing our ride through the Black Hills.

A universal affinity between bikers on the road is marked in passing by a subtle head tilt in Britain and a dropped left leg in France. In North America it was observed with either a peace sign or a tilted open palm, as if to give a passing high-five. For the most part, the gestures were the extent of biking camaraderie on the road, so when a couple pulled up next to us at a red light and invited us for a soda, we followed them to a nearby diner in Rapid City.

Kim and Mark explained that they had spotted the Flying Aga on the highway out of town and had been intrigued by our set up. As we made their acquaintance, they bought us cookies and drinks in the air conditioned diner before they took us downtown to a Native American shop. As a parting gift, they bought us some sweet grass to slake our curiosity about native customs, before wishing us luck and disappearing back into the busy streets of the city. We stayed a little longer in the shop where I set my heart on a beautiful glass-beaded bracelet. Although it was too expensive to justify purchasing, it would go on to play a part in our tale thousands of miles later.

After the unexpected break, we decided to head north to Sturgis, the location of the infamous annual motorcycle rally of the same name. We were a month too early for the actual event, but, as a motorcycle fanatic, Byron was keen to visit the legendary town anyway. For most of the year, the population was estimated at just six thousand residents, however, during the first two weeks of August it swelled to include almost one-million bikers from across the globe.

Despite our premature arrival, the town still offered traces of a party and buzzed with leather waistcoats and guttural live bands. After pitching the tent close to a few requisite Harley-Davidson bikes, we went to soak up the atmosphere in a wooden saloon bar where we washed down buffalo burgers and chicken strips with cool ale.

We set off in the relentless heat the next morning to ride further into the state. After leaving the creek in Cody, we had stumbled upon the small town of Byron in Wyoming and had decided to track down an Isabel to complement the find. Two days after locating it on the map, we spotted the large black letters of my name painted on a white water tower that was shaped like an enormous golf ball resting on an equally huge tee.

The heat was so intense that we didn't dare stop when we reached Isabel's deserted main street. We passed through in desperate search of shade and snapped a few photos from the saddle instead.

The quiet roads and closed shops indicated that another Sunday had come around, and we vowed to call time on the ride at the first sight of trees. The plan left us plodding on for many more miles until we lost another hour when we passed over the Missouri River into Central Time and quickly gave up on the search.

We settled for a site with few trees but a lot of grass and struggled to pitch the tent without regularly racing for shelter in the scraps of shade cast by neighbouring motorhomes.

The discovery of private cabin bathrooms and an air conditioned function room with a kitchen more than made up for the deficiency in foliage. We spent the evening in air conditioned bliss, using a real oven to cook a proper dinner while the 2012 Tour de France played out on cable television. We were joined by a couple who had quit their jobs to cycle around the country for a year. Theirs was a courageous feat, considering the climate and the additional hazard of exploding freight tyres, the remnants of which littered most roads and highways.

That evening, we decided to wait out the rest of the heat wave at a campground with a pool and, at first light, we set off to find the nearest contender. The suspension bottomed out repeatedly on the buckled road into Minnesota, and, at one point, we walked out of a supermarket to find the Flying Aga had toppled over on its side after the centre stand melted through the tarmac of a car park.

The bike prevailed through the obstacles and delivered us in one piece to a campground just outside Minneapolis. It had a pool, powerful showers, and a laundrette to see us through to the other side of the anticipated storm.

Every minute of the following day was spent within meters of the pool, which had also fallen prey to the heat wave. There was simply no escape, but the pool's warm water was still preferable to the sweltering tent and the mosquito plagued shade. Our clothes would be soaked the minute they touched skin, and our appetites disappeared as we turned to a diet of frozen drinks and ice cream.

Two sweltering days melted away at the campground before we heard about the nearby Mall of America. The third day was subsequently spent under the shield of the largest air conditioned complex in North America.

A week earlier, we had painstakingly relieved space on the bike after sending a parcel of luggage home from Cody, but we soon filled it again by investing in new hot weather clothes at the mall. We dragged out the rest of the day in the cinema and restocked on calories at an enormous food hall before risking a return to the campground when dusk fell.

Following an evening spent watching five separate Independence Day firework displays from the vantage of the campground, we decided we could face another day on the bike.

We crossed the breadth of Wisconsin early the next morning before setting up camp in the Upper Peninsula of Michigan. We arrived in Iron Mountain just in time to roast marshmallows with some fellow campers, before the almighty storm, that had been promised, finally let loose.

That night, the sky tore holes in itself while forks of lightning lit up the land as if the sun had risen early. A deluge of water pounded down on the tent, but it stood firm, and, when we ventured outside the next day, we were bone dry.

The air had cooled considerably, and the Flying Aga had received a thorough wash. It turned out that our neighbours in the surrounding RVs and motorhomes had been concerned all night for us, and, before long, we had been adopted as The Kids.

Debbi and Jon, who had shared their marshmallows with us the previous evening, lived in the nearby town and, over the following days, they would pop home and return to share homemade cookies and fruit from their garden with us. Our immediate neighbour, Jarrod, was a keen biker and, after studying some roadmaps with us, he came by one day with a Yooper sticker of Upper Michigan to add to the collection that was advancing across our panniers. A small family moved in on the second day and they invited us over to share a unique combination of brandy and ice cream. To top off the kindness at the aptly named Sunny Breeze Campground, the owners, Carol and Jerry, upgraded us to one of their log cabins on our final night.

There was an enormous, artificial ski jump in Iron Mountain, which we had been told offered a spectacular view across the region, so we stopped on our way out of town to have a look. Debbi and Jon had told us that there were steps leading to the top, and, after parking up, we began to climb them. The wooden slats quickly required the use of hands as well as feet to tackle their sharp incline, and, somewhere close to the top of the sixty-degree slope, we dared to turn around and look down.

We spotted people scaling actual steps that were built beside the natural hill finish of the jump, and it was suddenly clear that the structure we were poised on probably wasn't meant for climbing. Despite the realisation, we had made too much progress to stop, so we continued to the top where the view was as spectacular as we had been told.

A metal lattice platform revealed every detail of the fifty-four-meter drop below, and the stability of the structure quickly came into question. We found some steps leading around the back of the jump and wasted no time in commencing an upright descent. However, our earlier concerns about its stability were soon realised when we reached a section that had caved in and, soon after, discovered that the stairway led to a dead end.

We clambered back to the top platform and resorted to edging our way down the wooden slats, feet first. We dodged the splinters and protruding nails to return to solid ground where a glance back up at the structure brought on a wave of nausea that signalled our sharp getaway from the site.

We traced a route along the northern coast of Lake Michigan on a ride that was dotted with views of the sea-like mass of water and sandy beaches. Hours were then spent riding around in search of a campground until we eventually resorted to bargaining with motel receptionists and succeeded in getting a cheap room in the heart of Sault Ste. Marie. The large town bordered Canada and was home to an impressive lock system that joined Lake Superior to the other Great Lakes via Lake Huron.

With no tent to assemble, we jumped in the shower before heading out to sample one of the town's famous fish suppers. After watching an enormous ship pass through the lock just as the sun began to set, we joined a few fellow bikers for some beers outside their motel room. The surprise discovery that our room had come with air conditioning topped off the final night of our sizzling, second leg through the US.

CANADA

YUKON TERRITORY

NORTHWEST TERRITORIES

NUNAVUT

BRITISH COLUMBIA

ALBERTA

SASKATCHEWAN

MANITOBA

ONTARIO

QUEBEC

NEWFOUNDLAND AND LABRADOR

PRINCE EDWARD ISLAND

NOVA SCOTIA

NEW BRUNSWICK

• • • • FLYING AGA ROUTE

Maple Syrup and
Hospital Bills

Everybody we knew in North America lived in the east, excluding my cousin Lucas who had recently moved to the west coast, and we were rapidly approaching a month when we planned to visit all of them.

While studying in Edinburgh, Byron and his friends had formed an alliance with a group of students from Québec, and a promise to visit Jean-Francois and Boris the Blade in their homeland was about to be honoured.

Jean-Francois had invited us to celebrate his imminent wedding to Genevieve, but we had already committed to being in Connecticut on the date so we had arranged to join them for the end of the city's summer festival instead.

Three more days in the saddle eventually led us to Québec City. We had ridden east across the southern corner of

Ontario and past the north channel of Lake Huron before heading deep into the provincial forests. A stopover in a Canadian Forces base preceded a very close call with a naturist campground and a night in a trailer park before we reached the province of Québec.

We met Jean-Francois with his friend Mathieu in a multi-storey car park where we replaced our bike kit with civilised clothing, before loading all of our unlocked belongings into the back of his car. We left the Flying Aga parked alone in the strange city and spent the evening struggling to recall our school-learnt French with their friends who introduced us to regional beer and Québécois expletives long into the night.

When it finally came to leaving, everybody assured us that the bike was parked in the world's safest city and that it would still be in the car park the next morning. Desperate for sleep, we took their word for it and spent the night in the rare treat of a solid home.

It was the first time on the trip that we didn't have sight of the Flying Aga, and our sleep was racked with the guilt of having abandoned a friend. We knew our trip was nothing without it and, by the morning, we had vowed never to leave it unattended overnight again.

As we tucked into a mouth-watering breakfast of fresh fruit and French toast, complete with lashings of Genevieve's family maple syrup, she and Jean-Francois announced that they were expecting their first child. It was great news from a couple who had offered us our first home comforts following two months of living on the road and sleeping in fields.

With great relief, later that morning we found the bike exactly where we had left it and, after triple checking the wheel locks and the padlocks, we left it again and went off to explore the buzz of Québec in the full throes of its festival. As well as the language, the architecture and resolute ways of the city's population were reminiscent of its European heritage.

Jean-Francois had secured us tickets for the festival finale on the Plains of Abraham where we joined the masses in an inevitable festival scrum. We met up with more friends at the site, including Berube, who went on to entertain the crowds by fitting things into his mouth that weren't designed for the purpose, including beer cans and his own fist.

The next morning, we were introduced to a fine Québécois breakfast eatery where more fresh fruit was served up with waffles, pancakes, and maple syrup before we bid farewell to Jean-Francois, Genevieve, Mathieu, and Boris the Blade with sincere gratitude for showing us a terrific time.

We didn't get too far out of the city before we spotted a sign for a campground and quickly elected on an early finish. We set up camp between the trees on a hill in front of a huge stagnant lake where other campers were spending the weekend racing quad bikes.

Our plan to move on early the next morning didn't quite pan out after chronic chest pains left me in agony during the night. In a sleep-deprived panic, I woke Byron up to see if he could find a doctor. He raced to a nearby village shop where his attempts to be understood instigated a call for an ambulance. The pain continued to tighten around my chest, and, when the ambulance turned up, an agonising move onto a stretcher sent me into convulsions of retching. It was only when they ended that, I realised the strain had relieved the crushing sensation in my chest.

Exhausted, but suddenly liberated, the forty-minute drive to hospital didn't seem quite so necessary, although anxiety that we were about to find out something serious kept me quiet.

A doctor began an extensive check-up, and, together with the ambulance ride, I had soon racked up a $2,000 bill. While we waited for the test results, Byron contacted our insurance company, who agreed to foot the charges.

Relief that we were financially covered was soon matched by the all clear in the test results that showed nothing unusual apart from an apparently abnormal backlog in my digestive system. Grateful that it was nothing serious, we descended on the hospital canteen where Byron proceeded to eat two lunches to make up for a missed breakfast.

It was pouring with rain outside, and we were both woefully underdressed, but, once the hospital accountant received the guarantee of payment, she soon helped us source a taxi that would take us the expensive sixty miles back to the campground. The rest of our final day in Canada was spent in the tent, sheltering from the rain and sleeping off the surreal and panic-stricken events of the morning, hoping the first hospital visit of the trip would also be the last.

CITY BREAKS AND
HOME COOKING

64 DAYS ON THE ROAD | 8,105 MILES ON THE CLOCK

We crossed back into the US the next morning and stopped for lunch in the sun-soaked town of Rangeley, in Maine, where a sign declared that we were exactly 3,107 miles from the (actual) North Pole and the Equator. It didn't seem too far, but our less than direct route meant we wouldn't actually cross the Equator for another 170 days and almost 14,000 miles later.

Three more days saw us meander along winding mountain roads by day and sleep in the dense green forests of New England by night, until a cloak of torrential rain welcomed us to Connecticut.

We sought shelter and stopped for lunch in a fast food restaurant where a news channel was giving minute by minute publicity to the perpetrator of a massacre that had taken place in a Colorado cinema. The rain continued to fall when we returned to the road, and, less than five miles before our next stop, the bike cut out.

We free-wheeled into a restaurant car park and, as the rain soaked us to the skin, we stripped off the luggage, dug out the tools, and had a look inside. With cold feet, soggy gloves, and rain trickling down our necks, Byron discovered that the power cable leading to the battery had worn out and was broken.

The Flying Aga had probably been anticipating retirement long before we hauled it thousands of miles away from home to work long hours in a daily grind that were evidently wearing it down. After cable taping the connection back together, we reached the house of my aunt and uncle, Rita and Rolf, just as it conked out again.

Rolf had always been something of a legend to us as tales of his exploits made it across the Atlantic, so when we learnt that he was planning to celebrate his eightieth birthday by jumping out of an aeroplane, we were keen to be there.

We left the bike to rest on their drive and, after drying out and catching up on family news, we shared a lift the next morning with my cousin, Lucas, and Rolf's daughter, Kirsten. Tales of their childhood escapades that were far more interesting than anything we ever got told about while growing up entertained on the journey to the jump site.

An octogenarian undertaking his first skydive hadn't just attracted family to the airfield that morning. A local Fox News crew had been sent down to report on the occasion, too. While Rolf got kitted out, other novices and even regular jumpers lined up to have their photo taken with him. The coverage aired on the news later that evening and backed up the earlier allusion that a man of note had skydived that afternoon.

During the celebrations, Lucas had been experiencing chest pains that sounded similar to those that had led to my Canadian ambulance ride. We had suggested that a few antacids might help, however, the next morning we woke to find that he had taken himself to hospital and been diagnosed with a collapsed lung. Luckily, he hadn't waited to find this out after boarding a flight back to the west coast, which could have proved fatal, but, less fortuitously, he caught an infection and was hospitalised for over two weeks.

By the time we reached Rita and Rolf's, we had clocked up 8,000 miles on the road, and the Flying Aga was in need of a second service. Aside from a few minor ignition and cable problems, it had been running like a dream. However, during the service, a close inspection of the drained oils from the final drive and drive shaft revealed the presence of tiny metal splinters that were a sign of impending trouble.

Byron posted a message on an online motorcycle forum to find out the possible cause, and we were soon inundated with advice and offers of spare parts from the virtual world. The overwhelming response eventually led us to a specialist mechanic in Chicago. Unfortunately, though, he was about to have surgery but passed us on to another expert in Pennsylvania, who agreed to see us the following week.

In the meantime, we explored the wild and wooded region where Rita and Rolf lived, filling the week with visits to Lucas in hospital and some Long Island Sound outings in *R&R*, Rita and Rolf's trusty boat. We savoured the bliss of air conditioning and home cooked meals while the London Olympics played out on television. In another bid to create more space on the bike, we swapped our bulky sleeping bags for two much lighter blankets, before combing through the rest of our luggage in search of items that could be offloaded.

We were so close to New York that we booked a cheap deal online and set off towards the Big Apple for a couple of days. After weaving a route through an army of yellow taxis, passing hipsters, and hardened city dwellers, alike, we soon arrived in the heart of Manhattan. Unable to afford the hotel's secure parking fee, we ignored the scepticism of a porter who repeatedly declared that we would be crazy to leave a BMW parked on a New York street. Hoping to prove him wrong, we secured locks on both wheels before entrusting the twenty-four-hour manned doorway to deter any potential thieves.

The city was blistering hot the next morning, but we still covered a great deal of ground on foot. We trekked through Central Park before roaming the central grid of towering city blocks, venturing down the legendary Fifth Avenue, into Grand Central Station, across Times Square, past Madison Square Garden, and stopping everywhere in between.

The next day, we took a boat to Liberty Island before visiting the recently completed 9/11 memorial reflecting pools.

A huge black cloud had ominously crept across the skyline before a newsworthy, power-cutting storm struck later that evening. The cloud had buckled into the heaviest and most instantaneous downpour we had ever been caught in. Cracks of thunder bellowed through the city streets while spectacular forks of lightning zig-zagged across the dark sky throughout a long, wet walk back to the hotel.

Thankfully, the temperature dropped a few degrees, and the sun returned the next morning. The Flying Aga had survived its two nights on the mean streets, and, after checking out of the hotel, we took it for a ride through the city centre. After crossing the iconic Brooklyn Bridge, the rain set in again, and we made our way back to the suburbs of Connecticut.

The next day we set off again and rode north to Hammonasset State Park where we camped beside a potentially beautiful beach that we mostly hid from while the rain continued its vendetta against us.

The sky cleared the next day, and we continued north to Boston where my friend Becky lived with her boyfriend Rich. We knew that the metal, which Byron had found in the final drive and drive shaft oils, might stick a spanner in the works at any moment, but we were eager not to waste our time on the east coast.

We spent a perfect sunny weekend in the company of Becky and Rich, following the Freedom Trail, climbing the Bunker Hill Monument, and spotting the locations of an unexpected number of Boston-based films. We sampled our first frozen yoghurt and visited Becky's parents and their cat that apparently had just one neuron. We stumbled upon a late night, Shakespearean production on Boston Common and ventured through a lively Quincy Market before finally splashing out on a taste of East Coast lobster.

On Sunday morning, we woke to an excited call from our friend, Avy, back in London, who was caught up in Murray mania. Despite the time zones, we all watched in sync as the Scot smashed his way to Olympic gold.

We drove to the coast later that afternoon where an enormously long beach was swathed in a mass of sand-encrusted bodies and umbrellas. At an entry fee of $25 per car, whoever managed the gate was making a killing. Despite circulating rumours of a seal sighting and subsequent tales of nearby sharks, we braved our first dip in the Atlantic Ocean before soaking up the sun that had taunted us in our heavy bike kit for weeks.

Hours passed as we wallowed in the surf, but the relaxing afternoon came to an abrupt end when a strong wind began to whip up the sand. A distant black cloud closed in fast and soon propelled the thousands of sunbathers into a mad dash for the car park where we arrived seconds too late and were drenched in a flash.

In typical Sunday-evening-before-work style, we watched films and ate junk food in the comfort of Becky and Rich's apartment and, when they went to work the next morning, we made our way back to Rita and Rolf's for the final time.

After spending almost a month enjoying the company of friends and family, that evening marked the end of the first third of our entire trip.

HILLBILLIES AND
MOTORCYCLE CHROME

84 DAYS ON THE ROAD | 8,905 MILES ON THE CLOCK

With evidence of a potentially major fault inside the Flying Aga, we knew that persisting any further wasn't worth the probable future hassle. Although it would cost us more than we could spare, we were confident that checking out the problem as soon as possible would pay off in the long run. Surplus thirty-year-old parts would not come easy, and tow trucks or hospital bills would not come cheap, so a thorough examination was necessary if the bike and our budget were going to last to the end of the road.

After bidding a fond farewell to Rita and Rolf for the last time, we rode to Pennsylvania in search of the Rubber Chicken Racing Garage. Tom greeted us at his garage door, and, following a customary ribbing about the quantity of luggage we were carrying, including the recent addition of a double sheepskin seat cover that had been sent from Alaska, we stripped the bike of its excess load.

He got to work quickly and concluded that the drive shaft was faulty and that the cogs on the final drive were becoming misaligned.

Not only was the Flying Aga an old bike, but it was also European, and parts in the US were only traded among fellow enthusiasts or sold for much more than we were accustomed to paying. However, Tom was a renowned BMW restorer, and it soon became clear that the referral to him had been a greater stroke of luck than we had first realised.

He sourced a replacement drive shaft from a fellow rider, and, as the hours unravelled back in his workshop, it became clear that the job was going to run into the following day. The nearest campground was fifteen miles away, and our only form of transport was out of action on an operating table. As we considered our options, Tom and his wife, Paula, invited us to stay the night there, and we were chuffed to enjoy an evening of good food, margaritas, and more live London Olympic coverage.

The final touches to the job were made the next morning, and our worries were considerably reduced by knowing that the Flying Aga had a replaced drive shaft, fresh bearings, and re-shimmed cogs. Although Tom had also noticed that the drive splines in the final drive were wearing thin, he thought they would last to the end of our journey but warned us that they would need changing as soon as we returned home.

We were hugely appreciative for their help and hospitality and bid Tom, Paula, and the Rubber Chicken Racing Garage farewell before embarking on a ride back across the vast country.

A narrow road led us along a scenic route that was dotted with historic stone houses and pastoral churches that would not have been out of place in a rural English village. We ended the day in a campground on a small mountain where towering thick trees blocked any sunshine from hitting the mossy floor. Rain trapped us at the site the next day where a damp fog hung in the air and nourished a rainbow of toadstools.

We ploughed on through Pennsylvania the next day and pulled into a mountain overlook for a customary picnic lunch. As we sat hacking into bread with a pocket knife, a couple of bikes with tasselled leather saddlebags and polished chrome roared up beside us. Their riders were sporting leather waistcoats and cotton bandannas around helmet-less heads and they climbed off to welcome us to their self-proclaimed hillbilly country before explaining, with a snigger that suggested they knew more than we did, that the land of the rednecks would begin once we reached Texas. They soon roared off again, just as the thunder of another bike rumbled towards us.

A man wearing slightly less leather but cultivating a moustache to be contended with climbed off his bike with some difficulty. He pulled out a bottle of beer from his saddlebag and made his way over to us. It didn't take long for him to introduce us to The Kenasaki, an ingenious fusion of his name Ken and the Kawasaki make of his motorcycle. He had the name immortalised on the frame with a custom paintjob and, having failed to mask our growing fascination, he quickly settled onto centre stage.

Cracking open another bottle of beer, he recounted the colourful story of his wayward family before explaining that he once knew a guy from The Kingdom, as he called the UK. He couldn't remember his name, though, so, instead, described him to us with the possibility that the vague description might ring a bell. It was a long shot but made a pleasant change from people assuming that we were on first names terms with the Queen or the current national favourite, Kate Middleton. Eventually, we dragged ourselves away and left Ken to finish off his twelve-pack alone while we resumed our westerly bearing through the state.

A swell in roadside banners declaring that Mitt Romney was good and Barack Obama was bad accompanied our progress through Pennsylvania. Huge, isolated gun stores and anti-abortion billboards also popped up at random along the highways, and, no matter which way we turned, proclamations that "Jesus is the way" were emblazoned on car bumper stickers or sewn into the leather jackets of bikers.

Indications that Amish communities lived in the state also began to materialise in the form of horse and carts on the road that were ridden by men dressed in black and women dressed in plain dresses, none of whom would catch our eye or return a polite wave.

We camped on the banks of the Alleghany River that night and, the next morning, we visited the remains of what had once been the tallest railway trestle bridge in the world. Unfortunately, a fearsome tornado had blown half of the structure away during its restoration in 2003, but it was still an impressive feat of early engineering. After the brief stop, we continued our course and crossed into Ohio later that day.

We camped in a state park on the banks of Lake Erie and followed its shoreline into Indiana the following day. At some point, we passed a sign for the town of Hicksville, which summarised the best of what we had seen in the state.

As the day drew to a close, we struggled to find a place to camp, so resorted to finding a motel. The first few that we came across displayed signs declaring that soliciting would not be tolerated although, conflictingly, none of them offered rooms for a full night, so we kept searching.

We followed directions down a gravel track to another motel where it was immediately obvious that we wouldn't want to stay, even if they did have space. For some unknown reason, though, we followed through with the charade of asking for a room anyway.

A porch overflowed with the bodies of a few hefty men and a couple of similar sized women, all equally worse for wear. They turned in unison as we pulled up and stared vacantly when we did our best to feign interest in staying there. The leader eventually clambered over a collection of children that were wandering around barefoot in grubby nappies, and he wasted no time in telling us that they had no space before we wasted no time in thanking him and riding out of there. On the way to the exit, we passed some guys who were too wasted to give us a second glance while they waited patiently outside the doors of a couple of the rooms.

We did finally check into a motel that was free of dodgy characters but was lacking in hygiene. Everything, including the exterior door handle, was sticky. The next morning, we hightailed away from the depressing area and were close to leaving the state when we stopped to fill up with petrol.

A member of a Legion Riders chapter approached us at the pump and asked if we would like to join him in a flag line. A local wounded serviceman was being flown home that day from Afghanistan, and all available bikers in the region were meeting at the airport to provide a convoy for him. The gesture embodied a national resolve to prevent a repeat of the terrible reception that returning Vietnam War veterans had endured. It encompassed a resulting, admirable gratitude that the entire country bestowed on its service people at any given opportunity. The guy assured us that we would not be gate-crashing, so we took up his offer and followed him to the meeting point.

We joined just six other bikers, none of whom were quite as warm as the guy who had invited us. Our overloaded, muddy, 33-year old BMW didn't exactly harmonise with their well-polished chrome, and our heavy kit and helmets were probably less than a complementary addition, too. We tried to ignore the overpowering second thoughts about taking part and stuck with it, hiding at the rear of their small convoy, which was adorned with national and legion flags.

Other members of different chapters joined the ride out along the highway, and positions in the formation were reorganised to accommodate their standing. By the time we reached the airport, we were in the middle of about 250 other bikes. One of the organisers gathered the overwhelming turn-out for a meeting outside the arrivals hall where he sincerely thanked everyone for turning up, before explaining that the flight we were waiting for was delayed by at least three hours.

As we hung around waiting, the other riders gradually warmed up, and we made a few friends but, when news filtered through that the flight had been delayed even further, we realised that if we stayed we wouldn't make any progress at all that day.

We gave our apologies to the organisers and thanked the original guy for inviting us before setting off again, sorry to miss the grand finale of the serviceman's ride of honour but grateful to have played a small part in the build up.

We crossed back into Central Time in Illinois and gained our first hour back from the four we had lost on the ride to the East Coast. We traced the southern tip of Lake Michigan into Wisconsin where we found a rural retreat in Mukwonago to base ourselves and celebrate Byron's imminent birthday.

While more storms wreaked havoc overhead, we took a break from hand washing clothes and did some laundry before stocking up on groceries and carrying out repairs to the tent. The front tyre of the bike was still going strong, but the rear tyre had taken a hammering with the mileage and heavy weight, so we sourced a garage that ordered us a new one. While we waited for the replacement to arrive, we set off for Milwaukee to visit the Harley-Davidson Museum and mark Byron's 31st year.

After exploring the museum and chancing upon its storage room where hundreds of immaculate bikes sat alluringly untouched, we ate a hearty meal in its restaurant before going to collect the first new rear tyre of the trip. The celebration ended in a nearby cinema and was toasted with some local ale and a chocolate brownie before we returned to our collapsible home, which, at that moment, was pitched on the edge of yet another remote and deserted field.

MAN CUPCAKES AND MARINES

96 DAYS ON THE ROAD | 10,627 MILES ON THE CLOCK

Following the short break, we returned to the highway and made our way to Chicago in search of the starting point to historic Route 66.

The so-called Mother Road had been established in the 1920s and crossed the breadth of the country, serving as the migration passage from the industrialised east to the sunlit west. However, as time had passed, traffic on the road increased and necessary improvements led to its eventual replacement by an interstate highway in the 1980s. Use of the original route quickly declined, and the surface was left to crack and erode while trade to its towns and communities diminished. Despite the dire odds, though, its historic status and fixture in popular culture had kept it alive as the symbolic path to new beginnings and untold adventures.

Although it was in poor condition, and even incomplete through some of its eight host states, we were eager to ride the legendary route and set about finding the starting monument.

Our sizeable roadmap of the country was rendered useless when navigating built-up areas, and we had taken to preloading street maps on the iPad whenever necessary. It had been three weeks since we had last needed to do so, though, and we had forgotten all about the measure for Chicago.

We assumed that a monument would be easy to track down and had overlooked the fact that a once hopeful exit from the city might not be such a prominently marked feature.

On one of many stops spent scouring the roadmap in the hope of finding a clue, a bike passed us, then looped around and rode over to our spot in an empty car park. Scott was a member of a Chicago BMW riders club and had soon pointed us in the right direction, before resuming his Sunday ride.

The long search eventually led to an unassuming signpost that was tucked away down a side street. Following the expectant build up, the modest marker to the beginning of the historic passage went some way to typify our disappointment with the route itself.

We wound our way out of Chicago and through Illinois, making little progress after the hours spent riding around the city. We reached Missouri the next day and, after a long slog in the saddle, we struggled to find a place to sleep, after being greeted at a few campgrounds with signs declaring that tents were not welcome.

Eventually, we stumbled on a site that was home to a few old guys who were there to fish and showed little concern if we stayed or not. We pitched the tent before discovering that there was no potable water in the vicinity, and, after asking a few of the onsite residents where we could find some, a young lad quickly struck up a conversation about the Flying Aga.

When he heard our accents, he swiftly changed topic to tell us about the English bare knuckle boxers he had been watching videos of online and asked if we knew any of them. We quickly gauged that a wrong word could turn the mood after he went on to explain that his family were descendants of travellers from Britain, possibly, he thought, from a place called Romania. When we eventually got around to asking where we could find water, he disappeared and returned with a few bottles from his mum.

The conversation continued, and we were soon joined by a smaller kid who had appeared from nowhere. He wasted no time in clearing up the story behind his bandaged arm, explaining that he had been shot at close range with a ball bearing [BB] gun. He was proud to assure us that he had taken his revenge on the perpetrator after drawing two pistols and, illustrated with bent knees, shooting him in the "man cupcakes," cowboy style.

We left early the next morning and didn't see the modern day Tom Sawyer or Huckleberry Finn again. After a visit to

Saint Louis and a pause beside the Mississippi River under the steel Gateway Arch, we hit the road, desperate for the relief of fast moving air.

Despite the intermittent storms and rain clouds that had made their appearance during the month, the solid heat of the summer had continued to rise with a vengeance. We were still in Missouri when we spotted a motel with a pool and wasted no time checking in, before diving into the blissfully cool water.

A breakfast of oats, cooked on the road outside our room, set us up for a long day of riding. We made our way across the southeast corner of Kansas, before taking a descent into Oklahoma.

Having followed the original route with precision through each small town and across every crack and pothole, we were growing tired of the slow progress and the lack of captivating landscape. Although we were riding through states where petrol was at its cheapest, the fluctuation in speed was counteracting what should have been a cheap stretch and, by the fourth day, we began to understand the fateful demise of the once prosperous route towns.

By the fifth day, we were skipping turnings and sticking to bypass roads as the heat beat down on us. The terrain paled in comparison to the landscapes we had encountered during the previous three months, and the symbolic significance of the historic route was the only thing that kept us following it.

After labouring through Oklahoma, where the notorious tornadoes of the region remained under wraps, we soon entered the northern panhandle of Texas and enjoyed a rise in wind power that offered some relief from the stifling heat. We were fed up, though, and stopped at the first campground with a pool, where we elected to spend the next day basking in the sun, rather than baking in it.

The monotony of the ride had led to a fair amount of soul searching during the long and tedious hours and culminated that evening in what we thought had been a quiet, theological reflection.

When we woke up the next morning, a young family that had been camping next us, although at some distance, was driving out of the campground when the car stopped and the father ran back to our pitch. After some token small talk, he wished us luck before handing over a well-worn book, explaining that we might like to read it. Grateful for any new reading material, we waved goodbye to the car as it drove out of sight, before taking a closer look at the book.

It turned out he had left us with a well-thumbed copy of the New Testament, and we realised that we had arrived firmly inside the Bible Belt, where most people took their religion without reflection and were wary of those who did.

Byron spent a large portion of that day scrubbing away the dust and grime from every nook and cranny on the Flying Aga, while I made more urgent repairs to the tent. Late in the afternoon, we retired to the pool to work on what turned out to be painfully overdone suntans.

While we frazzled in the heat, a lone biker pitched his tent nearby, before introducing himself. Bryce had not long left the US Marines and was blowing off some steam that summer by travelling the country on his Harley-Davidson. He was the first biker that we had met during three months on the road who was our age, and it was quickly established that he and Byron shared a penchant for motorcycles and all things intrepid.

After settling in for the evening with some beers and camp-cooked spaghetti, we noticed that another lone biker had checked into a cabin just across from us. Derek turned out to be on the same countrywide Harley-Davidson trip and, by coincidence, was also a veteran Marine. Under a starlit Texan sky, a small motorcycle touring jamboree was soon in full swing, complete with head torches, cool beers, stacks of roadmaps, and two tobacco dipping and spitting Marines.

It was Derek's birthday the next morning, but he was heading east, back home to Boston. We were continuing west, so, after promising to send him a postcard, we parted ways. Bryce was heading in our direction and, despite warning him of the Flying Aga's speed capacity, he rode with us to New Mexico.

We stopped to leave our mark in the desert where ten Cadillac cars had been semi-buried at a slight angle in a straight line for reasons that were lost on us. However, the site did appear to have an immediate purpose of being graffiti'd by strangers, so we obliged with a discarded spray can.

According to Bryce's speedometer, we had soon cut his average ninety miles-per-hour speed to a steady sixty miles-per-hour. It confirmed a long held suspicion that our own speedometer, which had been pointing to an optimistic seventy miles-per-hour, had been exaggerating its readings. Luckily, Bryce also followed the school of thought to follow the tides on his trip and graciously plodded along beside us, regardless. After professing to enjoy the benefits of the fuel-efficient speed and the rare opportunity to take in the scenery, we were convinced that we had run into the best-humoured biker in the land.

We gained another hour after crossing back into Mountain Time in New Mexico, and Bryce treated us to our first skillet lunch in a twenty-four-hour roadside diner. He was on his way to stay with friends in the state, and, while we tucked into the sizzling feast, his friend, Jeff, rode out on his BMW R1200GS to meet him at the restaurant.

We prolonged the return back into the heat of the day by discussing all things motorcycle for as long as possible in the comfort of air conditioning. When a return to the road eventually became unavoidable, Jeff invited us to stay the night at his home with Bryce. Having expected to say goodbye to the guys after the meal, we were taken aback and accepted with much gratitude.

Like Brandon and Stephanie in Alaska, and Tom and Paula in Pennsylvania, Jeff and his girlfriend, Sonia, bestowed incredible trust, not to mention kindness, by inviting two road-grimy, travelling strangers into their home. They were not the last new-found friends to do so, either, and we owed a great deal to the universal biking camaraderie, as well as to the Flying Aga itself. We couldn't imagine that any other method of travel would have initiated so many unexpected experiences and friendships.

Having already slowed Bryce down on the way there, we didn't want to do the same to Jeff, as well, so we took his address and arranged to meet up a couple hours later. On our way through the state, we stopped for petrol and encountered the second motorcycle preacher of the trip.

A long-haired, larger than life biker approached us and quickly got around to asking if we had Jesus in our hearts. For the second time on the trip, we found ourselves searching for an answer that didn't come quick enough, and he went on to bless the Flying Aga, regardless. The same act that had struck us as bizarre fourteen weeks earlier, now seemed to encapsulate a significant part of US culture, that we had so mistakenly assumed would be similar to that of home.

We made our way into Albuquerque, where the traditional pueblo architecture and cactus strewn hills raised our excitement for the fast approaching next leg into Mexico and Central America. After arriving at Jeff and Sonia's house, we were thrilled to be given a bed for the night, and, after getting acquainted with their dog Mathews, they took us into town to sample a New Mexican meal and some strong, locally brewed ale.

The chance meeting with Bryce, Jeff, and Sonia had come out of nowhere and fully renewed our faith in an adventure that had begun to lose its spark since Chicago. The three of them unanimously affirmed our decision to break away from historic Route 66 and recommended a course that would encompass some of the country's most fascinating wonders of the natural world.

We all rode out in convoy the next morning, and, with a sincere hope to meet them again one day, we parted ways, as Byron and I left the historic route behind and headed into Colorado.

DUSTY ROADS AND SIN CITY

103 Days on the Road | 11,985 Miles on the Clock

A heavy presence of motorcycles indicated that another Sunday had rolled around as we rode north out of New Mexico. Dusty boulders and scrubland paved the route towards Colorado, where we weaved our way into green mountains and stopped to visit the Mesa Verde National Park.

Until the previous evening, we had been unaware of its existence but were soon exploring some of the most incredible, ancient cliff dwellings. Extraordinary family abodes and entire cities had been built inside cliffs and beneath mountain outcroppings by the ancestral Pueblo people who were thought to have lived there over seven hundred years earlier.

We joined a tour beneath the overhang of one cliff, where we scaled a vertical, thirty-foot ladder, which took us to a tiny gap between two colossal rocks. The narrow passage led into an excavated forty-room house where, despite its

109

partial reconstruction, original 700-year old wooden beams and plaster were still in place inside. Conserved corridors, balconies, fire pits, and solstice holes offered a staggeringly intact impression of an ancient life in the hills.

The tiniest of tunnels led to the exit of the dwelling, where, assured by the guide that nobody had ever fallen over the edge, we climbed back up the vertical cliff using original foot holes and some strategically placed chains.

The onward journey to Monument Valley should not have taken long, but we missed a turning in the middle of the desert and found ourselves on the wrong road in the wrong state. As we sizzled inside our riding gear, nothing but sand and rocks surrounded us on a perilously straight stretch of road. Despite the severe deficiency in landmarks, we somehow worked out where we were on the map and set off back towards the Four Corners, where the states of Colorado, Utah, New Mexico, and Arizona meet.

Not for the first time on the journey, we had been plunged into a sense of our own irrelevance when the desolate landscape had opened up. The entire region was incomparable to anything we had anticipated and its arid expanse was magnified all the more following the monotony of the previous week.

Each of the four states was made up of infinite miles of scrub brush that were occasionally broken by windblown rock formations that rose up from the flat land like giant totem poles and crumbling fortresses.

We looped the desert roads, passing bullet riddled signposts and bundles of tumbleweed, while whirlwinds of dust spiralled upwards in the distance until, eventually, the towering buttes of Monument Valley flickered through the heat haze on the horizon.

It was immediately apparent that shade was in short supply at the only campground in the valley, and we found the best of it under the gnarled branches of a solitary juniper tree. It was late in the afternoon, and, after pitching the tent, we followed the resident camp dog to explore the soaring red boulders of some nearby cliffs.

We reached the top of one narrow precipice just in time to witness a breathtaking sunset, which cast a mesmeric, rusty glow over the surrounding towers and flat-topped buttes.

The temperature fell with the setting sun, and we slept comfortably for the first time in weeks. We woke up early to watch an equally spectacular sunrise, before the refreshing cool air was replaced by another stifling hot morning.

After leaving the Navajo tribal valley, we set off towards the Grand Canyon. As the day broke into mid-morning, gusts of dust and sand blew across the Arizona desert, while grey clouds closed in overhead and a bolt of lightning forked across the road in front of us. A deluge quickly followed, and nerve racking thunder joined the lightshow.

Hailstones mixed with the rainfall, and Byron fought against low visibility and fast-flooding roads to get us to the Grand Canyon campground in one piece. While the storm raged on, we raced to the shelter of the reception canopy just as the loudest crack of thunder we had ever heard ripped through the sky. The park ranger assured us that the storm was a typical daily occurrence during monsoon season, exposing our naïve assumption that the summer months in a desert would mostly be hot and dry.

For the first time on the trip we pitched the tent in driving rain and sheltered inside it for another hour until, almost as fast as it had descended, the storm disappeared.

Having seen photographs and video footage of the site, we thought we knew what to expect at the Grand Canyon. Although the throng of tourists climbing out of buses and clamouring at the viewing fences went some way to diminish the atmosphere, we couldn't contain our awe when we peered out across the astonishing stretch of land. All of our assumptions became utterly redundant, and an overwhelming desire to absorb the exquisite scene sent us in search of a quiet spot.

As we wandered along the edge of the vast gorge, a couple of lads emerged from the undergrowth revealing a rocky path that had evaded the park fencing. We edged along the rugged track and scrambled down to a cliff-top plateau where we were transported to both peaceful seclusion and terrifying exposure.

The most extraordinary and uninhibited view glowed under the warm hue of sunset, and we sat in stillness for some time, spellbound by the scene. After a while, though, our dubious position on the protruding pinnacle eventually sank in, and a sudden awareness of the mile long drop that fell from three of the four sides of the table broke the magic.

Just as we began to peel ourselves away, a couple of professional photographers, carrying tripods and bulky equipment, came rushing down onto the ledge.

They walked fearlessly to the very edge of the overhang, where a visible lack of anything supporting it underneath had kept us at a distance. One of them stumbled as they rushed to set up tripods and fix lenses to cameras, and my heart leapt to my throat. All my fears of deathly drops looked certain to materialise, but, by an absolute fluke, he somehow regained his footing and, without even a second glance down, continued to snap away at the scene. In spite of his nerve, we backtracked along the trail without looking back until we reached stable ground.

A clear sky sent the temperature plummeting that night, and sleep came in fits and starts as the gamble of trading our sleeping bags for blankets back in Connecticut finally went against us. The only comfort that made the cold night tolerable was the prospect of checking into a Las Vegas suite the next day.

We were awake early in our frosty nest and set off before anyone else had stirred in the campground. As the day broke and we made our way through more fantastic desert terrain, we hit a wall of heat that far surpassed any temperature we had experienced to that point.

The landscape remained consistently spectacular, and the number of rocky cliffs increased as we climbed towards the Hoover Dam. We were on the verge of collapse when we arrived at its visitor centre and sat comatose in the car park, waiting for our body temperature to drop so that we could seek out the nearest refuge. The heavy air never did yield, but we eventually found the will to move and came across a café, where a fully functioning air conditioning unit left us euphoric.

After a full recovery, we edged our way towards the café exit and emerged back into the outside world, where the temperature was still overpowering. The engineering feat of the dam was even more exceptional after experiencing the debilitating heat that would have accompanied part of the five years it had taken to build. Standing at over two hundred meters [656 feet] tall, it was the largest mass of concrete we had ever seen, but, no matter where we viewed it from, all I could marvel at was how the workforce had resisted diving into the massive river below. We didn't last long at the site and were soon forcing our damp helmets back on for the ride into Nevada.

A growing preference for rural areas over cities left us without many expectations for liking Las Vegas, so we had only made a last minute reservation for two nights. Byron guarded the bike outside the hotel, while I went and joined an enormous check-in queue that was heavily biased towards a large group of young, well-groomed individuals. Taking in the latest change of surroundings, I noticed the luggage tag on one of the group's cases and was taken aback by an address that was very close to the flat we had left behind in London.

It turned out that the young gang were *X-Factor* contestants, and a girl checking them in was in the middle of making it very clear to the receptionist that nothing was to be charged to their rooms. She then led the eager bunch into the depths of the casino like a teacher on a school trip, confirming every suspicion that rock and roll was suffering following the birth of the televised talent show.

After failing to secure a deposit on our room with no less than four bank cards, we eventually got the key and discovered that valets were unable to ride motorcycles into their parking lot. Instead, they pointed us in the direction of a free, but unguarded, multi-storey car park, where we manoeuvred into a spot that lined up with a couple of surveillance cameras. While we deliberated over what luggage we could get away with leaving on the bike, a guy approached the highly polished Harley-Davidson that we had parked next to.

As if on cue, he told us that the panniers on his bike had been stolen the night before, and not a single person working in the hotel had been interested. The surveillance cameras had apparently shown nothing of the theft, and everything he had left in them was long gone.

Before he had turned up, we had just agreed to leave most of our belongings locked in our own panniers and top box but, after hearing of his misfortune, we knew it would be foolish not to pay heed to his ill luck. So a lock was secured to each wheel before we picked up our camping gear, the top box filled with our kitchen, the enormous sheepskin seat cover, two helmets, two jackets, two roll bags of clothes, and a black rucksack that was bursting at the seams with groceries, maps, and waterproofs. We lugged the entire lot past the hotel's busy restaurants, via its shops, and through its bustling casino in one single, awkward and uncomfortable walk.

The troubles of the hot and cumbersome day melted away as we walked into the suite to find everything we had dreamed of during the previous cold night. With floor to ceiling glass windows overlooking the city, an enormous king-size bed, a vast bathroom, fresh cotton towels, a three-piece suite, and air conditioning, it was hard to envisage leaving the room at all over the next two days. Our extensive luggage made no impression on its size, and we settled down to soak up the rare luxury.

After trying to use the percolator and turn on the television, it soon became clear that the hotel had other ideas about guests staying in their rooms for too long. There was a hefty charge to use everything that even the cheapest of motels threw in for free, so, after maximising the big bath and fresh towels, we ventured out into the hotel's casino.

The prospect of a comfy room and nothing to get up for in the morning soon turned a single drink at the bar into shots of tequila and free-poured cocktails. We had barely drunk alcohol since leaving the east coast and it quickly went straight to our heat-addled heads. At some point, we snuck away to the car park to check that the Flying Aga remained untouched, before returning to drink away more of our budget.

A few essential chores sent us into downtown Las Vegas the next day with very heavy heads. We changed the bike engine oil in a garage car park and purchased an increasingly vital Camelback hydration system to drink from when we were riding. By the time we were done, we caught the final hours of daylight beside the hotel pool, before hitting the infamous Las Vegas strip.

After successfully bypassing the bartender from the previous night, we made our way out to explore one enormous, iconic casino after another. We roamed the floors and soaked up the atmosphere as people won and lost on the tables and waited expectantly at the slot machines.

The streets were buzzing, and families were out en masse, and, aside from the touts who choked up the pavements to distribute cards offering anyone the company of a woman within twenty minutes, the place wasn't as overtly sleazy as we had expected.

We walked the strip until our feet could take no more and, after another quick check on the Flying Aga, we lost the rest of our spare change on some slot machines, before heading to bed.

Just before the doors closed on the lift up to our room, a weary looking woman jumped in and was followed by three men who had all seen better days. She asked them what floor their room was on, pressed the button, and, on arrival, followed them to their door, looking less than thrilled. Although the city had won us over, signs of its shady underbelly were everywhere.

The next morning we milked the comfort of the room for as long as possible, before facing the task of lugging our worldly belongings back through the hotel shops, restaurants, and casino into the sweltering car park. By the time we had packed everything back onto the bike, which had survived another night alone, it was past midday, and the temperature had surpassed forty degrees [104 F].

We headed deeper into Nevada through crushing desert heat, skimming Death Valley on the left and Area 51 on the right. Formidable winds buffeted us across the road, and we both struggled to lean against the force and remain upright, while Byron fought to keep us on a straight course.

As well as gambling, prostitution was legal in licensed establishments in the state, and a rich variety of so-called cat houses lined the highway with the same regularity as the bullet-riddled desert signposts. Some were concealed discreetly behind petrol stations, whilst billboards with the word *Brothel* written above a massive arrow that not even a cartoonist could simplify, directed traffic towards remote desert ranches.

In a wind ravaged, sweaty, and exhausted state we eventually called it a day at a small motel in Tonopah, where we spent a final night in the desert, before the hills of California beckoned the next day.

Coastal Ride and Golden Teeth

110 Days on the Road | 13,387 Miles on the Clock

We had intended to spend a couple of days in Yosemite National Park but had been spooked by reports of a circulating virus which had no known cure. Although the park was immense, and the chance of contracting the virus was minuscule, we were also ill equipped for hiking and decided that a ride through would suffice.

We were beginning to speed up, anyway, as our road insurance only covered us for four months in the US, and we had decided to leave when it expired less than two weeks later.

As we made our way down the main street of a Yosemite outlying town, we got talking to Jared. He was a fellow classic BMW owner who lived and volunteered in the park and was using the Internet in town to look up information on changing the clutch on his bike. After doing our best to help him out, we waved goodbye and went to find some food.

While we sat overlooking the shallow basin of Mono Lake, waiting for some burgers and chips to arrive, Jared reappeared to invite us into the park as his guests and to take a look at his bike. We hadn't accounted for the steep entry fee, so were thrilled by his offer to waive it and readily accepted.

The route through the park rose to over 3,000 meters [984 feet] and offered yet another glimpse of the country's most magnificent scenery. Huge cliffs and granite mounds towered above beautiful meadow valleys and alpine lakes. The road cut a snaking scar through grassy peaks, where clusters of evergreens poked through massive slabs of smooth stone and rock. By the time we arrived at the volunteer campground, we had missed Jared, who was maximising the Sunday to go on a hike but, instead, met his colleagues, who took us to see the bike in their modest tent village.

The majestic mountains of the park were soon replaced by dry rolling hills as we rode towards the coast. Before we left Texas, Byron had sent a message to a group on an adventure motorcycling forum, asking if any members had a garage that we could use to carry out another service on the bike. We had been inundated with offers of garages to use and rooms to stay in and eventually took up an invitation from Thor in San Francisco, who we were on our way to meet that day.

The sun had begun to drop on the late afternoon, and, as we cruised down a multi-lane, Californian highway, it fell directly ahead of us and dazzled our vision. Our reflective helmet strips and sunglasses combined proved to be poor competition, and Byron rode virtually blind, with only his left hand to screen the worst of the glare.

It was quickly marked as one of the hairier rides of the trip and was made all the more terrifying by the trucks and eighteen-wheelers that materialised from nowhere to hurtle past us. The sun eventually sunk below the horizon, and we made it across the bay in one piece before approaching the Golden Gate Bridge, where a thick fog whipped in from the coast to render us blind once again, and an icy drizzle dissipated the last of our body heat.

It was late in the evening when we pulled up to Thor's house. We had arranged the visit entirely online and were immensely grateful to him, but it was only as the exhausting day drew to a close that it occurred to us what a risk he was taking in inviting two strangers to stay in his home, with equal realisation that we were embarking on a scenario that we had been warned against since childhood.

However, our recent experiences with kind strangers and the universal biking camaraderie made us less concerned, so we stuck with the instinct that had led us to ask for help online in the first place.

Thor greeted us warmly, before pouring us some wine and showing us around his home. As an adventure motorcyclist, he had experienced the kindness of strangers himself, and we were far from the first travellers to whom he had offered a roof and a warm bed.

In addition to feeding us and driving us many times to the Golden Gate Bridge, which remained stubbornly shrouded in fog, Thor gave us more roadmaps to add to our stash. Tales of his own experiences over the border also went a long way to ease our growing qualms about the impending leg of our journey into Mexico. Sadly, though, we had set ourselves a time-frame in which to reach San Diego and, once the bike was serviced, we bid adieu to another new friend and generous host.

Over the past couple months our intercom system had begun to falter. The sound would rise and fall randomly, and my microphone had stopped working altogether. The protective foam on Byron's mouthpiece had also shredded on his thriving beard and, consequently, filled my ears with the deafening sound of the wind, so we decided to get the system fixed before we left the US.

It was manufactured in Europe, and, frustratingly, very few suppliers stocked the brand on the American continent. When we eventually sourced a seller, they were based fifty miles north, in Napa, so, after leaving Thor, we set off to meet them.

The landscape transported us into the rolling vineyards of Southern France, where sleepy towns and farms scattered the region. We met the supplier in the car park of a farm shop, where we discovered that a lot more new parts were needed than we originally thought, and, after the import mark up and added tax, we eventually paid close to what the whole system had cost in the first place just to get it fixed. The difference it made was immediate, though, and worth every cent.

After the costly fix, we rode straight back to San Francisco, where the negotiation of its gravity-defying steep hills took us on a rollercoaster ride of chores to collect spare bike parts and visit banks in Chinatown. We stopped in a few motorcycle clothing stores, where we hoped to buy riding jeans that would offer relief from the heavy-duty winter alternatives that we had been wearing, but we were disappointed not to find any that would fit.

The day of big spending meant we couldn't afford to stay in the city, and, by the time we began to make our way south, the sun had begun its daily descent. We rode fifty miles through the dark, before taking a chance on a slip road into Santa Clara.

Although our gambles had turned out well so far, any lucky charms ran out on this occasion. Too tired to keep searching, we pulled into the fourth motel that we came across and surrendered to our fate. The receptionist offered us two categories of room, and we chose cheap over quiet, before making the ultimate mistake of paying ahead of seeing it.

The courtyard was teeming with residents who seemed to live there permanently, and the door to our room looked like it had been kicked in a few times. After it fell open a little too easily, we stepped onto the remains of a carpet that stuck to our boots. The mosquito screen across the window had been slashed, and a thick crust of grime was exposed under a small fridge, when we later moved it to barricade the door. In the bathroom a smashed mirror, missing tiles, and a grim trace of excrement on the toilet seat added the finishing touches.

Although everything about it suggested otherwise, it still wasn't the cheapest room we had stayed in.

Just as we thought the worst had been uncovered, we overheard an incessant rant from a woman outside our door. When we eventually tuned into it, we realised her issue was with a bike that had been parked in her spot, and she was blaming everything from the management to racism for the oversight. It didn't take much to realise what bike she was referring to, so we went out to speak to her.

The tirade stopped mid-flow when she saw us, and she instantly calmed down when we told her that we would move the bike. We rolled it up to the wall under our slashed window, happy to have it as close to us as possible during the night. All the while, our forthright neighbour questioned us about the Flying Aga, which she thought looked suspiciously like a police bike. Through a mouth full of gold teeth, she then bizarrely went on to declare her love for us, which quickly bought her worse-for-wear boyfriend out of their room.

He looked us up and down through glazed eyes, obviously unhappy with what he had just overheard. However, instead of the showdown we were half expecting, he launched into a slurred warning about how much of a handful she was, with the sincerity of putting genuine rivals off the scent. Happily, their attention soon turned to one another when the woman apologised for her boyfriend and dragged him back into their room.

The raving that resumed inside went some way to explain the state of her dead-beat partner, and we ramped up the television volume in a futile bid to drown her out.

We woke up the next morning to hear her going on as if she hadn't slept at all. This time her problem was with a new victim, and they just happened to be standing directly on the other side of our slashed window. We packed up faster than ever before, and, while Byron sorted the bike out, I went to retrieve our deposit.

During a half-hour wait with a particularly burly guy from

New Jersey, I spotted a list of rules pinned to the wall that might have slowed down our hasty check-in the night before. It went into great detail about how, among other things, it was not the management's duty to take clients to court in the morning and that running out of cigarettes in the middle of the night did not classify as an emergency.

Following the disappearance of the cashier and receptionist, the prolonged wait only ended when a maid eventually counted out our deposits from her own purse, probably as a result of the New Jersey man's presence and not my own. Meanwhile, our gold-toothed neighbour had been grilling Byron about my absence with suspicion and was only satisfied that he had not done away with me in the night when I finally returned. She even hung around to wave us off as we hightailed out of there and never looked back.

A spectacular scenic highway led us south that day on a biker's delight of sweeping curves that hugged the West Coast cliffs. High arched bridges jumped from one ridge to the next, passing over powerful waters that crashed into beautifully wild beaches and coves below.

Fine pink pampas grass lined the entire route and dominated the surrounding wild hills, captivating my attention with the camera, while Byron sashayed through the twists and turns.

The necessarily slower speed on the winding route, combined with constant scenic overlook breaks, didn't do any favours to our time constraints, and we pulled into San Luis Obispo late that day, just two hundred miles away from where we had set off that morning.

A guy spotted us looking at our map on the edge of a street and it wasn't long before he was regaling us with tales of his escapades in Mexico. He and a group of friends had gone to surf there some thirty years earlier and discovered that they could sleep for free in local gaol [jail] houses. The Mexican law enforcers had apparently been happy for them to stay in the slammer in exchange for a share of the evening meals that they prepared while locked up.

We were uplifted to hear more encouraging anecdotes about the country and made a mental note of the scheme, although we were unconvinced that we would be entering quite the same place that he had visited.

After getting lucky with a cosy Latin motel that night, we continued further along the breathtaking coastal route the following day and eventually stopped at a peaceful rural spot where we planned to explore the state's rugged hills.

It was a weekend, and, although we slept soundly the first night, an extended clan of heavy-set adults and children soon turned up in a convoy of oversized pickup trucks. The notion that thin sheets of fabric were the only defence other campers had against the constant discharge from their truck radios and the row they made throughout the night was totally lost on them.

We escaped into the hills during the day, where we stumbled across beautiful hidden ranches and towns. We even came across an unlikely exhibition of vintage British motorcycles, before fitting in a trip to the nearest beach. Hoping to take a dip in the Pacific Ocean, we quickly found out that it was not such an attractive prospect while strong winds churned the open sea and whipped up the sand.

The rowdy group had packed up and cleared out on our return, leaving us in peace to cook a campfire feast and toast the anniversary of our first date.

The next night we stopped at a trailer park on the outskirts of Los Angeles, where the provision for tents fell to an all time low. We were given a pitch in the minuscule hedgerow at the back of the site, where we noticed a guy hosing down some of the most enormous snakes we had ever seen. Although a stick insect had sent Byron jumping out of his skin on the way to Boston, we had so far managed to steer clear of finding big spiders in the tent or poisonous snakes in our boots. The man put us at ease, though, after assuring us that the snakes hadn't just been found on the site but were pets that he was lending to a show in Las Vegas.

We were determined to miss rush hour traffic the next morning so left the site at an ungodly hour to visit Hollywood and central Los Angeles. After riding down Sunset Boulevard and into the Hollywood Hills, we witnessed a terrific morning view over the city, before making our way further down the coast to San Diego.

In the time that it had taken us to cross from the East to the West Coast, my cousin Lucas had flown home a whole six weeks after leaving for what he thought would be a weekend break. He had recovered from the collapsed lung and the infection and took us for a Californian seaside lunch to celebrate. Surfers were scattered on the beach and the waves, while we soaked up the sunshine before venturing downtown later that evening to toast our final stop on US soil.

There were a couple days left before our planned crossover into Mexico. Without insurance, currency, or visas for the imminent destination, we spent the following day riding all over town, attempting to sort out the finer details before our US road insurance ran out.

In another of many attempts to clear space on the bike, we packed up another parcel of our belongings and paid a small fortune to send it home. The act proved to be fatal, though, and, after apparently making its way to the correct address in England, for some inexplicable reason that we have never found out, the carrier sent our precious box back to the US, where it disappeared into the abyss of a US Postal Service warehouse, never to be seen again. We had foolishly included our diary of the trip to that date, together with marked route maps and various other irreplaceable items that we thought would be safer in a box back home than lying redundant in the bottom of a Flying Aga pannier.

Once everything was sorted for the onward ride, we enjoyed a final day in the country with Lucas, who introduced us to a range of extensive juice concoctions and the world of health conscious, exotic water.

He drove us all over San Diego, to its parks and beaches, including an optionally nudist beach, where a naked man with a lizard clinging to his arm instigated the single, most awkward scenario of the entire trip.

We spent a final morning watching the sunrise from Mount Soledad, before we headed down to another beach for breakfast and met a couple of Lucas's friends, who had gone for a typically Californian pre-work surf.

After the fitting finale, we bid a fond farewell to Lucas and made a beeline for the border.

In just four months, we had ridden 14,571 miles through thirty-two of the fifty United States and five of the ten Canadian provinces. We had glued one ignition barrel together, taped up a few cables, lost a small panel of bodywork, replaced the drive shaft and bearings, and changed one rear tyre but had otherwise encountered few problems with the trusty, thirty-three-year old Flying Aga.

We had managed to visit every existing friend and relative who lived in the two countries and had gone on to make so many new friends, that, when we approached the border to an entirely unknown land, it felt like we were waving goodbye to home.

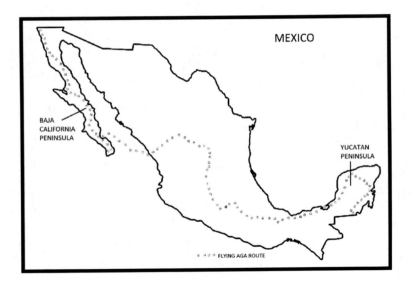

MEXICO

BAJA
CALIFORNIA
PENINSULA

YUCATAN
PENINSULA

FLYING AGA ROUTE

COLD BEERS AND PUNCTURES

122 Days on the Road | 14,571 Miles on the Clock

Media coverage of drug cartel activities had made such an impact throughout the US that total strangers had shown little restraint when relaying their preconceived notions of the terrible things that would happen to us in Mexico. Despite the occasional interlude of a positive account from someone who had actually visited the country, the torrent of foreboding had gradually exhausted our resolve to ignore the hype. Despite the fact that my own brother had lived in the country and had loved every aspect of it, it was the nay-saying that dominated our thoughts us as we approached the border.

Nobody was stopping vehicles from riding straight through the crossing, but we had been warned to get our paperwork sorted first or face being turned back when we tried to exit the country over 3,000 miles away.

Had we attained a better command of Spanish during some weekly, ninety-minute lessons back in London, the process would probably have been quite simple. However, we found ourselves running back and forth to a collection of different bureaus and booths, while armed officers rummaged through our top box and poked at the saucepans.

We did eventually make some sense of the procedure and paid a handsome, temporary importation fee for the bike of $200, which we were assured would be returned if the bike left the country when we did. With stamped passports and receipts for various other fees, we rode into the border town of Tijuana with vague instructions of where to find a vehicle permit office.

We immediately hit the hustle and bustle of the town, where the change in culture was absolute. People were walking everywhere in a scene that would have been unusual further north, where just about everybody drove a car. Small motorbikes with helmetless riders choked the roads, while dusty pickup trucks edged through the traffic.

We rode past vendors hauling colourful carts of chopped fruit along the streets until we eventually tracked down the well-concealed permit office, where a lone armed guard directed us to park in an empty courtyard. We had long ago fallen into the habit of keeping watch over the bike whenever it was loaded with luggage, so Byron went into the office alone, while I baked outside, too wary to leave its side and search for shade.

A group of guys who had been waiting outside the office wandered over to me after Byron disappeared inside. Although I nervously gripped a small tin of pepper spray that Lucas had given me as a parting gift, it turned out they were simply intrigued by the bike.

Although the Flying Aga had attracted some attention in the last two countries, it had usually come from bikers who related to the model or wanted to pass on a good route to ride. We soon learnt, though, that most motorcycles in Latin America were predominantly small and Chinese. Japanese or US-American bikes were not uncommon near cities, but the small motorcycles churned out by China were such an affordable means of transport that they dominated the roads and were the principal models that people were accustomed to seeing.

Adventure riding was popular throughout the continent but it was more usual to spot modern European or Japanese touring bikes that were better suited to the terrain and necessary endurance than a vintage European bike that turned out to be quite a novelty.

After Byron had been passed from one desk to another, he eventually secured the elusive vehicle permit an hour later, leaving just one more administrative task to complete before we could get back on the road.

We needed to officially leave the US by handing back our visas, so we went in search of the Mexican exit and US entry border point. After some wrong turns and clumsy enquiries for directions, we came to a multi-lane queue that backed out onto the highway. It had been so easy to leave the US, but it clearly required significantly more effort to get back in.

We weaved through the six lanes of stationary cars and trucks, dodging hawkers and food wagons, until we could weave no more, and I climbed off the bike to walk the rest of the way. An officer took the visa cards from me and, after I confirmed that we wouldn't be returning within the next six months, he gave me the customary look of concern. Too hot to care, I waved goodbye and traipsed back to find Byron and the bike.

We rode the wrong way back through the lanes of waiting vehicles, passing the same hawkers and food wagons, before exiting the queue straight onto the highway in the wrong direction. A few near misses and close collisions with comically indifferent drivers were successfully dodged, and, after correcting our course, we set off to find the coast road.

Exhausted looking men scattered the verge that separated the highway from an international boundary fence along the outskirts of town. They were thumbing lift requests to dusty trucks, while presumably waiting for darkness to fall so they could take a gamble on the fence. Heaps of rubbish lined the highway as we rode further out of town, and the occasional surprise whiff of sewage caught us off guard and made us retch.

The stunning coastal route soon opened up to twist along the cliffs and pass through small towns that brimmed with colour.

The day had been long and exhausting, and we pulled up to a cluster of motels that were charging more for a room than any that we had stayed at in the US. Worried we would never get the money back that we had paid to bring the bike into the country, we forfeited a night of comfort for an isolated, cliff top campground.

A group of surfers from California were the only other guests at the desolate site but they set off to go home just as we began to unload our tent. A thick fog soon closed in off the ocean, and we began to feel slightly vulnerable in our lonesome spot on the barren stretch of land

A very basic toilet block without door locks, paper, or lights made up the main facilities. Freezing cold water ran into two small sinks that were not far from a huge outdoor tank, where tiny pipes dribbled out more cold water for showering.

Needless to say, there was no sign of the picnic tables and fire pits that we had grown used to in Canada and the US.

We found a tiny café around the corner, where the girl running the kitchen soon rustled us up a feast of fresh tortas, tacos, and burritos that became the first encounter in our love affair with Mexican food.

As the evening drew down, a family pulled onto the empty cliff top and set up their camp directly next to us. It turned out they were missionaries travelling with a couple of US-Americans and, before long, they had given us a list of sites to check out on the Baja California peninsula.

They invited us to join them for dinner, and we tucked into fish tacos and marshmallows around their campfire, which did wonders for fending off the chill that had arrived with the thick fog.

When we returned to our tent later that evening, Fernando and Armando, the young twin boys of the site owners, came running over to speak to us. They laughed at our attempts to figure out what they were saying until it became clear that their endeavour was hopeless and they ran off. They returned some minutes later with a bundle of wood, and we realised they had just spent the best part of twenty minutes trying to sell it to us. Although we didn't want any, we raided our supply of biscuits to compensate their wasted efforts.

The fog had lifted the next morning, and we woke up to the most beautiful view of the ocean. The seascape was enhanced all the more when our neighbours pointed out a pod of dolphins leaping and diving along the coastline below us.

We had been in the country less than twenty-four hours and had survived a night on an exposed cliff top, eaten some of the most delicious food, befriended a local family, and witnessed what we took to be a good, aquatic omen. We were invigorated by the new day in the new country and, after packing up and waving goodbye to Fernando, Armando, and the neighbours, we headed south along the peninsula.

It didn't take long to arrive at our first roadblock. We were anxious that our high morale was about to be broken by a casual kidnapping or some form of extortion, but it turned out that the checkpoint was a military one and supposedly the safest variety. The military were embroiled in the long running war on drugs and had much bigger fish to fry than the occasional tourist, or so we hoped.

With automatic rifles slung over their shoulders, a couple of guards in desert camouflage and wraparound sunglasses waved us to a stop. They spoke extremely fast, and we made apologies for not understanding them, before making a terrible attempt at trying to speak Spanish. Both guards looked unenthused but, with little traffic passing through their spot in the middle of nowhere, they humoured us, and a few of their friends came over to see what the chat was about.

One prodded our roll bags with the muzzle of his rifle, while another looked on with amusement as his friend taught us a few Spanish swear words. Eventually, they got bored and waved us through so they could return to the shade of the only tree in the vicinity, and we set off with relief that the episode had been incident free.

Two hours later, we reached another checkpoint and received the same, fairly amiable reception. The guards indulged our poor attempts at small talk before dismissing us in favour of searching an implausibly overloaded truck.

The initial qualms that had accompanied us across the border were fading with every mile, and our attention soon reverted back to the sticky heat that continued to fry us alive.

After following the coast for some miles, the route veered inland and cut through dry rolling hills that were scattered with enormous cactus plants and scrub brush. The recent spell of stifling heat had kept the river overflow dips in the road dry, although rock and boulder debris from their last flood remained scattered across the otherwise smooth asphalt.

Vibrantly painted, low concrete buildings formed small towns along the route, which introduced us to the country's lethal speed bumps. In varying states of wear and tear, they had been laid without any apparent adherence to specifications of width or height. Most had faded to blend into the rest of the road, and few signs offered warnings of their existence. We found ourselves flying over them more than once, before landing with a crash that knocked the wind out of us in an ongoing annihilation of the Flying Aga's suspension and undercarriage.

A single-lane highway was the only paved road through the peninsula and it quickly turned to deep gravel when we followed a sign that directed us away from it, towards a campground. For three miles, Byron worked hard to keep the front wheel tracing the deep ruts and furrows of the track, while the heavily-laden, road bike veered all over the place.

The surface soon turned to deep sand, the worst of all conditions on which to ride any bike, but Byron kept us upright, fighting against the erratic tank slapping while battling the loss of traction.

The path eventually became a dirt track when we reached a tiny village, where the campground turned out to be a popular fishing spot. We picked a pitch beside a block of hotel rooms and set up the tent.

Although the bone shaking trail had led us to the sea, a visibly strong current and no beach cancelled out the prospect of a refreshing dip, so we resorted to the bar instead. It was Mexican Independence weekend, and an extended happy hour turned our initial order of a cold beer each into three cold beers and two free-poured margaritas. The drinks were soon complemented by a fresh fish dinner and Dino, a resident mariachi man with freakishly long finger nails, who serenaded us before demanding five dollars for his trouble.

After rising early the next morning, we had psyched ourselves up to tackle the dreaded rough route back to the highway when we heard a hissing sound coming from the bike. Close inspection revealed that a battery cable must have recently worn through its casing. It was shorting out on the bike frame and generating a minuscule plume of smoke that could quite easily have led to a fire, had we not spotted it.

With some frustration, we unloaded everything we had just packed away in order to remove the battery and tape the worn cable into a groove of a dissected plastic water bottle. It took a while to squeeze the cable and its new casing back into place, and, by the time the fix was complete, we had missed the cool window in the day.

Instead of pressing on, we decided to deal with the trail back to the highway the next morning and booked into the cheapest room at the adjacent hotel.

That afternoon, we joined the rest of the village for the Mexican Independence buffet and learnt our first lesson in Latin American timekeeping. We came to understand that turning up to a social gathering any less than two hours after the arranged meeting time would leave us bored and hungry while we waited for the rest of the party to arrive. Unfortunately for the rest of the party, while we learnt this valuable lesson, Byron exercised some liberties with the buffet, and the cooks had to throw a few more dishes in the oven before the village turned up.

We succeeded in setting off early the next morning, and Byron mastered the long assault course back to the main road. Free at last, we set off on the most incredible route through the core of the peninsula, where an enormous expanse of towering cacti and scattered boulders made for a magnificent ride.

We passed through a couple more military checkpoints, where the guards were more indifferent than ever and even failed to stop us as we rode straight through.

We were yet to come across a grocery shop, and, although an abundance of street food and cheap restaurants lessened the need, it meant that we weren't carrying any supplies in the middle of the desert. Eventually, a growing hunger led us to park up beside a tiny shack. We had already ridden past four similar huts with a reluctance to risk eating anything from inside, but the heat and hunger had worn us down, and we needed something to keep us going.

A swarm of flies had cottoned on that it was cool inside the small structure. They were crawling on every visible surface or lying dead on the floor and did little to boost our confidence in eating there. A weary man in a grubby T-shirt ignored us as we entered, but called to his wife, who took our order for the only choice she offered us. We hadn't understood what it was and we tried to guess as the man set about preparing it on an old, wood burning stove behind the counter.

It would have been easy to walk away and ride off, but we were becoming weaker by the minute so we shared a Coke while we waited, hoping it would prepare our stomachs for whatever was coming.

Of all the conceivable ingredients to be served in a desert, squid would not have been top of the list, but it came wrapped in tiny fried tortillas and was delicious. However, we were convinced that any kind of fish kept in a fly infested desert hut without a fridge would do few favours to even the hardiest of digestive systems, and we only ate a bare minimum before saddling up and hitting the road.

A few hours later, we arrived in Guerro Negro, the largest Mexican town we had come across since crossing into Tijuana. We had eagerly anticipated that a cheaper cost of living would be the upside of life south of the border, and our hopes were confirmed at a hotel where a room cost the same as a night's stay in a campground further north.

The prospect of an extended break from hot, sleepless nights inside the tent perked us up no end. The notion that we could avoid lengthy morning pack ups of equipment to get on the road while it was still cool was equally as uplifting. To top off the good news, there were no repercussions from the desert squid, and we slept soundly in air conditioned bliss.

Despite our plan for an early start while the air was cool outside, we discovered that air conditioning in the room had a greater appeal and didn't set off until the sun was high in the sky.

Passing through more mountainous desert, we crossed to the east side of the peninsula and reached the Sea of Cortez. We were hoping to find a beach paradise that we had been told offered free camping under palapas, which were tropical, open-sided, wooden structures with thatched roofs made from dried palm leaves.

The directions to the beach had been vague, and we rode into the oasis town of Mulege, which we had been told was closest to it, and made our way through its small winding streets to the banks of a palm lined river that led out to sea.

A dirt track ran alongside the river, but deep ruts filled with churned mud and seawater soon stopped us going any further. It seemed improbable that a paradise beach would be found at the end, anyway, so we turned around and weaved a path back out of the town. We followed the coast road to a petrol station, where the attendant told us the only beach he knew about was back in the town. Realising that our exit may have been hasty, we backtracked to have another look.

At the opening to the dirt path, we paused to consider whether it was wise to inflict another pounding on the Flying Aga, when a quad bike rode towards us. A tanned older guy riding with a beer in hand, swerved over to stop beside us. He didn't know about the palapa paradise beach, either, but, with a US-American accent, he warned us not to ride down the track as a hurricane had torn up the route a couple of weeks earlier.

He soon introduced himself as Marty, and we followed him to the local shop, where he loaded his bike up with beers and we bought our first Mexican groceries. Once we were all restocked, he offered to guide us down the dirt track to the beach, where he thought we could probably camp anyway.

We got to the same point that we had turned around at before, when Marty suggested we take a detour around the worst of the path, via a house that he was renovating. It sounded good, and we veered left to follow him up a steep rocky hill, where we passed a dilapidated building that had once been a US-American owned hotel. A cartel had apparently seized it and, in one weekend, they had let the local population ransack its contents of every single item, before leaving it to stand ominously empty ever since.

We followed Marty into the yard of the house that he was working on and felt a warning wobble at the back of the bike. It was the first puncture of the trip, which, quite frankly, had come a lot later than we expected.

Marty let us fix it on his porch and, while we got to work, he pulled up a couple of plastic chairs, cracked open some fresh beers, and directed a small fan at the bike to keep us cool. The fan was by far the most appreciated feature of the entire day.

Byron removed the punctured rear wheel from the bike, but, no matter how many different tools were employed, the bead of the tyre just wouldn't break from the rim of the wheel. When it seemed totally hopeless, Marty offered to take Byron and the wheel to a workshop in the town, while I stayed with our kit.

Not long after they set off, tiny red ants began eating my legs, and, as the evening closed in, an army of mosquitoes joined them. By the time the guys eventually returned, darkness had fallen and it looked like I had contracted chickenpox.

They had called in at three different workshops before finding one that was open to help with the wheel. A bent, two-inch nail had worked its way through the rubber of the tyre to slice a clean cut in the inner tube. The hole was quickly patched up, while the mechanics teased Marty about a recent robbery.

It turned out he was a keen fisherman and had triumphed in a recent competition to win a pool of entry fees. Unfortunately, his landlord had found his hiding place and stolen his winnings. There was no speculation about the accusation, either, because the landlord had done very little to cover his tracks, let alone deny the offence. He and his wife had immediately stopped going to work and had been spending their booty around the small town with little restraint. According to the mechanics, it was even common knowledge that the landlord had paid off the local policeman from the takings of the theft.

The incident was the reason why Marty was now ploughing everything he had left into converting his new place, where I had been waiting for them to return. He intended to create a palace out of the small house, while plotting a revenge that seemed to involve seducing the landlord's wife. If nothing else, the misfortune of the puncture was offset by our stranding in the crazy Mexican town with its colourful scandals.

Byron replaced the wheel on the bike, and Marty invited us to camp out in the shell of his new house. We jumped at the offer and, after throwing our gear inside, we all set off in his truck in search of food.

He drove us down to a shack that he called Mama's House, on the small beach where we had been heading earlier. It turned out that Mama was the mother of a family of good-for-nothing boys who all lived in the ramshackle home above their small restaurant. The structure was an incredible example of shanty-chic, built around thick stakes that had been set firmly in the sand and were linked together by an assortment of plywood, driftwood, bamboo, and fishing nets. The two-storey construction was topped off with a thatched, palm leaf roof in the ultimate display of ramshackle industriousness.

Mama hadn't been expecting customers, but she and Marty were good friends, and he soon persuaded her that we would eat anything she could rustle up. She made us some breaded fish and homemade fries that, like everything else we had eaten in the country, went down a treat.

We slept soundly that night among the sacks of concrete and scattered tools in the shell of Marty's new house, but woke up to find that we had both been feasted on by more critters and looked like we had caught chickenpox, mumps, and measles combined.

When we met Marty later that morning, he declared that the sea looked good for fishing and invited us to join him for an outing in his boat with his faithful dog, Trouble. He explained that there was a recuperating injured whale somewhere nearby that he wanted to see, and, with no plans to be elsewhere, we jumped at the chance to go for a cruise on the *Mary Jane*.

As a self-confessed forty-year-old with an extra thirty years of experience, Marty was no shrinking violet. Cold beers accompanied his lifetime of stories while we drifted out to sea and, until he went into detail about the incestuous habits of the local town, we had been soaking up the tales.

He navigated the *Mary Jane* to an isolated bay where his friend, Andreas, had lived alone for over forty years. With just a rowing boat to fish with and a palapa to sleep in, he lived on a peaceful beach for which he had apparently once fought off the attentions of a local cartel.

Andreas seemed like the most contented person on earth, swinging in his hammock in a cool shack that overlooked a breathtaking bay, where friends dropped by bearing gifts of beer, food, and clothes. He assured us that the whale had been seen in the area the day before, so we left him in his hammock and went in search of it.

We motored the length of the immediate coastline, skimming islands of rocks before drifting into bays. Somehow, though, the largest mammal on earth evaded us, as did the rest of the fish in the water, and we eventually returned to shore without a catch.

As if to demonstrate that the actions of Marty's landlord had more to do with being short-sighted than malicious, we returned to his house to find crushed beer cans and date shells scattered across the work site. The two guys carrying out the renovation had evidently taken Marty's absence that day as a cue to raid his fridge and his crop of drying dates. With a surprising lack of common sense to at least clear away the evidence of their idleness, they had also failed to make even nominal progress on the house. It didn't stop their protests the next day, though, when Marty refused to pay them. He explained to us that another guy who had laid his palapa roof had only weaved the palms into place without nailing them down, and when Marty refused to pay him until he came back to finish the job, he, too, had objected.

The apparent conflict that accompanied any attempt at progress while neighbours lingered close by, ready to take advantage, sounded exhausting but perhaps served as proof that paradise never came without a price.

After our fruitless fishing trip, Marty raided his freezer that evening and cooked up a banquet of seafood. His tales that had been cultivated during seventy misspent years ran through the evening and had us in stitches one minute and wide-eyed the next. We spent another night in the shell of his new home and, after a final breakfast the next morning, we waved goodbye with great affection.

We made our way out of the small town and along the coastal highway, where we traced the same course that we had taken the day before in the *Mary Jane*. Some miles after leaving the town, the road led us up a steep elevation, from where the palapa paradise beach suddenly appeared like a vision below.

It was exactly how we had imagined it: with white sand, turquoise sea, and nothing else for miles around, other than a few evenly spaced palapa shelters. The groceries we had bought with Marty had rotted in the heat of the top box the day before, and we had nothing else to sustain a visit. Having just roughed it for a couple of nights on a building site, we were baking hot, covered in insect bites, and in desperate need of a hot shower. So, we decided to keep the image of the beach firmly locked away for future daydreams and continued on the lengthiest ride we had completed in a long time.

The road led us south along the coast, before cutting inland through a desolate landscape where little else existed besides huge swathes of cacti and arid hills. It eventually looped back to drop us further along the same east coast that we had left behind that morning.

As we rode into the outskirts of La Paz, we spotted a hotel that Marty had recommended to us. We passed through its high-walled entrance into a clandestine complex that had been designed for maximum discretion. An anonymous booth quoted charges by the hour, and, after we handed over a payment to stay the whole night, the barrier was raised. No keys had been given and no personal details had been taken. The interior was set out like a suburban street with small apartments, each featuring a hedgerow and a garage.

We rode into one of the open garages, where a switch inside locked us in, and a small door led into a room that rivalled our Las Vegas suite. Complete with a huge bathroom, a big bed, sofas, and dining furniture, it made a change from the usual places where we slept.

The establishment was one of Latin America's many love hotels that dotted the outskirts of towns and highways in a sometimes nicer, sometimes grottier, version of the roadside motel. Their purpose was to offer complete anonymity to illicit lovers or unmarried couples in the predominantly strict Catholic countries. No doubt they made convenient locations for a few brothels, too.

The mattress of the bed was resting on a reinforced concrete block, and a switch beside it unleashed an outburst of passionate, Latino music from hidden speakers in the ceiling.

After a peaceful sleep in the private room, we set off to cover the short distance to the southern tip of the peninsula. However, another wobble from the back tyre stopped us in our tracks just ten miles from our destination.

In melting midday heat, we pulled onto the hard shoulder of a downward, highway bend. After offloading our luggage into the drainage trench, that was bizarrely full of butterfly carcasses, Byron unbolted the rear wheel. We couldn't get enough clearance to wedge it out from under the mud guard, though, and our options were limited on the corner of the fast road. As we struggled to think of a solution that didn't involve splitting up or leaving our worldly possessions unattended, a car pulled over ahead of us.

The driver was about our age and, with a beer in hand, he came over to introduce himself as Mario. Despite the language barrier, he understood our predicament and took hold of one side of the rear frame to help Byron lift the bike high enough so I could dislodge the wheel. He hung about to see what had caused the puncture, when the problem of breaking the tyre bead struck once again.

A mixture of poor Spanish and sign language soon explained the issue, and Mario offered to take the wheel to a nearby workshop for us. Simple workshops dealing solely in puncture repairs and tyre changes had lined the highway through the peninsula, and we were beginning to understand why there were so many of them.

Just after Mario made the offer, a girl emerged from his car, also carrying a beer. It turned out that they were cousins, and she proposed to stay with me and the bike, if Byron went with Mario to the nearest workshop. We couldn't believe our luck, and Byron set off with Mario, who had just made the universally recognised gesture to me, which implied that his cousin was crazy.

After comparing our separate encounters later that day, Byron and I pieced their story together. Mario had picked Carmen up from a club in town that morning because either their uncle or her dad had been taken to hospital. They were either on their way to see him or were on their way back from seeing him when they stopped to help us. Regardless of the finer details, it was an amazingly charitable gesture.

The inner tube was soon released from the tyre, and a metal shard was extracted. Byron had taken one of our new spare tubes to replace the punctured one, but it turned out that there was a nick in that, too.

While he attempted to ask the mechanic to stop resting the wheel on its brake disc, Mario took a telephone call and disappeared. By the time the two inner tubes had been patched up and the tyre had been reset on the wheel, he had still not returned. It occurred to Byron that he may have gone to pick up Carmen, and that I might be sat waiting on the highway alone. We had no way to tell each other what was happening, as we hadn't intended to split up at all during the trip, so were only carrying one emergency mobile telephone that was never turned on.

Back on the highway, I had quickly discovered the meaning behind Mario's parting gesture about his cousin. She was still drunk from her night out and was jumping about and waving at every car that passed us, prompting them to beep in encouragement and spur her on. I attempted to divert her attention, hoping that none of the beeping cars would actually stop, until a few of them did.

Fortunately, she sobered up enough to tell the drivers that we didn't need help and, despite the blazing heat, she then took a blanket from our pile of luggage and fell asleep beside the road.

Back in town, Byron was convinced that Mario and Carmen must have continued their journey and asked the mechanic to drive him back to the highway. Upon finding Carmen still with me and no sign of Mario, we stood around in confusion, before she woke up and spoke to the mechanic.

We couldn't understand them, but she was soon hugging us goodbye like old friends, before climbing into his truck. After asking where Mario had gone, she shrugged her shoulders as if it didn't matter, and the mechanic set off back towards town.

Seconds later, Mario's car pulled up. It turned out that he had gone to pick up another cousin, and, as we tried to explain what had happened to Carmen, the mechanic's truck reappeared. It was like a farce, but once everybody had returned to their correct vehicles, we couldn't thank the cousins enough for their kindness in stopping, let alone for staying to help us out. Before we knew it, though, they had cracked open fresh beers and, with a rearward wave, disappeared into the distance.

Three hours after the wobble, we found ourselves alone again. We had just wedged the mended wheel back into place, and Byron was tightening the bolts when a battered truck slowed down and stopped behind us. A glance up at the windscreen revealed that the vehicle was packed with a group of surly looking guys. We hoped that they, too, had just stopped to offer help, but armed with a tyre iron, just in case, Byron approached the driver, while I hung back and reached for the bear spray that had been our trusty, first line of defence since Canada.

I couldn't hear the exchange of words, but, before long, the truckload of sombre guys had broken into smiles. Byron had presumably told them that we had fixed the bike, and one of them reached into the back to pull out two cans of cold beer. He handed them to Byron, whose equal confusion and delight must have been evident, because they left a trail of hearty laughter when they promptly drove off. We couldn't have invented a more surreal few hours and took a moment to crack open the beers and toast the kind-hearted, albeit crazy, Mexicans.

With the bike fixed, we rode into Cabo San Lucas, at the southern tip of the peninsula. Designer shops, exclusive nightclubs, and a pristine marina had expunged every last feature of the Mexican culture we had grown fond of. The hotels had been priced to US standards, too, so we rode to the outskirts, where some semblance of Mexico returned.

After an evening spent feasting on street food, we took a walk around the main town the next morning. In a bid to escape the instant and unwanted attention of hawkers and street vendors, who were determined to sell us something, we paid to join a snorkelling trip. When it came to setting off, though, the broker transferred us to a booze cruise catamaran, assuring us that we would still get to go snorkelling.

The boat was packed with boisterous guys who couldn't get enough of the free beer and women, who were way past their prime for the dancing they were doing with the crew. Any sign of whales still evaded us, but we did see some beautifully vibrant fish when we eventually anchored in a bay.

We packed up early the following morning to loop the tip of the peninsula and head back to La Paz, where we planned to take a ferry across to the mainland. The deserted streets and closed shops signalled the arrival of another Sunday, and the possibility of empty roads made the prospect of the hot ride ahead less unpleasant.

We packed the bike and wedged on our stinking helmets before anything further happened. In addition to the two recent punctures, it transpired that the battery had run completely flat. Had we been carrying less weight, we might have attempted a push start, but in forty degrees [104 F] of heat we decided to hold out for a jump start.

Few people were around to ask for help, but as we topped up the battery fluid, we caught sight of a police car parked on the next street. Byron raced up to it and, after using our now standard mix of poor Spanish and hand gestures, he explained the problem, and they drove off to pick up some jump leads. The engine soon roared back into life, and, despite their preceding reputation, the policemen responded to our offer of a payment with a firm, "No, gracias amigos," before driving off.

As we had purposely avoided the northern mainland, where cartel activities were most rampant, it was difficult to work out if the "Mexico is dangerous" mantra had been blown out of proportion or if we had simply experienced a run of good fortune. After riding over 1,000 miles through the peninsula, we felt nothing but warmth for the country.

However, we would soon find out if our affection was to be long lasting when we crossed to the mainland.

We passed the Tropic of Cancer and rode through swarms of yellow butterflies before arriving back in La Paz, where we had already stayed once in the love hotel.

Somewhere on our journey through the US, we had come across the blog of Adam and Mackenzie, an Australian couple who were doing a similar trip to us on two Kawasaki KLR 650s. It turned out they had been riding roughly a week ahead of us since we began, and, after getting in touch with them, we had kept in contact ever since. They had told us about a hotel near the seafront in La Paz, where we could park the bike safely.

After we tracked it down, the manager waved us straight inside and indicated that we should park in the reception lobby. It was the first of many hotels where the owners thought nothing of motorcycles clogging up their interior courtyards and entrance halls.

When we stayed there a few days earlier, we had not visited the town but expected to find either a rough port, full of truckers and fighting sailors, or another US-Americanised resort.

It was a pleasant surprise to discover that it was neither. With boutique shops, local eateries, and a long promenade, where a group of men made their way from pillar to post with buckets of paint refreshing an already well maintained wall, it was clear that it was an upmarket seaside town.

That evening we ate in a restaurant where the chef occasionally appeared to throw a bucket of water over the stray cats that prowled its courtyard. After a delicious meal of fresh fish and seafood that cost less than the price of a sandwich back in London, we walked down to the promenade and watched another sunset.

The next morning we made preparations for the 250-mile sea voyage to the mainland. We bought ferry tickets to leave the next day and stocked up on seasickness pills, roadmaps, bike oil, insect repellent, and food. Then we spent two hours sitting on sticky plastic chairs outside a laundrette, waiting for our clothes to return to a respectable state. The days of coin slot washing machines had been replaced by service washes, where laundry was entrusted to strangers in the hope that it would all return in one non-coloured, non-shrunk, undamaged state.

For the second time on the trip we had been unable to take any more of the stench from our reeking bike trousers, gloves, and helmet interiors and had put them in for a service, too, risking the loss of any remaining water resistant qualities that they had once possessed.

We had been advised at the ticket office to arrive at the port three hours before the crossing, which we dutifully did in the peak of midday heat. The security checks had taken less than half an hour, though, and we were left to bake on the port concourse for the remaining two and a half hours.

Stray dogs scavenged around us while we learnt our second lesson on Latin American timekeeping. We waited patiently on a discarded rusty cylinder and watched the line up of overloaded wagons and double, eighteen-wheeler that looked worryingly un-roadworthy so close up.

Eventually, they loaded the ferry, and, just as the last of the trucks drove up the gangplank, another motorcyclist with a far superior aptitude for local punctuality rode over to join us.

Raoul was Mexican, which explained the timekeeping, and was heading home after a tour of the Baja Peninsula. Between his broken English and our broken Spanish, we struck up a friendship and rode onboard together. After parking in the bow of the ship, we set about unloading our onerous loose luggage, while Raoul made his way up onto the passenger deck.

By the time we had sorted the bags and strapped the bike down, the car deck had been closed, and a ramp had been lowered that separated us from any open doors.

Heat levels had passed uncomfortable long ago, and, with helmets, bottles, and bags to carry, we struggled up a narrow set of metal steps. They led us into a restricted part of the boat to another flight of stairs. All the while, we were hauling bags behind us and pushing helmets ahead of us, as any remaining energy and patience evaporated in the heat.

We passed through the crew quarters without seeing another soul before arriving on the top deck, where a couple of bemused engineers greeted us with surprise, before leading us to join the rest of the passengers.

After the long, hot wait outside and the exhausting hassle inside, we collapsed into the luxury of reclining seats and spent the next eighteen hours in air conditioned bliss. Yet another cautionary warning, this time about rowdy truck drivers and poor onboard conditions, was proved to be unfounded.

Street Food and Stray Dogs

134 Days on the Road | 15,952 Miles on the Clock

After a breakfast of eggs and strong coffee, the ferry docked at the mainland, and we were immediately stopped by armed officers as we rode out of the port. The desert camouflage uniform of the peninsula had been replaced by a marine print, and the previous indifference of the guards on the Baja had been traded for stern interest.

Our roll bags were prodded with the muzzles of their rifles, and we opened them up, as requested, before they peered inside then waved us clear. Raoul was waiting for us as we left the docks and he led us through a maze of bustling streets and heavy traffic to a petrol station, where we filled up the bikes before parting ways. He was heading south along the coast, while we were venturing inland.

Mazatlan turned out to be the rough old port town that we had expected to find in La Paz. Heavily congested roads and hectic streets were filled with ducking and diving stray dogs and people jumping to and from different buses. Masses of vendors descended into waiting traffic at every red light, while the air was filled with the sound of police officers blowing on whistles. Cables and telephone wires hung knotted and tangled like bunting across the chaotic arena, and, after eighteen hours on a quiet ferry, we struggled to work out which way was up.

A few policemen looked on indignantly as we took a wrong turning through one too many of their whistle signals, before we eventually reached a considerably calmer highway that led out of town. The entire carcass of a rotting cow jolted us awake just before we pulled into a military roadblock.

The desert and marine uniforms had been replaced once again, this time by woodland camouflage, and the demeanour of the guards was now totally sombre. A senior officer approached us and spoke very quickly. Our genuine inability to understand him didn't go down too well, but we persevered and dug out our roadmap to ask where we were on it. The map proved to be an icebreaker when the rest of the guards gathered around it to try and pinpoint our position. Although they had some trouble agreeing on the exact location of their roadblock, they soon confirmed that we were on the wrong road for travelling east.

We turned around and rode back towards the chaotic town, passing the stinking dead cow again before exhaustion got the better of us, and we pulled into the nearest love hotel.

After failing to haggle down the price with a cashier who was not quite as anonymous as her counterpart in La Paz, we entered a horribly seedy room. Everything was painted in a disconcerting rich red colour, including a faux-leather seat that came with its own guide for alternative uses. There was no natural light inside, and, with a duvet cover that featured miniature *Kama Sutra* images, a coarse red carpet, and fiery music blasting from the ceiling, it became the last love hotel that we resorted to. Surprisingly, considering the room, we collapsed into a deep sleep that lasted through the outer reaches of an almighty hurricane that struck the nearby coast that night.

In the morning, we woke up refreshed and with an urgent desire to put distance between ourselves and the grim red room.

Raoul had left us with a parting tip to ride Federal Highway 40, explaining that it featured a section known as Espinazo del Diablo, the Devil's Backbone, which offered a biker's delight of sweeping curves and incredible views. The route covered just two hundred miles but it ended up taking us eight hours to complete.

The road followed no end of tight bends and twisting, narrow lanes through the Sierra Madre Occidental mountain range. It climbed up steep gradients and across deep ravines, skirting the edge of sheer cliff drops, to coast beneath stunning, but formidable rock faces. The landscape was covered in vines and rich foliage from which elderly inhabitants would occasionally appear, wielding machetes and hauling bundles of sticks across their shoulders. Villages made of wooden shacks and small huts were nestled in the mountain slopes and on the edge of cliffs. It was a remarkable passage and kept us captivated for every minute of the eight hours.

The highway didn't come without a degree of risk, though. Its tight curves and narrow lanes weren't quite so enchanting when an occasional pack donkey was replaced by one of the same eighteen-wheeler trucks that had seemed so questionably roadworthy back at the docks.

Although an extensive engineering project was underway to create a shortcut through the mountain range, we could see that its tunnels and bridges were a long way off completion. In the meantime, the extensive twists and turns seemed to be the only viable trade route to travel east, and, despite the hazardous bends and vertical drop-offs, the truck drivers showed little restraint in tackling the road.

The heavy vehicles rarely slowed down as they encroached across both lanes to negotiate each tight bend and blind corner. Proof that drivers were close to insane was verified when one massive truck attempted to overtake another while they both advanced towards a blind corner. We found ourselves inches from the radiator of an accelerating truck cabin more than once, where a solid wall of rock or a petrifying descent offered the only alternatives if our brakes failed. The reason we avoided a collision at all was due to Byron's fast command of swerving on the terrifying corners.

As if the kamikaze driving and wandering animals didn't pose enough of a risk, our suspension deteriorated with every unavoidable plunge into the enormous potholes and ruts that scarred the road surface.

To top off the long list of hazards, a forewarning about robberies and the occasional murder on the route suddenly seemed quite plausible when a thick fog fell across the mountains.

We stopped halfway up one peak at a small family restaurant where a group of little kids ran amok, and the matron of the family offered us the only dish on the menu. We had no idea what it was but ordered it anyway and sat back to watch the fog fall, while the patron traipsed in and out with the carcasses of hunted animals. We were soon tucking into beans and meat chops of an indefinite origin, while the local stray dogs waited patiently for us to finish, and the flies that seemed to plague Mexico went about their usual business of annoying everybody.

Visibility returned after the break, and another military checkpoint soon appeared ahead. Our curiosity about the route and where we were on the map seemed to satisfy the sombre guards, and their rifle muzzles waved us on without much of an interrogation. Considering the government tally of drug war related deaths had reached close to 50,000 fatalities during the previous five years, it was little wonder that the military guards had no interest in pleasantries with tourists.

We finally reached Durango under a cloak of pouring rain and discovered a city that completely contrasted to the one we had left that morning. Landscaped parks, universities, and plazas lined the route while we ventured on a quest for an affordable place to stay.

Our pursuit sent us weaving through one-way city streets to the edge of town, where the paved roads ended and the locals gazed in curiosity at the apparently unfamiliar sight of tourists. We had crossed a time zone and lost an hour somewhere in the mountains, so it was later in the day than we expected when we reached a barrier at the top of a hill. A man guarding it advised us to go back into the city centre before it got dark, and we took his word for it.

After turning the bike around to retrace our route, the battery died once again. This time our position at the top of a hill cut out the need for jump leads, and I pushed Byron on the Flying Aga so he could fire up the engine and drop into gear while I caught him up and jumped on.

We rode back through the muddy streets before we returned to the network of paved, one-way roads. It was still raining when we swerved across three lanes of traffic to enquire about a room at the sixth hotel we had called in at. Finally in luck, the receptionist waved us around the back, and we parked the bike in a leaky garage, before traipsing mud and water up three flights of stairs to the sanctuary of a warm room.

As poor weather was forecast for the next few days, we packed up in the morning, hoping to escape it by riding south. However, when we set off to leave, we couldn't even jump start the bike battery and realised it was time to find a new one.

Jorge, the son of the hotel owner, ran a shop next door and had soon joined us in the garage to see if he could help. Between his English and our slowly improving Spanish, we were soon on the same page, and he offered to take us in his car to search the city for a new battery. Byron went with him, while I booked us in for another night at the hotel and hauled our luggage back up the stairs, trailing another path of wet footprints behind me.

Not a single garage in the city stocked the battery we needed, but Jorge refused to give up on the search and began calling people he knew to see if they had any ideas. He struck improbable gold with a friend who had been in a Las Vegas BMW dealership the very minute Jorge called him. He was a pilot and was scheduled to visit Durango three days later, so he purchased the battery we needed there and then. We were indebted to them both and had no idea what we would have done without Jorge's invaluable help.

With a few days to kill until the battery arrived, we set out to explore the city. An ornate cathedral stood at its heart in a plaza where cowboys sat at shoeshine booths, street vendors sold freshly chopped fruit from carts, and Mexican Independence decorations still hung from the lampposts. Policemen continued to fill the air with whistling, and an unusual number of Volkswagen Beetles clogged up the wide avenues.

We took a bus to an old film set where many a classic Western had once been shot. Cowboys, Indians, sheriffs, and can-can dancers performed to a Mexican audience who lapped it up, while we ate a feast in the set saloon, oblivious as to why the local crowd was crying with laughter but content with another mouth-watering national dish.

We met Jorge with his girlfriend one night and, after yet another delicious Mexican meal of tacos, enchiladas, and quesadillas, they took us to a lively mariachi show.

Not for the first time, we found ourselves contemplating that, had it not been for the Flying Aga, our tight budget, and a lack of planning, we would never have come across even a fraction of the terrific people and places we had stumbled upon.

Jorge dropped off the battery in the morning, and, after realising it would need at least twenty hours of charging, we booked another final night in the hotel. After trawling the streets and calling in at every tiny mechanic stall we could find, we bought a pricey battery charger in a shopping complex on the edge of town. While we set the new battery to charge, we purchased a C-clamp from Jorge's shop, in preparation for breaking the tyre bead during the repair of our next inevitable puncture, before spending the rest of the day writing the tenth entry for our blog and washing the bike.

The Flying Aga fired into life the next morning, and we said a fond farewell to Jorge and the hotel receptionist, who had spent the past few days teaching us Spanish in exchange for cakes. We had no space to carry the battery charger as well as the new C-clamp, and since our need for the charger had passed, we took a chance at returning it before we left town.

After explaining that we wanted to give it back to the same guys who had sold it to us the day before, they called their manager, who asked no questions and handed over a full cash refund. The day suddenly looked promising, and we felt hopeful for the next stretch of road, which we had been warned was a reputed hangout for bandits.

Although we learnt the Spanish translation of "bad people" from a wary petrol station attendant, the road turned out to be totally devoid of other traffic. Apart from clusters of workmen taking group siestas beneath trees and a few shacks selling melons and cactus fruit, the road was entirely nondescript.

We arrived in the city of Zacatecas in good time, only to ride around aimlessly for two hours in search of an affordable place to stay. Campgrounds had become almost non-existent in the country, and, although most hotels were extremely cheap, only a dedicated search would separate them from the more expensive tourist traps in cities.

We had planned ahead and looked up a hostel to stay in, however, the building we arrived at was locked up and not actually a hostel at all. A subsequent search took us on a rollercoaster ride of steep, narrow, cobbled streets through a colourful medley of neighbourhoods. We burnt some clutch scaling the hills on the outskirts of the valley town and gave the brakes a rigorous test when terrifying descents abruptly ended at death defying corners.

Eventually we found a small hotel, where vibrant art covered the walls and sculptures lined the corridors. A heavy wooden door led to our room, and we discovered an entire apartment that lacked only a kitchen inside. We unloaded the bike and wasted no time in setting off on our new favourite pastime of searching for food.

Depictions of skeletons and skulls, often dressed up in clothes or intricately decorated, were becoming a familiar sight in the country, where reverence for souls of the dead was as prevalent as any other spiritual following. We ate a delicious feast in a small restaurant, where the walls were adorned with more skeletal artwork than we had ever before seen in one place.

Later that evening, we took a walk along the cobbled lanes and stumbled on a callejoneada street party. The style of celebration was a spontaneous one that had originally been started by a student who instigated a wandering parade to mark the end of a school year. The idea had taken off across the country, and the unplanned callejoneadas would roam randomly through backstreets and passageways, dancing, singing, and playing instruments whilst picking up revellers along the way, who knocked back punch from small jars that were carried by donkeys. There were worse ways to spend a Tuesday night, and we wondered how its popularity had not spread beyond Mexico.

The city was encased in searing heat the next morning, but it didn't stop us hiking up its hilly streets, dodging hanging laundry and dogs that yapped from the edge of flat rooftops. We wandered through plazas and parks, passing an ancient viaduct and small cafés, where we stopped for a menú del día.

A menú del día was a set menu made up of a soup, a meat and rice dish, and a tiny desert. They never came with a choice but they were incredibly cheap and grew to be a firm fixture in our diet throughout Latin America.

Later, we took a cable car up to the topmost hill that overlooked the sprawling mass of vibrantly colourful buildings, before finding relief in the cool silver mines that lay beneath them.

That night we researched our next stop using an Internet connection in the hotel foyer. After a brief chat with the receptionist, she asked if we would be staying down there for long. Assuming that she wanted us to watch the place for a minute, we said we would wait for her to come back and thought nothing of the fact that she had taken the bundle of room keys and gone upstairs. On her return, she ignored us until we left to go back to our room.

A short while afterwards, we went out, and I noticed that the peso notes which had been in my purse were gone, and, for the rest of the evening, I racked my brains trying to remember where we had spent them.

It was only the next morning that I discovered the dollar coins, which had been in my bike jacket pocket since we had left the US, had also disappeared. Considering the jacket hadn't left the room since we arrived, it dawned on us that the girl must have let herself in the night before and taken them. A top that was similar to one I had been wearing, and which she had commented on, was also missing, and we both felt sick at the realisation that we had been deceived.

Luckily, our larger stash of money and passports were hidden in the padding of our stinking bike trousers and boots, where we were confident that no thief would dare go. Although it was by no means a major setback, the deception went a long way to dull our affection that had been growing for the country.

We left the Zacatecas with a bitter taste in our mouths and veered south towards Queretaro on an uneventful ride past fields of crops and rubbish-strewn roads, where occasional whiffs of sewage caught us off guard. We passed through countless small towns, where menacing speed bumps chipped away at the suspension, before another prolonged search for a place to stay played out along the cobbled roads of the latest colonial city.

We eventually found a small hotel, where the receptionist, Ruth, took us under her wing and restored our faith after the damage done by her counterpart in Zacatecas. She ordered us in a home cooked meal from her friend, before letting us loose on the hotel laundry room.

The next morning we soaked up the café culture in the city, where a majority of mostly Mexican holidaymakers kept the usual preying hawkers at bay. The streets were lined with impeccable pueblo buildings and concrete houses, each with heavy wooden doors that led through to beautiful outdoor courtyards and atriums. Cathedrals, parks, and plazas were buzzing with activity, while street food wagons and craft stalls lined the precincts and streets. Everything was spotless and full of character. Even when the sun went down, buildings that had been locked up during the day came alive with the sound of music and colourful parties.

On our way out of Queretaro the next morning, we got caught in diverted traffic, which took an hour to reach the arches of the city's enormous, ancient viaduct. The structure marked the start of the road to Mexico City, where machinery sat unattended on roped-off sections of new asphalt, the absence of workers indicating that another Sunday had come around.

Although there was less traffic than usual, the lack of any road markings brought mayhem to the highway. Boulders that blended with the road surface had been laid in place of dividing white lines and caused more than a few vehicles to swerve out of their way and into the path of oncoming traffic. Fresh tarmac switched without warning to unpaved gravel, while an occasional religious parade, complete with banners and effigies, clogged up the invisible lanes.

We had been in touch with an English rider who offered his Mexico City home as a hostel to touring motorcyclists. He had invited us to stay at the Garry Hostel, and we had arranged to meet him outside the city the next morning.

We hadn't planned to stay anywhere that night, so took a gamble on a town off the main highway and spent another two hours calling in at countless hotels that we couldn't afford or which didn't have an available room. Eventually we found one and reluctantly parked in a separate garage further down the street, before heading out for food. Everyone in town, including the staff in a café where we ate, was engrossed that night by a cliff-hanger on one of Latin America's notoriously cheesy, television soaps.

The next morning we stopped for breakfast in another café on the way to meet Garry. The prices were displayed above the counter, but, after eating, the owner handed us a bill for more than his sign quoted. With a smug grin, he passed off the difference to a rise in egg prices. His employee looked embarrassed, and it was clear that the proprietor was lying. Although we had planned to give more as a tip, anyway, inflated gringo pricing was becoming too regular for our liking, especially as the hikes usually came from the people who seemed to need it least. We were running late to meet Garry so, after making a small stand, we paid an amount that fell between what the owner was asking for and what his board had quoted, hoping that karma would do its worst.

Garry met us on the outskirts of the city, where he had kindly, and luckily it turned out, come to guide us to his home. We followed him through a labyrinth of roads, where more perilous speed bumps lay in wait and gaping cavities lurked in the cracked tarmac, where manhole covers had been stripped by metal thieves.

The lack of a formal driving test in Mexico soon explained the widespread risky overtaking, undertaking, tailgating, red light jumping, and haphazard stops in the middle of heavy traffic to talk to passing friends.

We descended vertical hills and weaved around the path of suicidal dogs before eventually arriving at the haven of his home. Garry had lived for over thirty years in the suburbs of the sprawling city with his wife, Ivonne, and their two children. They had built the home when the area was still rural, and a dirt track had led to their front door, but, by the time of our visit, the entire district had been paved over with well worn, winding roads, back-to-back graffiti gated houses, small shops, and lively markets, and we instantly fell in love with the hustle and bustle.

Mexico City had first been built by the Mexica people in the 1300s on a small island in a lake after a god had prophesied that their home would be found where an eagle holding a snake landed on a cactus.

Over a period of two hundred years, a strong and powerful hub developed on the site, which was later destroyed by the invading Spanish. Among other things, the conquistadors went on to drain the lake and build Catholic churches over the ruins of Aztec temples.

When we visited the area, the city centre was sinking into the drained lake faster than Venice and, with a population that had multiplied seven times in less than fifty years, it was facing unimaginable infrastructure problems. The city was indescribably vast and its complex network of roads and highways would have been near impossible to navigate, were it not for Garry. Later that day, we followed him into the centre and parked at his workplace, before setting off to explore.

We stumbled out of a crowded subway station into the central plaza and discovered that it was hosting a Homeless World Cup football tournament. The Scottish team had just won a match, and we soon learnt that the English team was about to take on the Germans, so we settled into the stands and watched our home team claim a convincing win.

Hordes of armed military and riot police seemed to match civilians one for one in numbers on the hectic streets of the city centre.

After a taco and enchilada lunch, we unearthed more history about the ancient cultures of the region in the vast anthropology museum.

As evening fell, we sat and rested our aching feet outside the Palace of Fine Arts, where we watched the people of Mexico City pass by. Following another crowded subway train ride back to meet Garry from work, we collected the bike and tailed him via a series of iconic city monuments and statues, before stopping at the Best Tacos in the World stall for dinner.

Rain set in the next day, and, after an unbeatable home cooked Mexican breakfast that included green tomatoes and lots of cheese, Byron serviced the bike for the fourth time on the trip. I got to work on another blog post, before Ivonne introduced us to a few longstanding Mexican soap operas.

Later that evening, they took us to their neighbour's birthday party, where we were greeted with two long glasses of tequila and the chance to practice our Spanish with their friend, Alfonso, and his family. Not long into the evening, Alfonso's daughters opened the door to reveal a group of musicians, who went on to play for the rest of the night, transforming the celebration into a bona fide Mexican fiesta.

Luckily, we had brushed up on our history of Mexico the day before, because Ivonne drove us out of the city to visit the ancient Teotihuacan pyramids the next morning. The site dated back to 100 B.C. and was thought to have been one of the largest cities of its time. Ivonne knew it well and had visited the ruins as a young girl before their later restoration.

Considering they were over 2,000 years old, the structures were immense. We climbed the steep steps of the main pyramids and explored inside some of the excavated temples, attempting to imagine an existence where human sacrifices and decapitation were part of everyday life.

On our way back into the city, we experienced what six million cars in rush hour felt like, without the benefit of a motorcycle to weave through the standstill. Ivonne pulled off the road early to wait for the jam to pass and drove into a suburb that had been home to the artist, Frida Kahlo. True to form, we spent the time there eating in a food market, drinking in a tea shop and eating again in an ice cream parlour, before watching an Aztec dance rehearsal long into the evening. We arrived back at their home later that night with infinite gratitude to Ivonne for showing us such a fantastic time.

A growing trend had begun to emerge, where expected short rides and brief visits were becoming much longer than anticipated. Our break with Garry and Ivonne had turned from two days to five, thanks to their generous hospitality. On our last morning with them, we followed their bike out of the suburbs and into the surrounding mountains, where we stopped for one final meal together before they ventured off on a camping weekend, and we followed the road south, passing the bubbling Popocatepetl active volcano on the way.

We had been advised to stick to toll roads in Mexico but had mostly ignored the recommendation in favour of better views along more scenic routes. That day soon changed our reasoning, though, as the potholed road took us through the centre of every single small town and village along the way. No end of speed bumps and suicidal dogs were joined by chickens, pigs, and donkeys in the road. We had covered less than two hundred miles in over five hours when the heat eventually wore us down. After pulling into the first hotel that we came across, we paid more than our daily budget for the benefit of staying in a room that hadn't taken the usual two hours to find.

We rode through over forty miles of sugar cane and corn fields the next morning to reach the base of the Sierra Madre Oriental mountain range. Crops of beautiful red flowers and palm trees had also dotted the route, where we joined overloaded trucks taking families to church and small motorbikes carrying a minimum of three people each.

The sun highlighted an abundance of green that spread for miles as we twisted and turned higher and higher into the peaks along Federal Highway 182. To top off the perfection of the day, the usual shroud of high altitude cloud cover and the crazy truck drivers were enjoying a Sunday off.

Older inhabitants of small mountain villages were hauling wood along the road using donkeys or back power, while younger men and women hacked away at the grass verge with machetes. Although the road was free of the usual hazardous trucks, wandering livestock and ferocious stray dogs kept us alert. Circling buzzards flocked high above us for most of the journey, perhaps waiting for the stray dogs to finally close in on their kill. Waterfalls spilled onto the road, where the Flying Aga took another hammering from deep potholes and unpredictable speed bumps.

Many hours later, we began a descent out of the mountains and into a tropical climate where the humidity escalated and replaced the smouldering but bearable heat with an intensity that sent perspiration levels soaring.

As the elevation fell away, the frequency and size of the mountain villages grew, and the means of using donkeys for transport was replaced by a return of small, Chinese manufactured motorcycles. Palapas and palm trees increased tenfold, while a plethora of oranges and dates were being traded along the roadside.

We slowed to approach one unusually visible speed bump in a village when a cheerful rider on a small bike pulled alongside us. An enormous sack of oranges was lodged between him and his girlfriend on the back and, as we took the bump together, he motioned for us to follow them.

The young couple were heading to the next big city and we stuck together for the rest of the ride. We eventually passed through more fields of sugar cane before reaching two enormous lakes that reflected the setting sun with perfection, marking the end of the mountains and one of the best rides of the whole trip.

Lillian and Alfredo saved us the usual search for accommodation by leading us to a hotel in the town of Tuxtepec, before disappearing into the busy evening traffic with their colossal sack of oranges. Once again, the room cost more than we could afford but it was mercifully air conditioned, and, when we stepped outside later that evening, the wall of heat had not let up and instantly made us grateful for it.

We took a toll route the next day that saved us from the speed bump-riddled villages, but still failed to offer much improvement on the cracks and potholes that punctured the roads of the country. There was little to see besides miles of waterlogged land and a few token construction workers who were napping beneath the trees.

Later that day, we pulled into Villahermosa and, after another customarily long search, we resigned ourselves to yet another high-priced hotel that was ominously guarded by armed police. We were resolute that this would be the last of the budget annihilating stays and set about basking in the luxury of hot showers, cotton towels, and air conditioning.

We roamed the streets later that evening and settled on a couple of plastic stools at an unassuming street taco wagon, which turned out to be one of the best food finds of the trip. Throngs of people waited in queues at the carts, which dotted the streets, while the busy traders worked like artists, slicing and dicing indeterminate cuts of meat from buckets on the floor. They tossed the meat through sizzling basins of fat before adding in miniature tortillas at the last minute to produce the most perfect mix of hot tender meat in crispy wraps that we had ever tasted. After waiting patiently while orders were called and money was exchanged, it came to our turn, and we indulged in far too many of them before returning to bed in a less than comfortable but incredibly content state.

CENTRAL AMERICA

BELIZE

GUATEMALA

HONDURAS

EL SALVADOR

NICARAGUA

COSTA RICA

PANAMA

• • • • FLYING AGA ROUTE

Sinkholes and Swindlers

154 Days on the Road | 17,446 Miles on the Clock

We followed the Gulf coast into the Yucatan Peninsula the next day. More potholes and hostile stray dogs were scattered along the route through sleepy fishing villages and past palm lined white beaches.

After arriving in the small coastal city of Campeche, we eventually found a hostel that was set back from the seafront and we shattered a makeshift ramp while navigating a high pavement to park in its lobby. There were just two spare beds in a tiled, windowless room at the end of a dark corridor, where metal bars had replaced the glass in the door window. Turning our back on the recent run of luxury stays, we snapped it up.

An open pipe trickled out cold water for a shower in the bathroom, where the toilet had no seat and a couple of threadbare towels featured the fading logos of nearby upmarket, tourist hotels. After discovering the snapped handle of a spoon that had been left as the only method of turning on the television, we carefully balanced it in the broken power switch that night and settled back into a cheaper way of living.

The sea beckoned in the morning, and the prospect of spending a day on a beach had us up bright and early. Unfortunately, our lack of forward planning had let us down again when we discovered a long wall separating the promenade from the sea. Not a grain of sand was in sight, and, despite the blazing heat, any desire to go for a dip vanished at the sight of the motionless, oily water.

With a change of tack, we set off into the town and discovered the most immaculate colonial city we had come across. A customary plaza and cathedral lay at the centre of a network of well kept streets, where square, stone buildings with heavy wooden doors had been painted in a rainbow of pastel colours. A day of eating coconuts, visiting cathedrals, and taking photographs of wooden doors followed, before we spent the evening in a restaurant that was heavily adorned with vibrant illustrations of skulls and skeletons.

The next morning, we went for breakfast in a nearby café, where the uncommon sight of a gathering of elderly men enjoying a coffee morning greeted us. The waitress apologetically explained that we had arrived too late for the baby shark tacos, and, unsure if something had been lost in translation, we were too polite to ask if she was serious. We stuck to eggs and fresh fruit, before nodding goodbye to the gentlemen's club and heading back to retrieve the bike.

Having shattered the ramp on the way in, we carefully eased it down the steep pavement curb that gave the nearby sea defences a run for their money, before setting off towards the depths of the tourist-ravaged Yucatan Peninsula.

During the long wait for our trip to begin, we had watched a BBC programme about a network of deep sinkholes called cenotes that were scattered across the peninsula. They were thought to have been caused by the same meteorite that had landed off the Mexican coast and wiped out the dinosaurs, and, since we were in the area, we decided to visit some.

Unusually, we even booked ahead to stay at our first backpacking hostel. With hammocks hanging at random from trees and suspended over a peaceful garden swimming pool, we couldn't believe that we hadn't stopped in at a backpacking haunt any earlier.

The town was considerably more chaotic than those we had stopped at over the past week and played host to an influx of peddlers whose survival seemed to depend on fleecing tourists.

We were taking in the main plaza the next day when a man asked if we wanted him to take a photo of us. We recognised his game immediately but were reluctant to offend him so went along with the conversation. His English was good, but we asked him to speak Spanish so we could at least get something out of the obvious charade and practice our steadily improving grasp of the language.

The guy launched into a story about his Mayan family who ran a craft shop in the town to help their community fund the education of its children. He explained that they struggled to compete against imposters who claimed to be Mayan and stole their business from tourists. There was no question that he was out to sting us for some cash, so we told him that we were travelling by bike and had no space to buy or carry anything extra but, despite Byron's objections and for reasons unknown, we still went with him to see the shop.

It was quickly obvious that the outfit was, as we had suspected, the crook in his swindling sob story. There was nothing authentic or craft-like about its cheap souvenirs that had clearly come straight off a production line, and, as soon as we arrived, the guy handed us over to his friend before disappearing back into the town.

We listened politely to a well rehearsed spiel that was delivered in fluent English, despite the supposed struggle of their community to educate its children in the most basic of lessons. We looked at his worn photographs of random people that he professed to be family, before the clinch came and he insisted that we buy something in return for the time he had spent talking to us. We told him we had no space to carry anything, but he was a big guy and didn't look too happy that this particular snare might not go their way.

Eventually, our lack of experience in such a situation let us down, and we caved in to his persistence. We bought the smallest bottle of liquor but were so annoyed with ourselves for doing so that we forgot to haggle, and their venture triumphed when we paid three times the going rate for the drink.

As we left the shop, I caught a glimpse of the guy who had executed the sale waving our notes in glee under the nose of a woman and felt sick. The cost hadn't been much, but it quickly sank in that we had knowingly been duped by people who were shamelessly capitalising on the plight of their fellow countrymen.

We decided it wasn't too late to rectify the error and went into a nearby shop to get a realistic idea of what the price of the bottle should have been, before daring a return to the scene of the crime.

Although we knew our money was long gone, there was a burning determination to let the swindlers know that their setup was not failsafe, and favour was on our side when we saw that the salesman was taken aback to see us again. The cultural dislike of confrontation had us leaving with a second bottle of the liquor, and, although it was hardly a victory, we left with hope that the minor altercation would dent their confidence in the scheme.

The next morning, we rose early and fought our way through the busy streets to the bus stop, where we caught a service to the outskirts of the jungle. An hour later, we reached a tiny town, where we hopped into the seat of a motorcycle rickshaw, whose young rider took us out to a cleared field where a number of men were gathered around waiting horses and wagons.

The primary industry in the area had once been the cultivation of an agave plant that is used to make rope and twine. However, when the production declined, a few industrious locals adapted the old plantation rails to run tours to three cenotes that lay along a seven-mile jungle loop. When we visited the spot, the tours had been running for a decade, and the livelihoods of the guides depended entirely on the enterprise.

We were soon settled in the back of a wagon that was drawn by a horse along the narrow, rickety rails into the thick undergrowth. Our guide pre-empted every fracture and loose section in the track, tipping the wagon seconds before we jolted over them, while directing his horse, who seemed to know what was coming without his help.

It was a single track, and we never did work out the etiquette that dictated the right of way. Sometimes we would pull to a stop and climb out of the wagon so the guide could lift the cart off the rails and let an associate pass by. Further down the same stretch, though, we would keep on going while another guide ushered his load off to let us trundle past. Despite a reported dispute between the locals, who had been running the rails for a decade, and a politician, who had just set up a rival business, we saw more signs of hostility coming out of the horse's rear than anywhere else along the circuit.

The cenotes had been used by ancient civilisations as the only source of fresh water in the river-barren peninsula and had been regarded as sacred gateways to the underworld of the dead. The flooded caves and sinkholes were, in fact, connected through incredible underground rivers that had formed following the collapse of limestone bedrock, most likely after the impact of the six-mile meteorite millions of years earlier.

The jungle tracks led us to three different cenotes that each sank to intimidating depths of over five meters [16 feet]. Two of the pools were hidden in caves that were only accessible by climbing through tiny openings in the ground, where rustic wooden ladders led deep beneath the soil. Jagged border rocks and boulders surrounded the sinkhole pools below, while shards of sunlight streamed through gaps in the cave roof, tangling with enormous clusters of twisted roots and vines that dropped straight down from the jungle to skim the water surface.

With their spectacular stalactites hanging eerily from the ceilings and stalagmites rising from the dark cave beds, where sinister black tunnels led into the unknown, it was easy to see how the sinkholes had been deemed as other-worldly.

After cooling off in the three different cenotes, where many a human sacrifice had once been made, the guide led us back along the rickety rails to the edge of the jungle, where we bid farewell to him and his trusty horse and watched them gallop off into the distance.

As they went, we spotted an enormous beast of a vehicle parked at the edge of the clearing and went over to check it out. It turned out to be a hybrid of half East German military tank and half German fire-engine and was transporting a German couple through the continent. It was so colossal that they were having to backtrack to the US to pick up bespoke [made to order] new tyres before they could resume their route south.

The couple told us about a fourth cenote just around the corner that they had visited the night before and recommended that we go and have a look. On our way to do so, we were blockaded by the motorcycle rickshaw riders, who approached us en masse and seemed adamant that we shouldn't go any farther. We couldn't understand their reasoning in stopping us, and, considering that we had understood the couple who had been to see it, we ignored them and walked on.

A trail took us through a small forest and past a rundown house before we reached another familiar circular opening in the ground. We stood contemplating the latest pitch black hole, fearing the top of a ragged rope ladder that led further inside and made the previous wooden contraptions look like grand staircases. The lack of any life nearby had us wondering who would notice if we never came back up.

We had decided not to explore the black void just as a bedraggled woman appeared with a few, equally miserable barefoot kids in tow. Although we didn't recognise what she said, we understood when she pointed to a sign that quoted a price to visit the cenote. Conscious that the source of the group's misery might be watching them from the creepy house, we emptied our pockets of change but declined a visit into the most sinister abyss of the day. After scampering back out of the forest, the motorcycle rickshaw riders were still nearby and looked relieved to see us return.

We spent the evening with Pete and Rach, who were travelling the continent with their young daughters, Tilly and Kiah, and an Australian couple who were stopping in our hostel to recover from a bout of potentially fatal dengue fever. They were the first English speaking friends we had met in a long time, and we all crammed into the tiny gallery of a hot and sticky pizzeria in town where we destroyed a fair few pizzas and beers.

The next day we made our first trip to the Caribbean coast and shared a palm lined road with vintage VW Beetle cars and dreadlocked cyclists, riding for as long as we could stand the heat. We passed Tulum and continued south along the coast, where glimpses of a tantalizing blue sea taunted us through the gaps between eco-cabins and boutique hotels. Eventually, we could take no more and pulled into the yard of one of the cabins, where a three-legged dog greeted us.

It was a peaceful haven, and we spent the final hours of the day dipping in and out of the unexpectedly choppy tropical sea, sharing the cabin's only patched up, worn-out sun-lounger, while the guests of the neighbouring hotel enjoyed soft cushioned recliners and the service of suited waiters.

Thunder rumbled in the distance the next morning, and a hammering rain made the prospect of the beach and the broken sun-bed less appealing. We were eager to reach Guatemala, anyway, to celebrate my birthday three days later in the jungle city of Tikal, so we packed up and, once the rain let up, we voluntarily left the Caribbean paradise to face the bedlam of our first Central American border crossing.

GANGS AND DIPPY EGGS

162 Days on the Road | 18,088 Miles on the Clock

We spent a final night in the Mexican border town of Chetumal before riding around aimlessly the next morning in search of the crossing to Belize. A few wrong turns were met with indignant whistles from the traffic police, but we eventually tracked down the exit out of Mexico.

Six thoroughly enjoyable weeks had passed in the final North American country of the journey, where two flat tyres, one flat battery, and one thieving hotel maid had been the extent of the terrible things that were supposed to have happened to us there. To ease our mixed feelings about leaving it behind, we were thrilled to receive a refund of $200 that we had paid back in Tijuana to temporarily import the Flying Aga into the country.

The paved road soon ended, and we came to a jumble of huts and buildings where tuk-tuk drivers transported Mexicans and Belizeans back and forth across a muddy quagmire. We couldn't fathom where to begin, but a young lad spoke to direct us, and, unusually, we understood him straight away. We had been immersed in Spanish for six weeks, and the sudden familiar sound of our mother tongue completely threw us.

As a former British Crown colony, Belize was the only Latin American country that, as well as Creole and Spanish, counted English as a national language. We weren't too certain that we liked it, though. Our still basic understanding of Spanish had helped us to retain a degree of detached ignorance that had sometimes been convenient in Mexico and had more than likely helped contribute to our fondness for the country.

With a thick Caribbean accent, the boy pointed us towards an office, where we purchased insurance before following a dirt track to a car park. A group of men shouted over to us that they would watch our bike, and, annoyingly, after losing the defence of poor language skills, their antagonistic tone was unmistakable. We had never taken the chance of leaving the bike unattended when it was fully loaded, so we ignored them and took it in turns to guard our gear.

They looked on resentfully, while I waited with the bike and Byron passed them to enter the immigration hall. While other people came and went, the group never moved. With the trusty bear spray to hand and armed guards patrolling the site, they weren't much of a threat, but it was irritating that we had so easily understood their hostility that would no doubt have gone unrecognised in Spanish.

Once Byron had the bike paperwork and his passport stamped to enter the country, we switched roles, and, despite no further exchanges, the tension had risen with the group. Their eyes followed me as I walked past them, an unsightly vision, with hair plastered to my head and a sweat stained back, which apparently did nothing to deter them because, once I was out of earshot, the lead protagonist shouted to Byron that he liked his woman.

There was no question as to the meaning behind the remark, so Byron took a gamble and stood up to him before he gained more confidence. Quick as a flash, he retorted that he liked the man's mother. It was a risky response, considering they were a gang of fairly well built Caribbean guys, but it paid off and left the man's posse in stitches, nipping his bravado in the bud.

When I returned from the immigration hall, the atmosphere had mellowed, and most of the men had dispersed. However, when the main guy saw me again, he decided to throw his weight about in a final attempt to save face. He approached us and aggressively asked to see our papers. His demeanour quickly attracted the attention of a few guards, who sent him packing, but the damage was done and he had tarnished the image of his entire country in our eyes. We were instantly eager to get back to the Spanish speaking territories, where such an exchange would never have got off the ground.

Three hours after reaching the end of the road in Mexico, we rolled into Belize, where a single-lane highway sliced through the country. With a land area of just under 9,000 square miles, we could have cut through in a single day but we wanted to spend at least one night there. The roaming livestock, machete wielding locals, and overloaded trucks that had accompanied us through Mexico continued to appear on the road as we made our way inland.

We travelled south through its countryside, passing beautiful wooden houses that had been built on stilts and were perched above well cultivated gardens and lawns. After a hundred miles, we bypassed its notorious capital city and famous coastline to cut west towards Guatemala.

San Ignacio lay at the end of the road that day, where a predominantly cheerful atmosphere contrasted with the cautiously bolted doors of guest-houses and the groups of men that appeared on street corners after dark. We avoided any more altercations and ducked from the path of one group into a small restaurant, where we feasted on meat pie and shrimp.

After returning to the same place the next morning for some very British dippy eggs and soldiers, the thought of another lengthy border crossing into Guatemala sent us rushing the short distance to get it over with.

Before we could pass into a new country, exit stamps from the country we were leaving were required on the temporary importation paperwork for the bike and in our passports. This was to prove that we hadn't illegally sold the bike while we had been there or overstayed our permitted visit. Occasionally, a questionable fee was charged, but otherwise the process should have been simple.

Entry stamps for the country we were entering were then required on fresh temporary importation papers for the bike and in our passports. A few more questionable fees were charged again, but the process should also have been simple. However, we soon learnt that Central American borders had perfected the art of confusing simplicity.

For starters, there was an immediate presence of tramitadores, who were independent fixers or middlemen, that knew the different requirements and the buildings where each step of a border crossing had to be completed. They descended in packs onto unsuspecting foreigners and falsely declared, while flashing questionable permits, that it was the law to use their services. They were usually men and were particularly skilled in selective hearing.

After we successfully left Belize with the appropriate exit stamps in place, we rode towards the entry into Guatemala.

Five tramitadores flocked towards us, and it took a lot of patience to convince them that we didn't want any help and weren't going to pay them. After shedding the last of them, we adopted our respective border crossing roles. I stood guard over our worldly possessions, while Byron, whose name was on the vehicle ownership documents, set off to untangle the red tape.

It soon transpired that we hadn't completely got our message across when an apprentice tramitador of about thirteen years old tailed Byron for close to two hours while he attempted to make sense of what was required to pass through the border.

Temporarily importing the bike proved to be the biggest drain on time and tolerance, as any sign of an official procedure always remained a mystery to just about everyone involved. At this particular border, forms were filled out in one unmarked office before they were verified by an official who declared that copies were required for a different official. An extensive search for the photocopy shack then took place, followed immediately by another search for a currency exchanger. Working out who exactly needed the copies came next and resulted in the revelation that they were, in fact, copies of the wrong form, and that a different form was required, which first needed a stamp from another office. Somewhere along the line, a passport stamp was also required, together with a photocopy of it.

The entire process was carried out in extreme heat in heavy clothing, while the exasperating apprentice tramitador tagged along and occasionally repeated what an official had already said.

By the time it was over, the boy was adamant that he had earned a fee for his assistance, but we were incensed that he was claiming credit for the feat that Byron had pulled off single-handedly and hadn't saved us any hassle at all. He was evidently a fast learner, though, because his selective hearing was unwavering.

He eventually gave up, and we got ready to leave, when an attack of conscience took hold. We tried to imagine a child that young braving similar chaos back home, harassing foreigners on the chance of earning some loose change, so, in acknowledgment of his nerve, we gave him a small part of the amount he had asked for, mindful that the gesture would do nothing to lessen the hassle that the next tourists would experience.

The final obstacle that lay between us and Guatemala was a police search. A few armed officers flipped through the pages of our diary, before attempting to take a couple of photos with our camera. After a glance inside our jam-packed panniers, though, they decided they had seen enough and left us to repack what they had messed up, before we cleared the gates to freedom.

Squashed Dogs and Shotguns

163 Days on the Road | 18,250 Miles on the Clock

The chaos evaporated as soon as we crossed into Guatemala, and a beautiful route lay ahead, where herds of humpback cows grazed in cleared patches of jungle and donkeys tucked into the grass verge beside the road.

Encounters that had once left us tense suddenly seemed trivial. We narrowly missed a close call with a runaway pig and saw a return of the perilous speed bumps that had briefly disappeared in Belize. We wrestled against roads that abruptly turned to gravel and left us in the wake of blinding dust when truck drivers sped past with little regard for their suspensions.

The border experience had either upped the ante, or we had finally acclimatised to the roads of Latin America. Either way, we arrived unruffled at a small hotel later that afternoon.

Most of the population of the Yucatan Peninsula and northern Central America favoured sleeping in hammocks and, although they were undeniably comfy, sharing one for an entire night didn't appeal, so we took a room with a standard bed.

After cooling off beneath an electric fan that could have either taken off or brought the ceiling down at any moment, we went for a walk to the nearby Petén Itzá Lake, where some horrifically malnourished dogs roamed the marshy shore. As if to illustrate their plight, one of them began to eat the excrement left by a fellow dog when we drew close.

A stone block jutted out into the lake nearby and was being used by some girls to scrub laundry while they concurrently took a bath in a scene that became a regular sight in the watercourses across Central America.

We were closing in on the Equator, where long evenings were fast disappearing, as darkness began to fall early. After watching a spectacular sunset fall below the water, we returned to the small village, where electricity was in short supply and, with little else to do, we got an early night in the mosquito plagued room.

Having arranged for him to take us to Tikal, we met the hotel owner, Umberto, at five o'clock the next morning. It was my birthday, and we were hoping to watch the sun rise over the ancient jungle city.

It was still dark when we set off, but we stopped to meet a few of Umberto's friends, who were not so prompt. They were guides at the site and were in no hurry to arrive before the sun rose. By the time they had stopped jumping in and out of the van and calling on friends, we had watched the day break through the streaky windows and arrived at the site in daylight.

Dense vegetation had lined the route into the national park, and yellow triangular warning signs had appeared along the road depicting the silhouettes of snakes, jaguars, monkeys, and, unexpectedly, turkeys. Although we had risen at the crack of dawn for nothing, the journey still got us excited for what lay ahead.

Umberto left us with his tour guide friends and, with a wink, he disappeared behind the café to spend the morning in a clandestine poker game with the other drivers who had brought tourists to the site.

Some of the Tikal ruins were well over 2,000 years old and were thought to have been left abandoned for at least half of that time. Over the later 1,000 years, the rainforest had reclaimed the land and encased towering temples inside rugs of thick jungle. Memories of the site had been reduced to legend among the Mayan people, who had continued to impart tales across generations about a lost city where their ancestors had thrived under a dynastic rule.

The city only saw sunlight again in the nineteenth century, when the tallest of its temples was spotted by a gum-sapper, who had been working high in the jungle canopy. The excavation of its temples, tombs, and palaces was still far from complete during our visit and huge, jungle-covered mounds indicated the presence of more pyramids and temples that were yet to be unveiled.

Our guides had grown up at the site and were soon pointing out hallucinogenic mushrooms that were still used in Mayan rituals and rites of passage, as well as animals and insects that our untrained eyes would never have spotted. They would let out uncanny imitations of the haunting howler monkey bellow or the sinister jaguar snarl, that always attracted a response from the depths of the jungle, probably from another well-practised guide.

They led us along a path that occasionally dipped into the tangled trees before returning to the beaten track. It was our first taste of exploring the interior of a jungle and, despite the less adventurous aspect of it being a tour along a trail, we were in awe of every twist and turn. A few spider monkeys swung through the branches above us, and several white-nosed coatis combed the undergrowth, while some racoons made a run for it when they heard us approaching.

At some point, we came across the ominous sight of a backpack hanging from a tree with a sheathed machete resting between its straps. Our guide ignored it and carried on walking until we came across its owner, who was raking leaves on the jungle floor. The guide stopped to chat with him for a minute when, without warning, he dived forward and shoved the groundskeeper out of the way.

It turned out that his leg had been inches away from a pit viper that was concealed in the bed of dried leaves. The guide explained that his brother had once been bitten by the species and, after a long and painful recovery, he had never returned to the jungle again. Using a stick to lift the snake above the ground, he showed us what to look out for, because, he explained reassuringly, not all hospitals stocked its anti-venom.

The incident occurred shortly after the guide had spotted a

tarantula the size of a large hand. It was the texture of rich velvet, and fine red hairs embellished its abdomen. The guide fearlessly picked it off the post it was climbing and offered it around to an impressive number of volunteers to hold it. At some point he remembered that it was my birthday and motioned me into the centre of the group, where he made an unsuccessful attempt to get me to hold it. After failing to convince me, he went on to dangle the spider in front of my face for a photo that was intended to look like I was about to eat it, however, I ducked and dodged with a shameful amount of genuine fear, and he eventually moved on to more willing targets.

We went on to spend hours scaling the historic structures, where ancient rulers, priests, and many a human sacrifice would once have ascended in pomp and ceremony, before blood and guts were spilt. A wooden scaffold and stairway had been constructed against the side of the tallest remaining temple, and we climbed high above the tree canopy to witness the most spectacular, panoramic view of the surrounding jungle.

As the sun rose higher, and the humidity in the forest became unbearable, we made our way back to the café to meet Umberto, who was finishing up his last poker hand.

We soon split from the rest of the tourists and made our way back to the tiny village, where we returned to the shore of the lake. One lady had replaced the girls from the day before to scrub laundry on the stone block, while another hacked away at a nearby tree trunk with a machete. Byron braved the water, while I soaked up the sun before it fell away early. Back in the hotel, a dubiously fitted shower head in the bathroom mildly electrocuted us both before we ventured into the dimly lit village.

The far from ordinary birthday was concluded in a small restaurant that overlooked the moonlit lake. As we drank cool beers and ate fresh fish, a loud cacophony signalled that a gang of frogs and toads were having a party of their own in the reeds below.

The next morning, the sounds from the nearby jungle woke

us at another ungodly hour, so we took advantage and set off on the road before the sun could do its worst. We made our way through village after village of palapa huts and wooden shacks, into the heart of Guatemala.

We crossed over rivers and passed alongside streams where whole families were bathing or scrubbing laundry on rocks. Barefoot women dressed in long colourful skirts and loose tops walked along the road balancing huge containers of grains and produce on their heads. Occasionally, a few machete wielding men would appear from the adjacent jungle and join them in their walk to the nearest village.

The same flora that we had seen in Tikal was enhanced by splashes of vibrant flowers, while mountains loomed ahead, dripping in thick blankets of foliage.

More than one runaway chicken sent us swerving across the road, while pigs, goats, and donkeys rambled in the hedgerows and herds of humpback cows were ushered to and from the fields by entire families. The road was well paved and free of the monstrous trucks that usually stormed past us. However, perilous speed bumps remained a permanent feature in every village and intermittently scraped across the bike's undercarriage or sent us flying.

We rode past young men and boys galloping bareback on horses and small motorcycles that usually carried one child resting on the petrol tank and at least one more squeezed between two adults on the seat. Wagons brimming with passengers or goods in their open truck beds passed us by, often with odd tyres and wobbling wheels. Labourers perched on the roof of truck cabins or sat on top of sacks of produce, and, every so often, we succeeded in turning their suspicious stares into waves.

Stray dogs continued to appear from nowhere and chase us with relentless malice. As long as we were in their sights, they showed a complete disregard for anything else on the road, which soon explained the great number of them lying hideously squashed along the route.

We stopped for lunch in a roadside café, where the menú del día was dished up to us the minute we sat down. A meat broth made of, among other things, a couple of chicken feet, was followed by beef, rice, and beans. It was good quality food and, judging by the number of labourers passing in and out of the establishment, it was designed to fuel a hard day's work.

We had reached the mountains that had loomed ahead earlier that morning. Their thick green coating was comprised of tangled vines and tropical trees that concealed any trace of the rock beneath. A mist began to descend on the area, and people poured out of a collection of trucks and buses in a nearby petrol station to haul tarpaulin over open roofs and exposed luggage. Their preparation proved to be a shrewd move when the heavens opened shortly afterwards and drenched us within minutes.

We eventually outran the rain and came to the end of the road, where a barge was transporting vehicles across the width of a river. We lined up behind a few wagons to wait as the vessel groaned its way from the opposite bank towards us. It was manned by a few guys sporting straw hats, who sent their outgoing load off as quickly as they ushered us onboard, before pulling away the second that we cleared the gangplank.

On the other side of the river, we rode directly into the heart of a busy market, where it appeared that the population of every village in the surrounding vicinity had assembled for a weekly catch up.

Stalls constructed of cane and tarpaulin hemmed the road, where people of every age were either buying or selling wares, chatting with friends, or quarrelling with siblings. People were climbing in and out of trucks or weaving through the chaos on tiny motorcycles and in tuk-tuk taxis, and not one person gave us a second glance as we meandered through the hustle and bustle.

The lush landscape was peppered with similar markets, and we picked our way through a couple more before the road led us to higher ground. We had just overtaken three precariously overloaded trucks, whose rear axles hovered inches from the road, when two adventure motorcycles appeared from the opposite direction.

Although there had been no shortage of bikes back in the US and Canada, only a handful were loaded up for extensive trips, and, since we had entered Latin America, it had been rare to see one larger than 250cc. The two that rode towards us were the very first heavily laden, sticker swathed bikes that we had seen since we arrived in Alaska five and a half months earlier. With the same delight of unexpectedly meeting a good friend, we pulled over and finally got to talk to some fellow overland motorcycle travellers.

They were Heidi and Bernd from Germany and were taking their two KTM bikes on a second tour, having already travelled across Asia. They were riding north from Argentina, and, as the three trucks honked their horns in victory when they overtook us, we exchanged tips on our respective routes ahead, before wishing one another good luck and continuing our separate ways.

Since crossing the border a few days earlier, there had been a marked increase in armed guards at the entrance to every shop, petrol station, and hotel. We had even caught glimpses of their standard issue, pump-action shotguns poking out the back of trucks ahead of us on the road. When we pulled into the mountain city of Cobán, the muzzle of one such gun stopped us at the entrance to a hotel, before its owner reluctantly let us through.

We were fortunate to get the very last available room inside, which, unluckily, sat directly off a huge atrium, where the Guatemalan youth basketball team congregated until late at night. On the plus side, it was free of mosquitoes and cockroaches, and, although the shower didn't electrocute us, it turned out to be our last encounter with hot water for a least another month.

We declined an invitation to watch a basketball tournament that evening in favour of food and soon found one of our favourite eateries of the whole trip. It was set in a minuscule room at the front of a small house, where a few wooden benches were laid out at the foot of some steps that led in from the street. The counter doubled up as the kitchen, where a single-hob, gas stove was set up to cook the food, and a bucket of water sat on the floor for washing dishes. One lady was finishing up her supper when we entered the cosy room, and she gave us a warm smile of contentment as she left.

A few girls, who had been playing out on the street, followed us in and took up their places behind the counter to offer us bistek y frijoles, a dish that consisted of a flattened steak and stewed beans. They served it up and hung about until their mother appeared and took over. Before we left, our query about getting breakfast there in the morning was met with confusion. We hadn't realised that it would be Sunday the next day, when just about everybody went to church.

We felt the long forgotten feeling of a chill the next morning when we set off early into the mountains, hoping to reach the border to El Salvador that afternoon. Although we were successfully travelling without much of a plan, Panama was approaching, where the road ended, and only a boat or an aeroplane could get us to Colombia.

The Darien Gap, which separates Panama and Colombia, is a mass of jungle and marshland. The only way to negotiate a route through was on foot or in an off road vehicle by those willing to risk the treacherous terrain and the threat of the resident paramilitary guerrillas, who had a penchant for murder and kidnapping.

Flight prices were beyond our means, but there were thriving operations of independent sailings, which capitalised on the absence of a ferry service. Tour operators and captains regularly ran five-day, miniature voyages across the Caribbean Sea between the two countries.

However, the bulk of demand for the passage stemmed from backpacking and overland travellers, and many of the organisers had apparently associated the adventurous nature of their clients with low expectations for comfort. Tales circulated about substandard safety equipment and the widespread practice of overfilling cabins and boats.

Less than a year earlier, an overloaded vessel had sunk off the Colombian coast, leaving its passengers to the fate of a small dinghy, while its consignment of their luggage and two overland motorcycles sank to the bottom of the ocean. The accounts had not gone unnoticed, and we booked our place on a substantial steel schooner that had been recommended by other motorcycle travellers who had gone before us.

Due to the sailing schedule of the boat and the need to time our arrival in Colombia with a visit from some friends, our crossing was due to sail less than three weeks after we left Cobán, and, for the first time on our trip, there was an urgency to speed up.

The ride towards El Salvador led through more of the lush mountains and small villages that we had passed the day before. We dodged the usual medley of roaming animals and took on the challenge of a few aggressive dogs, who would abruptly stop with uncertainty whenever we slowed down. Women continued to balance containers skilfully on their heads, and young men hacked away at the grass verge, while kids kicked footballs about and shouted in excitement when we rode past them.

As we made our way further south, the peaceful rural backdrop eventually slipped away, and the wooden huts and horses were gradually replace by houses and cars.

A group of tramitadores immediately spotted us when we approached the border to El Salvador, and, after jumping into the back of a waiting truck, they literally chased us to the crossing, where a mishmash of huts and buildings lay ahead.

We adopted a newly instated rule of ignoring anybody who wasn't armed and made a beeline towards a group of uniformed border officials, who had handguns tucked in their belts. As we climbed off the bike to speak to them, the tramitadores launched themselves from the truck and descended on us with a total disregard for personal space.

The air was smouldering, and their persistence did nothing to help our growing agitation, until we eventually matched their selective hearing with a brand of our own, and they slowly broke away.

It wasn't that the tramitador trade was short on business, because we had watched freight drivers attach hammocks to the undercarriage of their trucks and take naps, while they sent fixers to sort out their paperwork. It was simply that gringos probably paid over the odds if they could be snared. We didn't see the point of completing the challenge of the trip totally unaided, only to cop out of a few hassles at borders, which, however aggravating, had begun to improve our Spanish no end.

One last tramitador hung around after we spoke to the guards, who had stood back impartially during the ambush. He stuck his nose in our paperwork and generally wound us up, so we tried a new tactic. Instead of ignoring him, we told him that we were learning Spanish, and that it was a personal goal to exit Guatemala and reach El Salvador without any help. We had no idea why it worked, but he shook our hands and wished us luck before walking off.

With a sigh of relief, we took a quick look around to make sure he was the last of them and spotted a hunched old man nearby, who had obviously watched the whole scene unfold. As we caught his eye, he gave us the thumbs up and flashed a huge, toothless grin, as if to verify our victory.

The same palaver that had played out three days earlier, when we entered Guatemala, unravelled in reverse to exit the country, but, after paying a few quetzals for some dubious fees, we secured our exit stamps.

Prepared for more chaotic hassles, we rode a few hundred meters towards the entry to El Salvador. Of all the border crossings we would go on to conquer, the entry into El Salvador turned out to be one of the most hassle-free. The entire process took place under one roof, where offices and desks were clearly marked, and the officials couldn't have been more helpful. There was no sign of pesky tramitadores, either, and the only downside of the whole process was that they didn't have a passport stamp to add to our collection.

Volcanoes and Machete Commutes

166 Days on the Road | 18,709 Miles on the Clock

That night, we stopped close to the border in Metapan, where the guesthouses were barred and bolted, and armed guards were even more of a common sight than they had been in Guatemala. The private protection of businesses and properties had apparently become necessary when large numbers of nationals had returned home after being expelled from the US, following a crack down on inner-city gangs. Apart from a couple of shady characters wandering the streets that night, though, the people we met in the country were some of the friendliest on the journey.

The next morning, we retrieved the Flying Aga from a building site lockup behind the hostel and rode a short distance through coffee plantations and palm fringed hills towards a cluster of volcanoes. Vividly painted buses thundered along the roads, while whiffs of rotting waste continued to catch us off guard outside every town.

A wrong turn led us down a dirt track that we followed until we reached a gate, where the shaved heads of two dolls were tied to each post. Spooked by the sight, we abruptly turned around and hightailed back down the track to the main road, where we eventually found the turning to a nearby lake.

Over thousands of years, the lake had formed inside the enormous cauldron of an ancient volcano. We followed the road on a descent into the rich green crater, before embarking on a potholed, gravel track that traced its shoreline. Our fingers were crossed as we rattled and bumped along the path, desperately hoping that the Flying Aga would survive the latest assault on its old frame.

After checking into a hostel, where a beautiful garden backed directly onto the lake, we wasted no time in launching a rowing boat. We dragged it through a tangle of reeds and tree trunks, before paddling out to the heart of the cauldron, where we drifted in the afternoon sun and soaked up a spectacular view.

Later that evening, we wandered along the track in search of food and came across a lady cooking homemade fries and pupusas over hot coals outside the front door of her house. After eating an excessive amount of the thick, cheese-filled, corn tortillas, she flatly refused to take any more than a dollar from both of us as payment.

The next morning, we saved the bike from another pounding on the gravel track and took one of the region's gaudy buses up to an area that was home to three active volcanoes. A couple of armed policemen had joined us when we climbed onboard the service, that was transporting machete equipped farm labourers into the hills, and it didn't take long for one of them to single us out.

His rifle dangled over his shoulder as he stood in front of our seat, resting one hand on a gun tucked in his belt and the other on a truncheon. Considering he was on the verge of retirement, a surreal conversation unravelled in which he recited everything he seemed to have learnt about women from misogynistic hip-hop music. Conscious of the visibly armed people that surrounded us in the confined space, we did our best to humour him until the bus pulled up to the base of the volcanoes.

We lost the policeman when we joined up with a teenage guide, who was about to lead a group to the pinnacle of a 2,380 meter [7,808 feet] active volcano. Together with two much quieter armed policemen, an Austrian guy, and an El Salvadorian couple, we set off to scale Santa Ana.

The boyfriend in the El Salvadorian couple spoke English and filled us in on what we didn't understand from the guide. He explained that it was government policy for armed policemen to escort all tourist excursions, although he didn't elaborate as to why, and we didn't want to know.

The trek turned out to be a good test of stamina and began with a descent of the surrounding steep hills, where thick forests left the ground covered in fallen leaves and slippery mud. We crossed a few open meadows, before approaching the volcano.

Steps that had been fashioned from mud and rock helped to scale the lower slope, before a twisting path opened up above the tree line.

Unpredictable trails were scattered with boulders and had us rolling on ankles and stumbling to our knees every time our attention wavered. The police guards were a solemn pair and barely said a word throughout the day. One would scout the route ahead, while the other bought up the rear, and both took it in turns to disappear up vertical slopes, before emerging in silence, further along the trail.

We eventually reached the summit of the volcano and clambered up its sheer peak to the top. A mesmerising green lake lay deep inside the enormous crater, and, as we peered directly into the abyss, we learnt that it had last blown less than four weeks earlier.

The guards cracked their hardnosed act only once that day to dive in a panic towards Byron. He had encroached dangerously close to the edge of the crater after coming to the ludicrous conclusion that he would try and climb down for a better look. The swift change in their disposition cleared up any reservations as to his judgment, and, after seeing how long it took a few stones to reach the water below, everybody took a few steps back from the edge.

We were all determined to soak up the far from usual experience and sat for some time on the peak. Cloud banks closed in and froze us to the spot, briefly cutting off visibility before passing by and returning the emerald lagoon and the surrounding landscape to their full magnificence.

After refuelling on biscuits, we eventually left the site to begin the downward trek. Mastering the descent required a lot more concentration than the climb to the top, and, although our pace picked up, the ankle rolls and stumbles took on a greater frequency. We were exhausted and soaked in sweat by the time we returned to the start point, but it had been an awe-inspiring experience, made all the more adventurous by the fact that we had not seen another soul the whole day.

It took a few pupusas to replenish our energy levels, before we caught another commuter bus back to town. We sat near a lady who made herself comfortable, before pulling a chicken out of her bag and coaxing it to sleep on her lap. At one point, the bus stopped in the middle of the road to let two policemen onboard. They walked the length of the aisle, ominously looking everybody up and down, before stopping at the seat of one man. After uttering no more than three words to him, he got up without question and was escorted off. We couldn't understand what had gone on, and not one person from the group that he had been sat with said a word, even after he left.

After leaving the bus in town, we watched the chaotically colourful world pass by and waited for the service back to the lake. Street vendors cooked on open fires, while overloaded trucks and small motorcycles carted people home from work. Young boys hung from bus doors, yelling out routes and destinations, while hustling traders jumped on and off each service, selling snacks and drinks to the passengers. By the time our bus arrived, and we reached the hostel, it was dark, and we fell fast asleep the minute we lay down.

We left early the next day to fight against the rugged track that led us back onto tarmac, where eight men were attempting to re-erect a fallen telegraph pole using a battered pickup truck and some old rope.

After crawling tediously alongside miles of road works, we eventually rode through the capital of San Salvador, where everything we had deemed to be chaotic so far was amplified. We sweltered inside our heavy kit as we crawled through the streets that overflowed with vendors and hawkers, who clogged the roads with overflowing wheelbarrows and wagons of produces and wares.

After gradually weaving a path through the crowds, we rode straight into the red light district. The windows and doors of decadent small houses were flung open to reveal rooms teeming with half-dressed women, all smoking and drinking as they reached out and grabbed at passing men.

We continued riding through the mayhem, passing a gang of guys who chipped away at the ground with pick axes in what looked like hard labour on the beginnings of a new road. Progress was slow, but we crawled on and hit a jam of buses, where an army of vendors jumped from door to door, selling their merchandise, before trying their luck on the queues of waiting traffic.

At some point, we got lucky with a clear run out of the city and, after pinpointing the nearest coastal town on the map, we raced towards it with visions of sunbathing and surfing. Although the route had brought an end to the congestion, the otherwise decent surface was pock marked with lethal craters that added to the usual obstacles of stray dogs and wandering pedestrians.

We arrived at the town on the coast only to discover that it consisted of just one street. A restaurant had been built on what might once have been the hint of a beach, but there was nowhere to stay and little else around for miles. Our hopes were scuppered, and we backtracked to the main road, hoping to stumble across a town where we could get food and a bed for the night. The heat was horribly uncomfortable, and daylight had very nearly departed by the time we finally got lucky.

We checked into a hotel in La Union where a frayed hammock had been slung across the length of the room, and a small, sheet-less bed was pushed against the back wall. A barrel stood beside the toilet, and a smaller bowl floated inside it for scooping out its cold water contents to either wash with or to flush the toilet. The light in the room seeped through patterned, holey bricks that stood in for windows. Despite the minimalism, the room still had cable television.

We fell into another deep sleep until loud chanting came blasting through the glassless holes in the wall at five o'clock in the morning. It turned out to be the El Salvadorian Navy on exercise, and, once they had woken us up, we couldn't get back to sleep. Instead, we hatched a plan that would take advantage of an early start.

We decided to cross the border that morning and ride straight through Honduras, then cross another border into Nicaragua, where we hoped to spend a few days looking for turtles and surf. The distance on the map told us the mileage was easily achievable, but the two border crossings on the way offered less certainty. However, a rest on a beach was calling, and the challenge had been set, so, as the day broke, we set off with blissful ignorance as to what lay ahead.

WRONG TURNS AND
ROAD CRATERS

170 DAYS ON THE ROAD | 18,990 MILES ON THE CLOCK

Half an hour later, we reached the first of the two borders, where the usual charade of tramitadores, unmarked offices, and photocopy shacks lay in wait. Byron tackled the chaos to sort the paperwork for leaving El Salvador, while I stood guard and answered some unlikely questions from a few traders who were milling around.

One group had been staring at the Union Jack sticker on the bike's front mud guard for some time before asking me if I was German. Others didn't bother to hazard a guess, but, when I told them we were English, they looked puzzled. They began reeling off every English speaking country in the world, other than the logical option of England itself, to determine which one we came from. Great Britain and the United Kingdom didn't help their confusion either and simply had them going back over the same list of countries in an attempt to guess which of the English-speaking Great Britain or United Kingdom countries I meant.

The poor geography wasn't limited to passers-by. We had noticed that the previous few temporary importation documents for the bike listed Byron as an Irish national. Having failed to find any reference of our actual nationalities on their computerised list of options, the officials had decided that the word *Ireland* would suffice from the United Kingdom of Great Britain and Northern Ireland title on our passports. Once we had noticed the error, Byron even had a look through the list himself and couldn't find a correct definition. So, following another lengthy ordeal to exit one border and enter another, the bike left El Salvador and was ridden into Honduras under Irish ownership.

The lush landscape and volcanic skyline continued through Honduras. Herds of humpback cows ambled in thick grassy hills, while stray dogs continued to pit their lives against fast moving vehicles.

The quantity of craters in the road quickly began to exceed any level of tolerability, and we fought hard to determine the intentions of countless oncoming trucks or cars, whose attempts to minimise impact with the holes frequently brought them over to our side of the road at full speed.

Presumably as a means of disposal, piles of refuse were alight in the fields outside towns and in ditches beside the road, while a presence of tiny roadside dwellings, erected from castoff planks of wood and torn tarpaulin, signified an increase of abject poverty.

Outside the busy town of Choluteca, we joined a road that we thought would lead us to Guasaule, the nearest border to the coast. When it began to approach some mountains, though, we stopped to ask a few workmen if we were on the right route, and they soon told us we were heading towards San

Marcos de Colon, another border further north. According to the plan that we hatched earlier that morning, there would only be enough daylight hours to reach the Nicaraguan city of León if we crossed at the Guasaule border. Going to the San Marcos de Colon border would add an extra ten Honduran mountain miles to the ride and a further seventy Nicaraguan mountain miles to the otherwise flat ride from Guasaule.

On top of the extra mileage, the workmen told us that there had been a massacre of four people a few days earlier at the mountain crossing. Although we had learnt to take the advice of locals with a pinch of salt, when it came to information they gave on neighbouring cities or countries their sincerity had us a little worried. However, at that point we were still not completely sure that our wrong course was a problem, so we kept riding and stopped for a customary picnic in the mountains.

After a proper look at the map, it was clear that we wouldn't make it to León in daylight if we continued to the mountain border, but there was still a good chance of completing the one day challenge if we turned back and corrected our course. We flipped a coin three times to settle the decision, and, although it told us to persist with the mountains, for some inexplicable reason we chose to ignore it and backtracked towards the original target.

Roughly ten minutes after setting off, a huge repainted US-American school bus approached us in our lane at full speed. There was no other traffic on the road, and, unusually, few potholes were in sight, so we couldn't understand what the driver was doing. We were a larger presence on the road than most local bikes, and our heavily laden frame heightened our visibility, so we assumed the driver would move once they saw us.

We slowed down to give them time to do so, but the bus didn't deviate, and nothing gave away what was happening behind its heavily decorated windscreen. We kept clear of the lane it should have been using in case it swerved at the last minute, but it didn't, and we only evaded it by skidding down a steep grass verge just as it passed us.

My previous reprimands for some of the more obscene gestures Byron had been throwing at reckless drivers were forgotten, and we united in giving the back of the bus our wholehearted rage. To add insult to the encounter, before our very eyes, the vehicle moved into the correct lane just yards up the road.

After we recovered from the shock and exhausted a catalogue of gesticulations, we eventually found the correct route to Guasaule. Although it had evidently once been smoothly paved, it was a minefield of the deepest and widest craters we had ever come across.

Traffic weaved a path from one side of the road to the other, risking head on collisions in an effort to preserve wheel rims, suspensions, and neck muscle. Barefoot men and children raced out of the undergrowth, wielding shovels and outstretched hands while miming the action of filling in the holes. Some truck and car drivers flung coins to them from windows, which they scrambled to find before returning to the undergrowth to wait for the sound of the next approaching motor. Although a few token holes had been packed with rubble and soil, we had a sneaking suspicion that the shovels were deepening a few more craters than they filled.

The ride was a game of wits and by far the biggest challenge to that point. Attempting to distinguish the next crater from the shadows cast by the neighbouring trees, while also second guessing the judgement of oncoming drivers, was exhausting work, and I was only on the back. Ironically, though, we battled through the worst of it and came to within a few miles of the border, when we sailed straight into one of the gaping holes before catapulting directly into another, much deeper one. The wind was knocked out of us, and the Flying Aga came to a crippling halt.

A herd of bulls loped past us, led by a young lad of about ten years old, who didn't even flinch at the catastrophe that had just hit us.

At first glance, we couldn't spot any discernible damage, and it appeared like we might have had a lucky escape. The Flying Aga wobbled when we took it to the side of the road, though, so Byron had a closer look and, for the first time on the trip, he looked genuinely beaten.

The front wheel was not only bent, but a section of it had buckled from the rim by a good eight inches. Further inspection showed the suspension had finally met its match, where both rear shock absorbers seemed to have exploded on impact. To top it all off, the latch that secured the top box to the bike had snapped clean away. Nothing about the situation looked good, and our hearts sank as we scanned the area.

Overgrown fields and the beast of a road were all that surrounded us. We hadn't bought any currency when we entered the country, our water supply was low, and we had eaten all of our food up the mountain, where we should have taken notice of the coin flip. We were lost for words and stood staring at our broken steed, unsure whether to laugh or to cry.

The sun had begun to drop in the sky, and our only option was to get to the border before we were left stranded in complete darkness. So, with no alternative but to fire up the engine, we spent an hour limping the few miles to the crossing, where we hoped to find a place to stay.

We paid some fairly unwarranted fees to exit the country that, in just three hours, had nearly run us off the road and destroyed our bike. Then, due to an eagerness to shut up shop for the night, we tackled more surly guards and one short-changing currency exchanger to enter Nicaragua in slightly less time than a usual border crossing.

LAID UP

A distinct lack of anywhere to stay at the border left us chancing further mileage on the wrecked bike. We winced at every wobble it took on a slow, four-mile ride to the nearest town.

Somotillo was not exactly a tourist trap and had been dealt more than its fair share of shady individuals to hang around on street corners. We pulled up to one of its few guesthouses, where a man who liked the look of our ailing bike, arranged for a room to be made up for us. After learning of our predicament, he then went to find a friend, who he thought might be able to give us a lift in his truck to the nearest city. Although our mechanical dilemmas had been gaining momentum, by some means they were consistently offset by the kindest of strangers who materialised from nowhere.

Within minutes, a crowd of men had gathered around us to offer advice. Like the first guy, they were a decent group and were soon helping us to push the bike into the guesthouse, where we parked beside an armchair and in front of a television in the owner's livingroom.

The room we checked into was a rough brick and corrugated-iron shell. Two single beds had been pushed together beside a cornered off toilet, where a lack of running water was compensated for by another barrel. Any free space on the floor was taken up by an enormous broken television that had us clambering over the small beds to reach either the toilet or the exit.

We threw our bags into the room before going in search of food, when a particularly well-built fellow guest came out of his room and asked where we were from. It turned out that he had lived for a long period in the US and spoke perfect English, when he ran a finger slowly under his nose and told us that he could sort us out with anything that we needed. Conscious that we should avoid offending him, we politely passed on the offer but got chatting, anyway, and found out that every room in the guesthouse was taken up by the group he was with. They were prospecting for gold in the area and worked for the man who had arranged for us to take the room.

Their boss soon returned with a quote from his friend with the truck, and, although it was a reasonable offer, we were anticipating a hefty repair bill to fix the bike so, instead, decided to chance one final, very slow ride to León the next day.

Apart from a rundown supermarket, nowhere else was open to buy food, so we settled for bananas, crisps, and water for dinner. It wasn't long before exhaustion struck, and we fell into the two single beds, which promptly collapsed. A quick look underneath them revealed that half of their slats were missing, so we shifted them about and carefully got back in. Just as we began to drift off, a squeaking noise filtered down the rafters. When it was joined by the sound of scurrying, we realised the source was not coming from birds, as we first hoped, but from an industrious family of mice that was running along the top of the walls.

Since the early naval wake up call, the day had been horribly long, and we had no idea what the next one would bring, so we surrendered to the rodents and the broken beds and hoped that sleep would set in quickly.

It came in fits and starts until the morning broke and revealed just how industrious the little family had been. Their droppings were scattered around our pillows, across the broken television, and on the limited floor space. The shelter was still preferable to sleeping beside the road without provisions or water, but, after seeing the droppings and the grime on the floor, we were keen to move on.

After making the best of the cold water in the barrel to wake up and wash with, we retrieved the bike from the living room. The boss, who had arranged the room for us to stay in, was asleep on the sofa, and his friend was in a hammock. We realised that they must have given up their own room for us that night. We didn't get a chance to thank them, as they were snoring peacefully when we wheeled the bike back to the road and set off as the sun began to rise.

It took five hours to ride seventy miles on that beautiful morning. Although it was blighted by anxiety that the front tyre could burst at any moment, we rode slowly, and the early dawn activity along the way kept us engrossed. People led their livestock out into the fields, while others cycled past them with buckets and machetes slung over shoulders. We barely kept up with tiny motorcycles, each carrying at least three people to work, and horses that were pulling carts of wood. Vendors served breakfast on roadside fires to people queuing for buses, while others were still asleep in hammocks inside small, tarpaulin-covered huts.

We crossed our fingers as we wobbled all the way into León, praising the Flying Aga for enduring the handicap of a busted suspension and a broken wheel to get us there in one piece.

We anticipated a long stay, so found a hostel where the owners gave us a good rate and agreed that we could park inside if we paid upfront for a week. It was our second backpacking hostel, and everybody was speaking English, but, for once, we didn't care. At ten o'clock that morning, we were sitting in its café, drinking coffee and chatting to a US wildfire fighter. By eleven o'clock, Byron was navigating our broken steed up a set of steps using another wooden plank as a makeshift ramp.

He rode the Flying Aga in from the street below, then took it up another interior flight of steps, twisting the handlebars just in time to narrowly avoid colliding with a hefty pillar. We parked right in the middle of a small courtyard, immediately outside what became our room for the next fifteen nights.

A group of workmen were building a new shower just beside our parking spot and seized the opportunity to shirk the job in favour of watching Byron strip the bike that afternoon. The inspection confirmed the worst with the suspension, and Byron was pretty certain that the front wheel would need replacing entirely.

Using some epoxy resin and the hand axe we had been carrying as a peg mallet, he did what he could to straighten out the buckled metal. However, nothing could be done for the suspension, so he bolted it all back into place while we set about deciding what to do. After enquiring about parts and welders in the small city, where no building stood higher than two storeys, it soon became clear that the chance of finding anything suitable to fix a thirty-year old, German bike would be a small miracle.

We still had at least 10,000 miles to go before we reached the end of the road, so cutting corners would have been foolish. Instead, we spent the next three days trying to find a solution in the world of online adventure motorcycle forums.

While our problems were consigned to the virtual world, we explored the bustling streets and markets of the small city. As the days passed by, we got to know the hiding places of the resident tortoises and witness the hostel cat give birth to a small litter. We lived in hope that the construction of the hostel's first hot shower would be finished before we left, but the workmen moved excruciatingly slow. Their friends, who cleaned the dorms every morning, were no better and spent entire days mopping the tiled floors back and forth.

We signed up for Spanish lessons at a foundation that was researching a chronic kidney disease, which had struck the workers of nearby sugarcane farms. Our mornings were spent attempting to retain more Spanish than we had managed so far, before we volunteered with the foundation for the rest of the day. Byron also joined the hostel's own charity and played football with an overwhelming number of young street children, who we would spot later in the evenings, smoking on the streets and sleeping in doorways.

On the first Sunday of our stranding, we climbed into the hostel's rickety, flatbed truck to bump and bounce along a rural track with a group of fellow guests. We ducked from flyaway branches and hung on for dear life, all the way to the base of Cerro Negro, the youngest volcano in Central America. We were each handed an orange cotton bag and a brightly painted wooden contraption, before we set about scaling the coarse black slope, where a minor stumble would instantly slice knees and scrape away layers of skin.

Halfway up the steep incline, a strong wind blasted us into the slope, and a group of dark clouds drew close. Visibility dropped rapidly, and instructions filtered down from the leader to retreat. The storm was heading straight for us, so we clambered down, fighting the wind and the driving rain, before reaching the base where total calm prevailed. We sat waiting for the guides to round up the less eager defeatists and coax them down the jagged rocks, as we watched the outbreak pass by overhead. Visibility returned as quickly as it had disappeared, and a debate ensued as to whether we should climb back up again, despite the encroaching end to daylight. The verdict was unanimous, and we retraced our steps through the razor sharp rocks to scale the active volcano, once again.

The wind fought hard to blow us away when we eventually reached the ridge of the Cerro Negro crater. The sky had cleared, though, and an untainted display of natural beauty lay before us. Grassy knolls and volcanic peaks spread for miles in every direction, glowing in the warmth of the setting sun.

It was a year ago that Garth had died, and, as we fought against the powerful weather, there was something about the moment that made us hope that he was somehow able to share the exquisite view, wherever he may have been.

We stood at the edge of the crater and pulled on the orange boiler suits and scratched laboratory glasses that had been in the cotton backpacks. We had braved the truck journey and the two consecutive treks to willingly launch ourselves down the volcano's almost vertical, 500-meter slope on little more than a plank of wood that would reach speeds of up to sixty miles per hour. It was an act that would do more to affirm life than any other Sunday afternoon activity we could recall.

Following a five-minute demonstration of how best to approach the challenge, we lined up at the top of the slope to tackle the descent one by one.

Screams of fear and delight accompanied the plummet of twenty daring souls as a stream of dust and volcanic ash kicked up in their wake. Some took a direct route straight into the radar of a waiting speed gun, while others fatally fought against the momentum and went flying off the boards to collide with the brutal volcanic surface.

Clear vision was non-existent through the scratched lab goggles, and, as grit and gravel flew at my face and shot up my nose, I hung onto the steering rope of the board and did my best not to move a muscle. Somehow the frozen-with-fear position worked, and I jumped off at the bottom in one piece, spitting out shards of volcanic rock as I looked back up the long distance to the top.

The tiniest dot that was Byron wasted no time in setting off, and, with ambitions to beat the speed gun, he moved like a bullet to the halfway point of the slope. He must have dropped a foot or touched the surface, though, because he abruptly flipped through the air and took a horrific, head-first dive onto the harsh rock. I held my breath, willing him to get up, while everybody who had taken similar tumbles drew in sharp gasps and compared war wounds where entire layers of skin had been ripped off.

Luckily, Byron was soon back on the board and making his way down, flipping and colliding with the surface to reach the base with an entirely scraped and bloody scalp. It had been exhilarating, but we realised that help would have been a long way off had anything more serious occurred. With a beer to numb the pain, we were whipped by branches through the bars of the open truck as it traced the rural track back to town in the dark.

In the meantime, a great deal of progress had been taking place in the online forums. We had been inundated with offers of cheap sales and even donations of spare wheels and suspensions. However, the cost of shipping and the need to hire an agent to release anything from customs into Nicaragua was, by our means, crippling, so we held out for a local solution.

On the fourth day after smashing into the Honduran double-whammy, we received a message from Aaron in Miami. He explained that he was flying to Nicaragua two weeks later and offered to carry the parts we needed on his flight. Aaron was, without a doubt, the absolute epitome of the kind stranger. Receiving his simple message lifted our spirits immeasurably and substantiated a growing sense that somebody was looking out for us.

Since Aaron was not leaving for two weeks, we had time to purchase a new suspension from Kurt in Michigan and a second hand wheel from Chris in California. An international plan of action saw Kurt send the suspension to Chris who forwarded it with the wheel to Aaron. Meanwhile, we sat tight with our broken bike and waited to meet Aaron, whose generosity was saving us at least a month's budget.

We were determined to make the most of the long wait, so we continued to pass the same lady every morning who sold us a bag of chopped fruit on our way to Spanish lessons. Byron continued to play football with the street kids, while I helped with marketing at the foundation.

We paid for another week at the hostel and met no end of people who drifted through its doors, including Jesus, who went off to buy a horse so he could travel bareback through the country, and Tim, a stand-up comedian. We also met Annalisa and Andy, who were on their way back to Britain after spending six years abroad, and Adam and Mackenzie, our fellow bloggers, on a Kawasaki adventure.

We explored the cathedral roof, from where a view of low, red-top buildings filled the gap between the distant volcanoes that encircled the city. We roamed the lively streets, passing horses pulling carts and children asking for ice creams. Sandinista murals of the country's revolution, some thirty years earlier, adorned buildings, and we visited a museum, where a veteran of the uprising insisted on guiding us around, even though he knew we could barely understand him.

Young kids would wander the streets by night, calling out "money, money, money" at just about everybody who crossed their path, while they banged drums and twirled effigies that depicted some of Nicaragua's many popular legends.

After surrendering to a mass game of flip cup in the bar one evening, we joined Annalisa and Andy to clamber into the small hostel wagon, whose front windscreen was shattered after the driver stood on it weeks earlier. After driving with his head poked out of the side window in order to see, the driver dropped us at a nearby club, and we made a beeline for the bar, where all manner of local rums and vodkas slowly destroyed us. At some point in the early hours, both Byron and Andy simultaneously slumped and reminded us why we had resisted late night revelry for so long.

Back at the hostel, a power cut had plunged the windowless rooms into darkness. Any drop of comfort that a few, well placed fans usually offered had also disappeared, and our plan for the first lazy morning in weeks was scuppered when the electricity remained cut off the next day, transforming our airless room into a small oven.

We reconvened with our new partners in crime, Annalisa and Andy, that afternoon and climbed back into the small wagon with the bashed-in windscreen for a drive to the outskirts of town. A large gathering of locals met every Sunday afternoon at a cock fight, and a resident Dutch guy had made some sort of arrangement with the organisers to let a small group of tourists attend each week.

The venue was in somebody's backyard, where a simple ring of mud had been fenced off with a circle of upright wooden planks. Four rows of staggered, makeshift benches were erected around its periphery and wobbled dangerously, as the predominantly male audience balanced on them to watch the action. The unassuming arena was covered by a now familiar corrugated metal roof, from which a clock was attached to a luminous light and suspended above the ring. Stacked cages sheltered the prized birds close to the enclosure, and small cliques of men assembled at a distance to coordinate the most complicated betting process of which we had ever heard.

Homemade snacks of enchiladas soon made their way out to a few tables, where our Dutch guide filled us in on the rules and customs of a Nicaraguan cock fight.

The birds were selected at birth by their owners and were kept and trained with the same dedication that was shown to racing dogs or horses. They were often a key source of income for a family and fought rounds, rather than to the death. Owners treated them like a prized possession, and the sight of men sucking blood from a bird's nostrils to clear its airways during a fight was equally fascinating and grotesque.

Local rum messed with our concentration, and, above the din of the hollering owners, the tipsy spectators, and the squawking roosters, it was difficult to follow the rules. It was soon clear, however, that they were taken very seriously when a disagreement erupted between two hefty spectators over who knew them better. Old school fisticuffs were threatened by white-vest-sporting, outstretched-fist-waving, overweight, sweaty men, although, disappointingly, an actual fight never materialised.

Among the comparatively shorter and seldom bald men of Latin American, Byron's lack of locks was accentuated by his height. So when an uncommonly bald local man spotted Byron in the crowd, he immediately took a shine to him and embarked on a series of exaggerated displays of affection. He shouted out to his "brother," while caressing his own head in acknowledgement of their bond. However, as the elderly guy got progressively drunk on the lethal rum, he tripped and knocked himself out. Their brotherhood was quickly forgotten when he spent the rest of the afternoon looking dazed in a chair, while his friends took care of him.

The next morning, we learnt that our new suspension had made its way to California and, together with the new wheel, it was on progress across the country to Miami. Although everything now looked hopeful with the bike repair, we realised that we were not going to reach Panama in time for the sailing we had booked to take us to Colombia.

There was no option but to cancel our spot on the substantial steel schooner and begin a fresh search for a boat that could safely take us and the bike on the five day ocean crossing. Eventually, we resorted to a considerably smaller yacht that had reports of a fiery captain but of good food and safe standards. It was due to set sail on the same day that our friends left Britain, meaning we would miss some of their two-week visit but would still at least get to see them.

Although it was the longest period that we had settled in one place for six months, time had passed quickly in León. Before we ventured off again, we took a final trip in the back of the trusty hostel truck to visit the nearby Pacific coast in search of the surf and turtles we had been looking for when disaster struck two weeks earlier.

The truck dropped us at a mooring, where we climbed into a rowing boat that took us across a small inlet. A sandy path at the other side wound through trees to an isolated spot, where a lodge and very little else existed. The sea was rough and perfect for more advanced surfing, but we were priced out of the market for lessons, so settled for swimming instead. We ate fresh fish and swung in hammocks, before the sun disappeared early and a plague of mosquitoes made a meal out of us.

The lodge's horse and cart soon drew up on the beach to take us back to the inlet. As we wound through the trees along the dark track that we had walked earlier that day, the hooves of the horse and the wheels of the carriage sashayed so silently across the sand that it felt as if complete peace had fallen across the world. We reached the inlet and idled through shallow water to a waiting rowing boat. Although we had not encountered surf or turtles, on that still evening we at last found a brief taste of the tranquillity we had hoped to find since the day we agreed to do the trip.

The boat took us across the inlet and, after piling into the old truck, we spent the drive back to the town watching fireflies and wishing on shooting stars with untroubled, happy hearts.

We learnt that the construction work outside our room was scheduled to end the day that we left the hostel. Hammocks hanging from the rafters and a hot shower would have topped off the extended stay perfectly, but it was not to be. After bidding adieu to our new friends, Byron navigated back down the makeshift ramps to the road outside, where broken glass littered the tarmac. Even if the final sixty-mile ride didn't finish off the busted Flying Aga, another puncture might well have been the last straw for us.

We wobbled slowly along the sixty miles, arriving without further damage in Managua, where Aaron greeted us into his home. It turned out that he and his fiancée, Connie, were getting married in the New Year, and, together with the substantial weight of our new suspension and front wheel, Aaron had also carried the glass bowls for their wedding table centrepieces and a Christmas tree on the flight. The man was a hero in our eyes, and when he explained that he had visited a British store in Miami to pick us up tea bags, baked beans, and jam we were blown away. To illustrate just how much he embodied the universal biking camaraderie sentiment, he had carted the entire consignment with a broken leg.

We changed the wheel, fitted the new rear suspension, and secured the broken top box with bungee cords to the brackets. Aaron then drove us all over town to help search for an extra long bolt to replace one that we discovered had bent during the pothole collision. To top off everything he had done for us, the gesture that confirmed him as a lifelong friend came when he asked a more than willing Byron to ride his DR650 motorcycle from a friend's garage back to his house.

Once the Flying Aga was restored to full health, Connie and Aaron invited us to join their friends for a barbecue and to stay the night. So, our Honduran catastrophe concluded with an evening under the stars eating jerk chicken, drinking fine Nicaraguan rum, and enjoying great company.

The next morning, we fired up the revived Flying Aga and waved a fond farewell to Connie and Aaron, hoping they would take up our offer to visit us in England some day.

As if to test the extent of the bike's recovery, we took a wrong turn somewhere on the road out of the city and ended up on a very long detour that veered off asphalt and onto an unpaved track. We dipped and bobbed along the route, which did very little for the restoration of our nerves, while we ate the dust that was kicked up by approaching and overtaking traffic that was risking far higher speeds than we dared.

The trail passed clusters of haphazard townships and the now familiar sight of machete wielding men, labouring grandparents, and burdened, but skilfully postured, women.

It eventually led us into the countryside and turned from gravel to house bricks, before joining back up with the highway, two hours after we had set off. It had been a nerve racking test for the newly recovered bike but it also gave us a final chance to see rural Nicaragua before we reached another dreaded border and left the beautiful country behind.

NEAR DESPAIR AND
TOW TRUCKS

It was another Sunday, and there was slightly less chaos at the border, although the process still took two hours. Happily, the entry into Costa Rica was situated under one roof, and, although the return of road insurance made a dent in our spare change, we passed through fairly quickly. We hadn't beaten darkness, though, and, by the time we rode into the new country, a plague of mosquitoes had begun their nightly feast.

Freight and cargo vehicles were stacked back to back for miles along the road, presumably waiting to pass through the next morning. Drivers congregated in groups or swung listlessly in hammocks beneath their vehicles, while a few ladies of the night wandered the long line, touting for business. We rode past the waiting trucks for what seemed like miles, all the while straining to see through the darkness and spot the headlights of oncoming vehicles.

Since entering Mexico, we had been warned not to ride at night and had so far avoided doing so. Until that evening in Costa Rica, we had assumed the advice related to false roadblocks and gangs that operated in the shadows. However, as we cleared the line and hit the open road, we realised that it was more likely due to the presence of hurdles that posed enough of a risk during daylight but were potentially lethal obstacles at night. Wandering animals, small motorcycles without headlights, deep potholes, and menacing road bumps suddenly became bullets in a dangerous game of Russian roulette.

We pulled into the nearest windy town, which confirmed our fears that super cheap rooms and affordable meals had reached an abrupt end. That evening, we received a message explaining that the boat we were rushing to catch from Panama had been overbooked and that we had been placed on another crossing that left four days later. Although the delay cut away more of the time that we would spend with our friends, it did mean that we could take up an offer from Lucas to visit his friend's house, just two hours away.

Shortly after setting off the next morning, another wobble of the rear wheel struck with the now familiar sensation of a sinking heart. Flat tyres shouldn't have posed such a hassle or delay, but the position of the customised panniers and the rear mudguard made removing the rear wheel trickier than necessary.

Since the last two punctures, Byron had worked out that taking the front wheel off first and tilting the entire machine forward to balance on the front forks created the necessary clearance at the back. However, the position of the panniers and the new suspension meant that access to the rear wheel bolts was still only achievable after the exhaust had also been removed. None of the process was possible at all until we had removed the top box and unstrapped the roll bags, so that we could burrow through the panniers to dig out the tools.

Once the bike was primed, we could take a look at the problem. Using our newly acquired C-clamp, the bead of the tyre could be broken from the rim of the wheel. Extracting the inner tube was no problem, but locating the cause of the puncture could take some time, especially if the culprit was lodged deep inside the tyre rubber. Once we had identified the problem, we could either patch the damaged tube or use one of the spare tubes to return into the tyre.

Hefty tyre irons, water, and washing up liquid then helped ease the tyre bead back over the rim of the wheel. Finally, enough air pressure was required to reseat the tyre on the wheel. If all had still gone well by that point, the rear wheel, the exhaust, and the front wheel had to be reattached before the tools and luggage were repacked, and we could get back on the road.

Although we had stopped on the main highway, the frame of a bus shelter lay ahead of us, and we rolled the bike onto its concrete base before unloading the luggage. Ingeniously, Byron looped our luggage straps around the frame of the shelter roof and through the pannier brackets. The method suspended the rear half of the bike above the ground and eliminated the need to remove the front wheel. Once the exhaust and the rear wheel were off, it took a while to locate a shard of glass that had most likely been picked up on the road when we left the hostel in León.

To our utter dismay, the operation also revealed another casualty that we must have overlooked during the Honduran debacle. We discovered a slight bend and a hairline fracture in the rear wheel but, with few options, we could only duct tape up the crack and hope that it would stay sealed until we could find a more permanent solution.

While we were struggling with the latest fix, a few local kids and a couple of guys had gathered to watch us. We had attempted to talk to them at first but they only seemed interested in how we proposed to sort out the puncture, so we got to work while they watched in silence. After a while, the older man had obviously seen enough and continued his journey with a couple of the children, leaving a younger guy behind. He softened a bit when we passed around some snacks and he began showing us some horrendous scars that covered his legs, explaining, we think, that they were the result of having crashed his bike while carrying a machete.

After we replaced the inner tube and eventually got the tyre secured onto the wheel, our inadequate hand pump wouldn't generate enough pressure to fully inflate it. For all the tools we were carting around with us, we had ruled out packing a compressor pump because they took up too much space.

After a lot of deliberation, Byron followed the young lad into a nearby field on the understanding that a farmer might have a pump. Time ticked on, while I sat with the bear spray in one hand and an axe in another, willing them to reappear before it got dark. When Byron eventually did come back, he was walking alone and shaking his head. Nobody could locate a pump, and the farmhands didn't think the farmer would be back for at least two hours.

We conceded that we needed help once again, and, while Byron resumed his efforts with the hand pump, I began flagging down vehicles. Most of them simply waved back while they drove on past, while a few unlikely suspects did pull over. Huge HGVs and eighteen-wheelers held up the traffic, while I shouted up to their drivers from the edge of the road asking if they had a pump. Some climbed down to see how they could help, but none of them were carrying what we needed.

Meanwhile, the young lad had returned to loiter in the background with his friends, obviously annoyed that Byron hadn't waited for the farmer, but doing nothing to help otherwise.

As time ticked away, and the situation began to look more hopeless, we weighed up the odds of having to stay at the spot for the night. However, as long as the sun still shone, we were convinced that all was not lost so kept pumping and waving.

Three hours after the initial wobble, a man pulled up in a car and came to talk to us. Steven wasn't carrying a pump, but, like Mario in Mexico, he offered to take us and the wheel to a nearby garage. We were fearful of leaving the bike alone or splitting up again, so when he suggested that he could take the wheel for us and bring it back, we eagerly handed it over to him with great appreciation. The kindness of strangers had struck again.

With nothing to do but sit and wait, we did just that under the watchful eye of the group of locals, who genuinely appeared to have nothing else to do. After forty-five minutes, it began to dawn on us that we may have been hasty in passing our immediate fate into the hands of a total stranger. If Steven didn't return, we would be facing an entirely new level of setback.

Just as doubt began to take a hold, it was replaced by guilt when he pulled up with the freshly set wheel. We couldn't have been more grateful to him, and, after he gave us his contact details, he continued his journey with a smile and a wave.

Our silent audience edged closer when he drove off, curious to see the final stage of the operation. Once the wheel was reattached, the exhaust was secured and the bike was lowered from its bus shelter suspension, we packed up every scattered tool and piece of luggage. None of the spectators said a word, until, four hours after coming to a wobbly halt, we think they asked for a tip as we rode away.

By the time we located the house of Lucas's friend, Tony, it was dark and nobody was in. The property was set off the main highway in a semi-residential area, and we knew that someone was expecting us, although about five hours earlier. We waited for an hour on the lawn outside the building, hoping somebody might turn up, but, when nobody showed, I went in search of a telephone and got lucky in a pharmacy, where the manager called the number we had been given. With no idea what the person on the other end of the line had said, I went back to find Byron who was slumped on the grass, homeless and hungry.

We decided to wait and see if the call amounted to anything, and, after half an hour, a housekeeper cycled up. He let us in and told us that Tony had given us the place to stay for as long as we wanted.

Like many Latin American buildings, a substantial house lay behind the unassuming boundary wall, and we had the pick of four different bedrooms that were set up to comfortably sleep a party of sixteen people. An oven, a fridge, and a washing machine in the kitchen were the icing on the cake.

Although the building harboured more than its fair share of mosquitoes and cockroaches, we had soon put them in their place, before settling into the rare luxury of having an entire house to ourselves.

We cooked up a feast with the oven and put every item of clothing we owned through the washing machine, including our now rancid, sweaty gloves and bike trousers. The sun stayed behind the clouds and kept us from braving the swimming pool, but we used the time to write the next entry for the blog and to give the bike a wash. We also repaired the latest punctured inner tube, and Byron fixed the brake light that we discovered had worryingly stopped making a connection with the brakes a couple of days earlier. Time was creeping up on us, though, and, after two nights, we reluctantly bid farewell to the housekeeper and set off to explore more of the country.

A new rear tyre and an air compressor were at the forefront of our minds, and we rode towards the capital in search of them. We stopped at every workshop in the small villages and towns outside San Jose, but none stocked the size or durability of tyre that we needed, let alone a compressor that was small enough to fit in our bulging bags.

A few hours of riding around the city centre eventually led us to the first BMW dealership that we had seen since San Diego, back in the US. Its workshop had a rear tyre in stock that would fit our old bike, and, although it wasn't made of the harder compound that we were looking for, we took it anyway and hoped it would last us to South America. After it was fitted, we checked into a small family hostel nearby and enjoyed the first faint trickle of a hot water shower in over a month.

We had wasted a lot of increasingly precious time the day before, so set off early the next morning in search of tropical beaches and wildlife.

An extensive detour on our way out of the city equipped us with a compressor pump to finally complete our flat tyre repair kit. With the successful purchase in the bag, we ventured towards a mountain road that could well have been beautiful, were it not for the driving rain and encroaching mist.

As we made our way along it, and the route rose higher, the temperature plummeted. Although it had been overcast back in the city, the climate had been pleasant, so we were poorly dressed in just T-shirts and jackets and stopped in a rare lay-by to throw on waterproofs before setting off again, still hunched and shivering against the cold.

Byron weaved the bike along the narrow road, conscious of oncoming freight vehicles as he strained to see through the mist. Our visors streamed with rain on the outside and steamed up on the inside, and, to top off the escalating misery, the Flying Aga began to sputter. It stammered intermittently, then quickly deteriorated into fits and starts before eventually conking out entirely.

We stopped precariously close to a blind corner, where the road offered the only flat surface in sight. Somehow we avoided any collisions with the rapid flow of traffic and wheeled the bike down the steep grass verge, where I stood and propped it into the slope, while Byron got to work.

The irony was excruciating. We had literally just purchased the last crucial device to help fix the recent regular flow of punctures, only to find ourselves stuck up a wet mountain with an entirely unrelated problem.

Byron tested the wires and cables running to the ignition before he found that the spark plugs were failing to spark. He changed the HT leads, which generated a weak response, and, being conscious of an urgency to get to safer ground, we decided the swap would suffice to at least get us away from the perilous spot.

When Byron went to replace the plugs, though, he found the threads in the two sockets were shot. After half an hour of careful screwing and unscrewing in the rain, some metal splinters from the right-hand cylinder head spark plug thread fell into the engine, and, for the first time on the entire trip, Byron refused to ride the bike any farther.

Anything that wasn't supposed to be in the engine had the potential to do some severe damage, and we knew it wouldn't be easy to get someone to fly down from the US with a new one in their luggage. After the hassle and money it had taken to replace the final drive in the US and to get a new wheel and suspension to Nicaragua, we weren't keen on tempting fate, so, once again, we set about flagging down help.

By sheer chance the mechanic that had fitted the new rear

tyre the evening before had given us his business card as an afterthought when we had left. It was the only life line we had to get us out of the predicament, and we dug out the one mobile telephone we had been carrying for emergencies.

We were halfway up a wet, misty mountain, though, and we couldn't pick up a signal. Darkness was about an hour away, and, in our position at the side of a steep verge, with a narrow road on one side and thick hedgerows on the other, there was little chance that any traffic would see us once daylight disappeared. We shivered in our damp clothes and took it in turns to keep the bike propped into the steep verge, while the other flagged down traffic.

Daylight fell away rapidly, and visions of snatching at sleep in the undergrowth, while the other kept the bike propped upright, were a miserable prospect as the rain continued to fall. Despite the increasingly dire circumstances, as the least mechanically gifted half of our duo, I trusted Byron's resolve not to turn on the engine.

A couple of cars did pull over, but when we asked the drivers to try the mechanic's telephone number, none of them could pick up a signal, either. Although they agreed to call the number on our behalf once they descended the mountain, we held out little hope that any of them would actually do so.

The predicament was the closest we had come to experiencing total despair. While we fought to keep calm, a sense of panic crept up on us that we had never fully faced before. Eventually, we came to the realisation that our best hope would be to catch the attention of a charitable trucker, who might be able to transport us with the bike to the nearest town.

Wagons and trucks took no notice of our waves as they cruised past the wet corner, but a highway patrol truck raised our hopes immeasurably when we thought the driver gestured that he would turn around. There was still no sign of him a good twenty minutes later, though, and an overwhelming sense of gloom returned, as it finally felt like our run of luck had come to an end.

Just as we began to plan for a night on the wet mountain, a pickup truck pulled over, and our hearts raced with hope. The driver came out to talk to us, and we managed to explain the situation in broken Spanish. Our relief was incalculable when Jose agreed that we could put the Flying Aga in the back of his truck. However, when he pulled out the flimsiest plank of wood for us to roll the heavy bike up the four-foot elevation, our optimism dwindled. Even without our experience of breaking similar planks to escalate the curbs of pavements, it was no surprise when it immediately bowed under the weight of the Flying Aga.

Jose didn't give up, though, and motioned for us to freewheel back down the hill, while he brought up the rear. It worked perfectly until we reached an end to the downward slope about ten minutes later.

Darkness had fully set in by this point, and, although we felt totally beaten, Jose persevered and dug a tow rope out of his truck. He tied it to our front fork and his rear bumper, and, although it was risky, particularly on the narrow road, it was our best option. I climbed into his cab, and we both held our breath as he slowly towed Byron and the bike along the dark road.

Miraculously, we avoided meeting another vehicle the entire way to a truck stop, where Jose cut the towrope and wasted no time in continuing on his way. We were indebted to him, and, through his charity, we sensed the strongest affirmation yet of an unspoken hunch that, somehow, Edward and Garth might have been looking out for us.

The truck stop was like an apparition. We had never been so happy to see an open-front, breeze block shelter or to smell hot broth and cheap coffee. We were shivering uncontrollably as we rolled the Flying Aga under a canopy, when a guy began speaking to us. He reverted to perfect English when our Spanish faltered and offered to ring the mechanic for us. It turned out that the dealership ran a twenty-four-hour rescue service, and, after arranging for them to come and collect us, like Jose, the man disappeared into the night.

The dire situation couldn't have turned around quicker, and, with hope on the horizon, we peeled off our wet layers and squeezed into as many dry clothes as we possibly could.

Truck drivers, families, and minibus passengers streamed in and out of the open front building, while we tried to get warm for four hours. Although we had just narrowly escaped an entirely different outcome, we began to dread the money that would be drained on the imminent BMW tow.

Johnny, the mechanic who had given us his card, eventually arrived, and all of our worries evaporated when he strapped the Flying Aga to a trailer and we climbed into his heated truck. On the way back into San Jose, he explained that the mountain we had just encountered was known locally as Cerro de la Muerte, the Mountain of Death, and that we'd had a lucky escape.

It was past midnight when we reached the city, and Johnny dropped us back at the hostel we had left that morning. Johnny offered to take the bike straight to the workshop at the dealership, where he told us we could work on it for free the next day. He even waited while we unloaded our bags before he made his way back into the night with our trusty, but, once again, broken steed.

We arrived at the workshop the next morning to find that Johnny had given us our own workbench and free rein to do whatever was necessary. A few of the mechanics were soon offering tools and paraphernalia to help clean out the damaged thread and fit a new helicoil.

While they were at it, Byron and the mechanics also checked on the drive splines in the final drive that Tom had noticed were wearing thin back in Pennsylvania, in the US. A unanimous conclusion was drawn that riding all the way to the bottom of Argentina with the drive splines in their current state would be a close call. The dealership stocked minimal parts for a thirty-three-year old bike, though, so Byron stuck to the task at hand and fished out the metal debris before fitting the new helicoil thread repairs.

We thanked the team profusely and settled the bill for the tow with the manager, who honoured Johnny's word and didn't charge us for anything else.

Meanwhile, we had received another message from the agent who was arranging our passage to Colombia. The boat they had moved us to was delayed by a further four days as a result of storms moving across the Atlantic. On the one hand, the news granted us leeway to sort out the bike, but on the other hand, it cut our time with our friends, Abby and Alice, down from an original two weeks to just four days.

We set off again the next morning and steered clear of the Mountain of Death, making a beeline for the coast road, instead, which turned out to be well-paved, very wide, and at sea level. The sun shone gloriously for the first couple of hours, and the tension that another potential breakdown might strike us down began to melt away with every uninterrupted mile. Just as we thought we were home free, though, the bike began to cough and choke.

We stalled and sputtered mid-highway for some time before giving up completely. The only saving grace that prevented a tumble into despair was the contrast in conditions to the day before. The sun was shining, the road was straight, and a substantial hard shoulder offered a stable platform to take a look at the problem.

We unloaded the luggage into the highway trench, while eighteen-wheeler trucks, cars, and buses roared past us. Byron tested the HT leads, the spark plugs, and the ignition again, before methodically going through just about every electrical connection we could think of. Nothing was visibly wrong, and we began preparing ourselves for another return to the city, before a final check revealed the connection between two of the ignition coils was loose. After re-crimping the connections and electrical-taping them tight, the engine fired up first time, and we gave the onward direction one last shot.

The rest of the journey was fraught with the anxiety that a rear wheel wobble or a recurring stutter would force us into another lay-by, but we reached the outskirts of a coastal national park without further incident.

Minutes after checking into a small hostel in Uvita, a heavy seasonal downpour let loose outside, and, to avoid any more miserable soakings than were necessary, we settled indoors for the evening at an in-house, hammock cinema, while the rain hammered down on the metal roof and drowned out most of the film.

The next morning, we left the small hamlet on foot and followed a network of paths and dirt tracks in search of the ocean. We passed runaway livestock and playing children before eventually stumbling upon a mass of towering palm trees, where we caught the familiar salty scent of the sea. We weaved a path through the solid trunks of the forest, clambering over giant, fallen leaves and coconuts, before emerging onto the most unspoilt beach we had ever seen.

The sand reached for what seemed like miles to the left and right of us and was sandwiched between the tropical forest and an imposing stretch of Pacific Ocean. A morning mist hovered above the scene, in which every shipwreck survival tale materialised before our eyes. It was breathtaking, and we perched on the edge of a washed up log, captivated by the untainted beauty.

The heat was on an upward spiral, and we set off back to the hostel to retrieve our swimming gear, vowing to return immediately and spend as long as we could in the exceptional setting. We bought ingredients for a picnic on the way and reached the hostel just as another downpour dashed all immediate plans for a day at the beach. While the rain raged above us, we used the time to check over the bike and set up a small launderette inside our room.

Alas, the bad weather was unrelenting and hammered away at the roof long into the evening. By the end of the day, we had exhausted all possible distractions and chores, so resorted back to the hammock cinema.

The sky had cleared by the following morning, and, although the idyllic beach beckoned, we could only think about getting to the port in time for the boat trip before any further dilemmas made us miss the crossing. So we forfeited a second visit to the beach of our dreams and dodged a stray monkey and a low flying turkey vulture to reach the border with Panama later that day.

A further three hours were spent wading through red tape and negotiating queues, before we crossed into our final Central American country.

WHEEL WELDING AND
A FATED OPOSSUM

195 DAYS ON THE ROAD | 19,867 MILES ON THE CLOCK

Shortly after riding into Panama, we passed a policeman standing by his car in the middle of a two-lane highway. Breaking a speeding law in any country would have been quite a task on the Flying Aga, so we thought nothing of his waving when we passed him in the flow of heavy traffic. We heard his siren a few hundred meters further down the road and looked back to see him blazing towards us. Still unconvinced that he was after us, we kept riding until he locked onto our tail. It was the very first time on the trip that we had been pulled over outside of a roadblock, and we wracked our brains to think of what we had done wrong.

The officer pulled out his speed gun, and it was immediately clear that we hadn't done anything wrong at all. Cars had been whipping past us, while we had plodded along behind a truck, but it was apparent that our obvious tourist status had isolated us from the crowd. Ten weeks had passed since we crossed into Mexico, and, despite all the cautions of bribery and corruption, this was our very first suspect encounter with a police officer.

We did our best to get the point across that the bike was incapable of speeding, explaining that if, in fact, we had been, then he had missed all of the cars that had been overtaking us. His expression gave nothing away, though, and only once betrayed a flicker of confusion at the photocopy of Byron's driving licence.

As his poker face continued, we began to doubt if resistance was a wise move in a country that we had been in for less than an hour. Our baffled act at being charged with speeding eventually seemed to be winning, though, and we could see him slowly begin to lose resolve. We came to a stalemate, where he stared expectantly and money probably should have changed hands, but we stared back innocently. Finally, he got bored and waved us off. It took all we could muster to keep our cool and ride away calmly, when we felt like celebrating at having successfully evaded our first bogus allegation.

Much like the rest of Central America, the landscape was striking. Thick clumps of grass covered rolling hills for as far as the eye could see, while small birds gathered around humpback cows as they grazed in fields. Villages and towns played havoc with our mileage estimates, and, after crossing into another time zone at the border, it was much later than we realised when darkness fell.

The army surplus bag that was screwed into the front screen had gradually been pushing down and loosening the bike's headlight so that it was pointing directly towards the road surface below, instead of lighting up the route ahead. We had only ridden once at night in Costa Rica and had since forgotten about the problem. Nothing worked to keep it focussed on the road, so we eventually pulled in behind a truck and tailed it all the way into Santiago.

The darkness had brought a nip to the air, and we were cold to the bone by the time we reached civilisation. We had arranged to stay at a guesthouse and arrived to find that it was based in the attic of a family home. Undeterred, we soon lugged our bags up a perilous ladder into the loft, where we fell asleep within minutes.

Our time in Panama was now on a tight countdown, and we were determined not to waste it, so we clambered out of the loft early the next morning and set off towards the Panama Canal.

We joined other snap happy tourists just in time to document the passage through the canal lock of a truly enormous cargo ship. The heat had returned with a vengeance that morning, and we couldn't bear it for long in our kit, so we set off soon after the event, hoping to cool down once we gained momentum.

With a variation that summed up most of the trip, the climate that had crippled us some two hours earlier turned to a cold drizzle as we rode north towards the Caribbean coast. The light rain quickly ripened into a full scale downpour, and we came to an abrupt standstill at a roped-off section of road.

An entire slice of mountain had slid away, taking the road and everything that lay in its path with it. There was no way through the debris, and, as far as our map showed, it was covering the only route that led to the small port where we were supposed to meet our sailing.

Luckily, a few military guards overheard us asking for directions, and one of them gestured for us to follow them. Their truck sped off, and it took every ounce of concentration to keep up with it on our tired bike in the pouring rain. After thirty minutes of backtracking along the same highway we had already travelled, we spotted a hotel and made a sharp exit from the road, fairly certain that the military truck had forgotten about us anyway.

We trailed water and mud into the smart hotel bar, unsure what our plan was, until we discovered an Internet signal. We picked up yet another message from the agent, who explained that the boat would not leave for a further two days, due to the continuing storm. Although the news meant that there was no further urgency that day, the delay cut the original two weeks that we were supposed to travel with Abby and Alice, who were now already in Colombia, to an almost pointless two days.

In the hotel bar, a captain of a boat overheard us asking for directions. His vessel was moored in the same port that we were trying to locate, and, when we showed him the map we were using, he looked confused. He explained that an empty section on it had actually been the site of a well-paved highway to the coast for some time. We cursed it for sending us on a wild goose chase and thanked the captain, before setting off back into the rain.

We found the new highway and passed a military roadblock that was manned by the guards who been leading us earlier. They looked confused as we sailed past them half an hour after disappearing from their tail, but they still waved as we rode by.

We turned off the highway just before the coastal city of Colon, veering east to ride along a flooded road beside stretches of a furious Caribbean Sea. Lush rolling hills and soaked shanty towns cropped up along the way, before we finally reached the hostel, where we would spend our last days in Central America.

The agents organising our boat trip turned out to be a European couple, who had sailed the world for fifteen years before settling in Panama and buying the hostel and the boat we were due to travel on. The rest of the passengers had already arrived and filled up the outdoor wooden dormitory, so we took a newly built room in a concrete structure, where hot water and a comfy bed lay in wait.

The hostel brimmed with life in its coastal jungle setting. The haunting sound of howler monkeys woke us each morning, while a cacophony of toads erupted each night, and three enormous hounds slobbered away the hours in between. An orphaned green parrot hopped around eating just about anything it could reach, while beetles, insects, and spiders scuttled in every nook and cranny. Exquisite tropical flowers filled the garden, while banana plants and palms flourished in the seasonal rains.

We hit a windfall when we learnt that the owner of the hostel was able to weld aluminium, and he sealed the fracture in our rear wheel. It was the last of the breaks that had blighted us since Mexico, and fixing it before we embarked on a new section of the continent proved to be a great weight off our minds.

It was an equal relief to discover only four other passengers waiting for the crossing, rather than the crowds we had been warned of. Fanny and Markus were both Swiss and had been travelling a similar route to us. Lake was a Guyanese-American, who was also transporting a motorcycle that he had ridden from Florida with just one small rucksack for luggage. Andrew was an Irish backpacker whose repeated requests not to be called Andy fell on Byron's deaf ears. They were all about our age, and, luckily, we got on well, considering we were about to spend five days together in the very small confines of a forty-five-foot sailing yacht.

In true Latin American style, nobody was sure when exactly we would be setting sail, as the boat was yet to return through the stormy seas from Colombia. The next two days were spent packing and repacking, stocking up on last minute supplies, and speculating as to how much space there would actually be on the boat for the six of us, plus two motorcycles and two crew members. Just as dusk began to settle on the second evening, and we resigned ourselves to waiting another day, the boat docked in the small port and set the wheels in motion for loading the luggage onboard.

Having lazed around for most of the day, we were suddenly thrown into a frenzy of activity, rushing to get everybody's belongings to the waterfront and onto the boat before the sun went down. We frantically undid all of our careful packing in about twenty minutes, when it became necessary to detach the front screen and right pannier from the Flying Aga in order for the bike to fit comfortably onboard.

We had read tales and watched footage of motorcycles being loaded onto boats for the passage between Panama and Colombia, so we thought we were more or less prepared for the process. However, as we had learnt along the way, photos, film footage, and written accounts never do complete justice to experiencing an event first hand.

Darkness had caught up with us by the time the procedure began, and we wheeled the Flying Aga halfway down a concrete jetty to position it parallel with an elongated rowing boat. The hostel owners had employed a group of ten strong, local men for the task, and some of them stood in the boat, while the rest lifted the bike towards them. Once it was onboard, Byron sat on it to keep it upright, while two of the team held it firm at either end. The same process played out for Lake's Honda CRF250, and, with the two bikes loaded, the long boat slowly motored out into the dark marina.

It pulled up to the stern of the yacht, where a winch was assembled using the rear, raised grab rail. A few of the guys held the rowing boat steady against the yacht, while ropes were secured to one bike at a time, and, with sheer brute force, they were hauled onboard.

Despite our complete trust in the owner, who had a confident Germanic authority over the entire operation, we still breathed an enormous sigh of relief that neither motorcycle had met a watery demise. The owner secured each bike to the port and starboard rear grab rails before wrapping them tight in tarpaulin to create two enormous, bulging weights at the back of the yacht that we prayed wouldn't move an inch until we reached Colombia.

As we enjoyed some cool beers under a starlit sky, movement in the shadows of a wall caught our attention. Something had been scurrying back and forth across a light fitting, where the wall met the ceiling, and we aimed a camera at the area to take a few photos. The images showed what looked like a giant rat, but, with no idea what the creature actually was, we called the owners over to ask them. It turned out to be an opossum, and the owners' ominous groan of annoyance told us that it was a pest.

The species had apparently made an orphan of the hostel parrot, and, when it reappeared on the light fitting, a swing of a machete preceded the creature's abrupt demise. The action simultaneously severed the light cables in the hostel and plunged the building into darkness. Needless to say, the light mood quickly changed, and we all judged it to be a good time to get some sleep.

We woke up the next morning to the aftermath of a fire in the dormitory, where the rest of the passengers had been sleeping. An unplugged television had spontaneously combusted in the early hours, and, although it was hastily put out after waking everybody up, the terrifying alarm didn't stop an excessive amount of dawdling and delays to our sailing.

Once fishing hooks had been purchased and we had returned to collect forgotten passports from the hostel, we finally climbed aboard the sailing boat for our first extended sea voyage.

After being welcomed to Mexico at a cliff top campground by a pod of dolphins, we were bid adieu from Central America by their lone Panamanian cousin, who emerged from the marina just as the captain lifted the anchor.

SOUTH AMERICA

GUYANA
VENEZUELA   SURINAME
COLOMBIA   FRENCH GUIANA
ECUADOR

PERU

BRAZIL

BOLIVIA

CHILE   ARGENTINA   PARAGUAY
URUGUAY

• • • • FLYING AGA ROUTE

TIERRA DEL FUEGO

Seasickness and Mutiny

199 Days on the Road | 20,371 Miles on the Clock

We motored slowly through the marina and out towards the open sea, when the captain advised everybody to take a seasickness pill. We still had some left from our Mexican ferry journey so took one each with no idea as to how vital they would become.

Just before we hit the open sea, we both foolishly went below deck where the air was stuffy and the motion of the boat was at its strongest. It wasn't long before we topped off the error by settling down above deck at the aft of the boat, close to the two bike bundles.

Ten solid hours of unstoppable, chronic nausea commenced before any trace of the pills had a chance to kick in. It rendered us utterly incapacitated, and the slightest movement of a muscle sent us crawling hopelessly to the splintered platform at the back of the boat, where we hurled into the deep blue sea. We were incapable of talking at all and could only lie in mutual dread of the next onslaught, all the while holding out for the evening, when we were due to anchor in the shallow bay of an island.

After the first hour, there was nothing left inside us, but the slightest shift from an uncomfortable position or the faintest utterance of a word continued to send us racing to the creaking platform. Unable to move from the back of the boat for fear that we were so empty our internal organs might be heaved up next, we drifted in and out of consciousness as puddles of seawater formed around us, and the glaring sun burnt any exposed skin.

We spent nine hours laid up and suffering between the bike bundles until a light rain became torrential, and waves began to crash over the gunwale. They washed across the deck where we were lying, and the risk of getting swept overboard with the next swell forced us to join the other passengers in the shelter of the steering pit. Byron fared better with the move, which saw me dive immediately to the side of the pit and retch overboard from a new vantage point.

Despite the stormy weather, moving without vomiting was hopeless, so I lay in the narrow walkway outside a cabin window for the final hour, praying for the day to end. Although none of the other passengers had suffered in the same way, in empathy they brought out waterproof jackets and towels as defence against the elements in the exposed spot.

Eventually, the torture came to an end, and, under the cover of darkness, we drifted into the bay of a San Blas island, where the anchor was finally dropped in still water.

Instant relief flooded through us, and it almost felt like the past ten hours had never happened. Although we were utterly exhausted, the nausea had completely dispersed.

We spent the evening resting in the steering pit and gazing up at a starlit sky, thankful for the reprieve. Tiny creatures secreted phosphorescence that swirled through the sea around us, and, although a few lights glimmered on the small island, we were totally encircled by the peace of the natural world.

We slept soundly in the more bearable movement of shallow water and woke the next morning in the most contrary of climates to that of the Decembers we were used to. Byron dived straight from the boat into the warm ocean, and the rest of us quickly followed suit. We swam to the shore of the island, where soft white sand covered our feet and crystal clear water lapped at fallen coconuts and driftwood. After such a harrowing journey to get there, we were determined to make the most of the two day stopover in the San Blas islands.

The San Blas is an archipelago of over 370 islands that are independent of Panama and home to the Kuna people, who had built the dormitory back at the hostel where the television had spontaneously combusted the previous morning. Originally from South America, they had moved towards Panama when the Spanish arrived on the continent. They lived for some time in the jungle of the Darien Gap, but disease and limited trade had eventually driven them from the mainland and out to the islands. Trade opportunities with passing ships and freedom from disease had offered them an improved way of life, and they had stayed ever since.

Only a small number of the islands were actually inhabited by the Kuna, while hundreds more lay scattered across the ocean, unoccupied and ripe for exploring. The islands fluctuated in size from one that literally consisted of a patch of sand and a solitary palm tree, to others that were home to hundreds of residents.

We ate breakfast back on the boat before sailing to another island that sat so close to sea level that, from a distance, a collection of colourful wooden huts appeared to float on the surface of the ocean. A few makeshift piers jutted out from the main bulk of land, and we climbed from the boat's dinghy onto a tiny beach between one of the haphazard walkways and a ramshackle pig sty.

Despite its remote location, little girls fearlessly ran rings around us, while one guy, who was listening to thrash metal on a portable stereo, greeted our captain with a fist bump. Apart from a few older women who wore brightly patterned clothes and beautifully intricate beads on their calves and forearms, everybody was dressed in T-shirts, jeans, or shorts.

Nestor, the father of the fearless young girls, greeted our merry band warmly and invited us to sit outside the hut that formed their family kitchen. He took food from the captain to prepare a meal inside, where streams of light shone through gaps in the wooden walls and a single saucepan simmered above an open fire that blazed on the sandy floor. Coconut shells hung to dry from the rafters near a small selection of pots that were suspended above the floor on wooden sticks. Disappointingly, fish was not on the menu, and he served up the rice, beans, and meat supplies from the boat, before we went to explore the island.

We followed the sandy passageways between the wooden huts that engulfed the island, passing women gutting the day's catch and young kids playing football in the narrow lanes. Older children were embroiled in a game of volleyball in the island's main square, while teenage girls sauntered past everybody with indifference. Narrow, carved-out tree trunk boats and canoes came and went, bringing fishermen home and carrying families from one island to the next.

It didn't take long to discover that the ramshackle piers led to the island's only toilets, where crudely constructed, open air closets rested on stilts above the sea, and toilet seats opened directly into the water below.

Bewildered by Markus's and Byron's attempts to scoop up fish using baseball caps and discarded shoes, we ended the day with some children who showed them how it was done with a tiny hook and line.

After stocking up on snacks and sweets for the onward journey at one of the island's two tuck shops, we weaved a path back to Nestor's hut just as a seasonal rain shower set in. We waited for the captain to return, but eventually Nestor ushered us into his carved out tree canoe and paddled us to the yacht, where the captain and his first mate had snuck away earlier with the dinghy.

They had prepared one of many mishmash meals that were covered with plastic cheese, and, as we ate, the last lights were extinguished on the nearby island. That night, we settled in for another peaceful sleep in our cabin that doubled as the ship's larder and was starting to reek of ripening produce.

Everybody bypassed the token onboard facilities the next morning and dived into the sea for a wash before the captain wasted little time in lifting the anchor. We were soon sailing towards another island that was less inhabited and boasted the most beautiful shoreline. Soft white sand covered the beach, and a shipwreck played host to some exquisitely coloured fish and coral.

We soon learnt more about the savvy Kuna people, who would appear from the shadows to charge a dollar for each fallen coconut a visitor picked up. Our captain reeled off other examples of their shrewd acumen that included an ongoing negotiation between the tribal chiefs and the Panamanian immigration officials, who used one of their islands. A deal was yet to be agreed after the Kuna chiefs had quoted a five hundred dollar fee to remove each palm tree that was growing on the small airstrip used by the Panamanians.

Using the lines and hooks that the owner had given us before we left Panama, the boys in our party were soon trying to rectify their fishing failure from the day before. After no success in catching dinner, though, we set sail again to an entirely uninhabited island, where we planned to idle away the rest of the day.

We paddled the small dinghy out to its shore, where all signs of human life soon disappeared in a forest of coconut palms. It was the epitome of a desert island, and we spent yet another unusual Sunday clambering over fallen tree debris, dodging piles of coconut husks, and sidestepping hermit crabs. We soon stumbled upon a small white beach that was too enticing to pass by, and, with the rest of our gang of would-be pirates, we settled there for the final few hours of the day.

A team effort that involved shimmying up palm trees and knocking down loose coconuts produced a small harvest that we hacked into with pocket knives. We also took it in turns to return to the boat and ransack the larder for biscuits and supplies to take back to our new base that provided a welcome getaway from the double act crew.

When the captain wasn't teaching his girlfriend and first mate how to sail, they spent the days wrapped in nauseating displays of affection, while smoking joints and drinking beer. Despite the carefree charade, though, the marijuana had obviously made the captain incredibly paranoid, because he interpreted almost any query from his passengers as antagonistic. Without warning, he would launch a hostile defence against the slightest of questions, immediately turning the mood of the boat on its head.

Andrew had lived on a boat in Ireland and, on our first evening at sea, he noticed that the navigation light used for sailing in the dark was broken. Time and again, the captain flatly ignored his concerns about the fault, insisting that the owners knew about the problem and that it posed no risk to sailing, because he used a radar system. The rest of us didn't know any better, but Andrew was visibly worried, and the captain constantly belittled his doubts.

We only found out later that the original captain of the boat had resigned just days before we sailed, and the one who took us across the ocean had simply been an acquaintance of his. The owners hired him as an emergency replacement, and, although he got the boat across in one piece, he didn't seem too bothered about its consignment. Fortunately, we found new friends in our fellow passengers and united in a mutinous plot, while we ate fresh coconuts and crackers on the beautiful secluded beach.

Eventually, the sun began to drop, and we dragged ourselves away from the tranquil spot. We swam back across the dense coral, narrowly missing the pink bowl and long tentacles of one of the jellyfish that infested the island seas during the winter. Silhouettes of fishing canoes and Kuna boats drifted peacefully across the darkening sea, while we ate our last plastic cheese meal in calm water. Seasickness pills were ingested before we all descended below deck and willed sleep to set in, before the concluding forty-hour stretch to Colombia began later that evening.

We had slept lightly before the winds picked up out at sea. Although the seasickness pills fought off the hideous retching, a constant fear of regression left us in a delicate state, while dry mouths, hollow stomachs, and insomnia soon emerged as side effects. Together with the erratic movement of the boat and the sound of the crew racing about above deck, I spent a restless night dreaming up deliriously vivid catastrophes. The hours to morning were filled with nightmares where the bikes rolled off the back of the boat and sunk to the depths of the ocean, or where the two bikes unbalanced the boat and capsized it.

The dreams were only interrupted once when the boat bent horribly close to the water. Everything that wasn't screwed down, including us, went flying into the bulkheads, while the crew raced below deck, professing that everything was under control.

We climbed above deck the next morning, exhausted by the night but still mercifully free of seasickness. The rising sun had brought calm to the water, and the waves lapped peacefully at the side of the boat. The captain was characteristically unresponsive to our questions about the conditions during the night, but, despite his attitude, we now had a renewed faith in his ability at sea.

A resolve to remain nausea-free was all that occupied our minds for most of the day. We ate endless dry crackers and kept sight of the horizon, watching for whales, dolphins, and mermaids as we sailed on autopilot, while the crew slept off their busy night.

The hours ticked away while no landmarks or other boats broke the monotony. All we had seen for 360-degrees was the curvature of the planet in the clear sky above and the surrounding ocean. As the day grew long, a delirious sense that we had made no progress at all from the centre of a huge dome began to set in.

The highlight came when a pod of dolphins propelled themselves like torpedoes towards the boat. They flipped and dived ahead of us for a few magical moments, killing the tedium in one fell swoop, before they swam away one by one, to make the day of some other lonely sailors.

Another broken night of sleep in rough seas followed, but the water eventually fell to an almost flat calm the next afternoon. We had successfully avoided a return of the seasickness, but the pills and constant motion of the boat left us jaded, while the salty wind and burning sunshine had us all longing to cool off in the deep blue sea.

The water was so calm that it took little persuasion for the captain to drop the sails and turn off the motor. We didn't realise how noisy the boat had been until an immediate stillness prevailed, and we drifted silently in the middle of the ocean. We had got what we asked for, but a pang of doubt hit us as we peered down into the inconceivable depths below.

Ignoring the mounting trepidation, we launched ourselves overboard and left Lake to single-handedly take charge of the boat. The captain and his first mate had joined us, and, in the excitement, nobody had thought to lower the rear ladder. Apart from Lake, who couldn't swim, our only means of keeping the boat close came from a single line that the captain had kept hold of.

Not for the first time on the journey, our existence on the planet suddenly felt utterly insignificant after diving into the middle of a sea that sank to mindboggling depths of four miles. The brief encounter was awe-inspiring, and we swam as far from the boat and as deep into the abyss as we dared, while our hearts beat faster than ever before. We were conscious that the sharks and whales, which had eluded us so far, could have put in an appearance at any moment, but the terrifying prospect only intensified the thrill.

Aware that the situation could turn at any moment, we called up to Lake in jest and cried out that he was our only hope of survival. With evident unease at the responsibility, he jumped fully dressed off the boat to join us. Although he had a life jacket on, considering that he couldn't swim, we were dumbfounded by the bold move. The boat was now totally empty, and, had the captain lost hold of the line, it would only have taken seconds to begin drifting away from us.

Suddenly mindful of the endless void below us, I clambered onto Byron's shoulders and hauled myself onboard to drop the rear ladder for the others. It took a while before they all climbed back up, but we eventually set off on the final stretch of the miniature voyage.

An unexpected skyline of high rise buildings and towering skyscrapers appeared on the horizon a full six hours before we reached the marina of Cartagena. The captain had earlier estimated that we would not arrive until five o'clock the following morning, so we assumed it would be no problem to sleep onboard and unload our belongings the next day. However, he had other ideas, and, true to form, when we requested to stay onboard he grew agitated. He showed total disregard for the fact that it was dark and none of us had arranged anywhere to stay, not to mention that we had no way to sort out our passports so late at night.

To add to our growing dislike of the man, he had not employed the group of men that the hostel owner had assured us would be there to help unload the motorcycles. Not only was he booting us off late at night, but he also expected everybody to assist in unloading the bikes, despite half of the passengers having nothing to do with the two vehicles.

His uncle had joined us, but he did little to raise the complete lack of confidence we now had in the captain. We did everything we could think of to express how unhappy we were with his cheapskate plan, asking him to wait until morning when it was light and we could employ the brawn of a few more men. In spite of our fears, he began untying the bikes, anyway, leaving us little alternative but to join in or face watching him single-handedly send our dreams plummeting into the black waters of the Colombian marina.

With frustratingly little power over the situation, the boys helped to winch the bikes into the woefully unsuitable dinghy, all the while wishing we had gone ahead with our planned mutiny. With a consignment of six men propping up a heavy motorcycle, the rim of the dinghy dropped almost level to the surface of the sea.

Lake's Honda went first and made it in one piece to dry land, before the Flying Aga followed and, true to our concerns, proved to be too heavy to unload at the other end. The dinghy had to be motored around the marina to berth on a small beach, where the air from the inflatable vessel was released in order for the bike to roll off. A trio of passing policemen assisted in lifting it over the promenade wall, luckily without requesting to see its importation paperwork or questioning why it wasn't being unloaded at the official dock.

It was eleven o'clock at night by the time the rest of our luggage made it to the promenade and the captain left us on the street without our documents, passports, or any idea which direction we could find a room for the night.

It had been part of the deal for him to sort out the paperwork, and he promised he would return it to us the next day. However, ditching us late at night in a city where it turned out to be illegal to ride a motorcycle after 11 P.M. had not been part of the arrangement.

Familiar Faces and Fiestas

204 Days on the Road | 20,371 Miles on the Clock

The others went ahead in a taxi to find a hostel, and Lake followed them, while we put the Flying Aga back together at the side of the road. It was nearly midnight by the time we were repacked and ready to find where they had gone, and we cursed the captain for not letting us stay onboard.

On entering the old town, Lake had been pulled over by the police. With his lack of luggage, they most likely took him for a local, rather than a typical overloaded tourist who didn't know about the 11 P.M. rule. We stumbled upon him in the one-way system of narrow streets that were buzzing with revellers. As the most laid-back person we had ever met, it was no surprise that he had not declared his lack of knowledge about the motorbike curfew to the police. Instead, when the officers asked to see his paperwork, he offered to buy them dinner, thinking it would be less hassle than explaining why he didn't have a passport.

We arrived just as he was ordering them burgers from a nearby cart, and he tried to save us from the same questioning by motioning to us to keep riding. The officers were equally keen to keep us away after realising that Lake was, in fact, a tourist, who they probably shouldn't have been fleecing. Revellers gathered around to see what was going on, and, amid the chaos, Lake explained that he would catch us up. We were still none the wiser but were too tired to think straight and assumed that we had interrupted some sort of transaction. So, when one of the policemen offered to show us the location of a hostel, we followed him. He dropped us on the street where we knew Abby and Alice had arrived earlier that day and where the other boat passengers had gone in the taxi.

It was close to one o'clock in the morning, and, other than a usual late night crowd, there was nobody around to ask advice about parking. The first two hostels we tried didn't have anywhere to leave the Flying Aga, but the third agreed that we could squeeze it into a gated passageway that was set off their main entrance. As we navigated up another steep curb using a plank of wood, Andrew appeared and came over to help.

We were trying to squeeze our wide bike into the narrow walkway when, led by the same policemen he had been buying burgers for, Lake pulled up. It was only when the officers had swiftly ridden off that Lake filled us in on what had actually happened.

After talking the hostel manager into giving him a room and letting him park his bike inside with ours, Lake took a turn on the plank to ride into the small lobby. None of us had eaten since lunchtime, so, once the bikes were secure, we went in search of food, and Andrew went back to the bar. In an exhausted, sunburnt, and salt-encrusted state, we wandered through a small red light district and ended up in a sketchy café to eat whatever they would put in front of us.

Meanwhile, shortly after we had left him, Andrew was accosted by more policemen, who asked him to accompany them to their headquarters. He had been talking to a couple of dodgy individuals in the bar and assumed the policemen thought he had bought drugs from them. Incensed, but powerless, Andrew went with them to a nondescript office, where they asked him to remove his shoes and empty his pockets. Convinced they were about to set him up, he refused, and, luckily, they eventually let him go.

Back in the café, we did our best to appear inconspicuous among the groups of shifty locals and cursed the captain again while we ate greasy, gringo-priced burgers that were coated with more plastic cheese.

After a pitiful few hours of sleep that were broken by the bizarre rocking sensation of still being at sea, we eventually retrieved our passports and paperwork the next day. The process had not been free of more hassles, though, but we finally bid good riddance to the captain after a minor showdown.

Despite the unnecessary aggravation he had caused, we were fortunate to have enjoyed a tremendous experience in the lead up to the final leg of our adventure. We were at last in South America, and an overwhelming sense of relief flooded through us at having reached the destination that had been in our sights for the past six weeks.

After finally meeting up with Abby and Alice, who had already spent twelve days travelling through Colombia, we savoured a precious two days with them in the blisteringly hot city. Having only just caught up after seven months, it was with a cheerless goodbye that we waved them off on the third day, as they returned to a snow covered England ahead of Christmas.

By then, Lake and Andrew had also gone their separate ways, but Markus and Fanny were still in town, so we met up with them to witness a Christmas light switch-on in the sun-drenched Caribbean city. The old city of Cartagena was set away from the towering office blocks and skyscrapers that had loomed on the horizon out at sea. It was brimming with life, and, after a cheap fish supper with Markus and Fanny, we ducked as hundreds of thoroughbred horses, ridden by Panama-hat-toting farmers, trotted through the narrow streets in an annual race. A music festival played out in one of the many plazas, while other horses pulled wagons of tourists and locals through the cobbled streets. Old men played cards in leafy squares, while colourfully dressed women sold chopped fruit and fresh arepas from carts. Exquisite colonial buildings lined the network of picturesque streets, and an enormous fort overlooked the coast in the distance. At the top of our road on the outskirts of the old walls, call girls and drug dealers whispered to us every morning as we passed through the less exclusive areas, contributing to the old city's rich diversity.

Our energy over the previous six weeks had been poured solely into reaching Colombia, and, although we had no onward plan, we did have some time in which to piece one together. My parents were due to visit the city a few days later, and we elected to take a small break from our route south, to travel east along the coast before they arrived.

Three hours on the road introduced us to the most terrifying driving of the trip, and we arrived in the city of Santa Marta in an overheated and dishevelled state. Every vehicle we had come across appeared to be in a race that we didn't know about. Drivers that pulled out to overtake would often be overtaken themselves mid-manoeuvre, creating three lanes of traffic on single-lane highways. Usually the operation was carried out in perilously close proximity to oncoming vehicles, and any space to potentially backtrack was quickly filled by other drivers. We frequently faced cars that drove straight towards us in our lane without deviation, and they only ever pulled over with milliseconds to spare.

A further three hours of riding aimlessly around the city failed to find a hostel with spare rooms or parking, so we went to try our luck in a small fishing village a few miles east.

Taganga was teeming with hostels, palapa huts, and bars, and its working beach was packed with fishing and diving paraphernalia. We had stopped near the seafront and were wondering how best to decline the persistence of two policemen and a hostel owner who had just shown us around a cat infested, mothball-scented room, when Andrew from the boat randomly appeared. The three salesmen didn't take too kindly when we seized the opportunity to follow our friend to his hostel, instead.

We bounced over rocks and skirted deep potholes to the edge of the village, where a small fortress had been built at the foot of a cliff. Andrew led us through an ornate wooden door and into a traveller's paradise. Hammocks hung from a top deck that overlooked the nearby bay and sun loungers surrounded a swimming pool at the centre of the courtyard. A games room, wireless internet, hot showers, air conditioning, and a roaming blue and yellow macaw completed the extravagance. The hot water showers alone would have been enough to tempt us, and we checked-in immediately, paying the same price that the mothball and cat infested hostel had been asking.

The place was run by an army of heavily tattooed, ex-military staff, who assured us that the Flying Aga would be safe parked outside because, they explained, everybody knew not to mess with them. We soon learnt that the abundance of tourists and backpackers in the picturesque fishing village was down to a lively night-life and a selection of readily accessible, extracurricular substances.

Having reached the age of knowing better, we declined the harder goods on offer but made the most of the comfort. We ate a lot of fresh fish, drank a lot of cold beer, and enjoyed a few hot showers, before meeting a guy who had been travelling for six weeks but was yet to leave the fortress. We took his tale as our cue to get off the beaten track and said our final goodbyes to Andrew, who was heading south.

It was still unbearably hot, but we grudgingly swapped swimwear for heavy bike gear before setting off further east along the coast. Small villages came and went along the road as the wind picked up and knocked a few degrees off the searing temperature. We approached the small village of Palomino and quickly spotted a Canadian plated BMW F650. The rider lived nearby and told us about a secluded resort on the beach, so we went to investigate, as he rode off on a trip to the capital city.

We turned off the main road and followed a muddy track through wild foliage, bouncing in and out of ruts and potholes, until we came to a clearing where palm trees towered over a blend of fine grass and sand. A couple of wooden cabins had been built close to the adjoining beach, and a jolly lady came out from one of them to greet us. The huts were fully booked so, for the first time since Mexican Independence weekend on the Baja Peninsula, we crow-barred the tent from the depths of the panniers and camped.

The beach was flanked by palm trees and driftwood debris in another textbook, castaway setting. A strong wind whipped up the sand and sent huge waves crashing into the shore, keeping the mosquitoes at bay but preventing a swim.

We were closing in fast on the Equator, and, by six o'clock that evening, the entire area was lit only by a star-filled sky and a full moon. A Colombian family invited us to perch on a few logs beside a campfire, where coconut husks, dead palm leaves, and driftwood kept us warm until we retired to the comfort of our little tent.

The wind had dropped by the next morning, and the full brunt of the heat was released. After eating a breakfast of plantain and eggs, we hacked into a few fallen coconuts before following a rural track into the nearby town. A main street was lined with tiny stalls and simple cafés, where we ate a chicken and rice lunch before stocking up on groceries and fresh fish.

We were alone on the site that evening and, when the sun dropped, we lit another campfire and commandeered the small outdoor kitchen. After mixing a few embers from the beach fire with some books that had been left as kindling, we soon had a modest barbecue going. Under the glow of some precariously balanced candles, we grilled a rustic feast of fresh fish, vegetable kebabs, and homemade coconut rice.

Two nights spent camping on the coast had revitalized us, but the ride back to Cartagena soon unravelled any good the short break had done. Despite the affable nature of every Colombian we had met so far, a whole new breed emerged on the northern roads, where a perpetual race continued to play out. Regardless of what lay ahead, no driver was content to be stuck behind any other vehicle, and, after one too many close encounters, we pulled over at a roadside café to catch our breath.

Almost as soon as we parked up, a well dressed man sauntered over and questioned us about the bike. Although our Spanish had improved, our command of the language was still feeble in the face of fast local chatter. The difficulty in keeping up with what he was saying was not helped by the heat or our hunger. As he continued to talk, we edged towards the counter where some fans were whirring away. He moved with us and, after we had ordered our food, he ushered us back outside to sit down. We couldn't understand why he had taken over but he was a big guy and seemed to have some sort of authority, so we took a seat at a table outside.

After clocking the young men joining him for beers and the number of people who passed the café and nodded acknowledgment to him, we speculated over who the group might be.

When he came back to join us, we finally understood that he had been offering to buy us our lunch. He soon introduced us to his son and nephew, who were in the party of young men with him, and, before our lunch came, they had written down their contact details in case we had any troubles in their country. It was our first encounter with Colombian hospitality, and we learnt that a polite decline simply didn't translate. So, in a hot and hungry state, we accepted lunch from the group of men who, despite our assumption that they might be the local mob, surreally went on to discuss an upcoming Madonna concert.

Judging by the copious empty beer bottles that filled their table, the guys were on a bit of a bender and left us to eat when our lunch was served. They returned when we had finished, this time to give us an entire catering platter of apple pastries from a stash that had just been delivered to them, most likely as part of the food for the party they were warming up for. Our polite decline fell on deaf ears again, and, when we climbed back on the Flying Aga, we took the platter of pastries with us, wondering who would be in trouble for giving away the dessert.

We soon made our way back into Cartagena, where the population of Colombia had descended for Christmas. After returning to the same hostel and parking in the same narrow walkway, the manager explained that two people, who were also travelling by motorcycle, had called in before we had set off along the coast. They were heading north and had left him with their roadmaps and a travel guide to pass on to us. We never got to meet them, but the guide and maps proved to be invaluable as the weeks progressed.

Having seen few other adventure motorcyclists during the first five months of the trip, the sight of box panniers covered in stickers and roll bags bungeed to top boxes was becoming more frequent as we all funnelled through the route between Panama and Colombia. The laden bikes were always ridden by similarly over-dressed-for-the-weather riders, who wore full face helmets and were caked in mud and dust. As with the couple who had left us their maps, though, it was rare to cross paths in the same place at the same time, so it was a happy surprise to hear that Bryce, who we had met in Texas when he was touring the US on his Harley Davidson, had just arrived, fresh off the boat.

We had been following his progress ever since October when, after modifying El Calvo, his Honda XR650, he had taken the plunge and begun his own journey south. We knew that he wasn't too far behind us but hadn't anticipated that we would cross paths again, until we found ourselves delayed after the damage caused in Honduras. He had just arrived from Panama, and we wasted no time in meeting up exactly sixteen weeks after waving goodbye to him, Jeff, and Sonia in New Mexico.

With a lighter bike carrying just one lone ranger, Bryce had found himself in a few more scrapes than we had encountered. Not counting the inevitable, mechanical hiccups, he had ploughed into the back of a bus, been bitten by a dog, and his riding partner had been run over by a truck in El Salvador. When Bryce wasn't riding, he had also been run over by a speed boat and inadvertently drugged.

It was fantastic to catch up with him that evening, and, after a breakfast filled with more anecdotes, he overtook us on El Calvo to continue riding south, while we went off to meet my parents, who had also just arrived in town.

Rosemary and Owen had waved us off on a dreary night in London seven months earlier, so it was quite surreal to see them again on the sun drenched, Colombian Caribbean coast. As much as we didn't want to think about returning home, it was a tremendous pleasure to see them in the city that was fast becoming synonymous with reunions.

My Colombian sister-in-law, Vanessa, was visiting her family in the country, and, although my brother was stuck back in London at work, my parents had flown over to combine a Christmas holiday with meeting her family and seeing us. They had arrived from Bogota that morning, and, although Christmas was still a week away, it felt like it had come early when we saw the items they had somehow managed to squeeze into their luggage. As well as some essential new motorcycle parts, including fork seals, new gaiters and ignition points, we had never been so excited by the sight of teabags, Wrigley's Extra chewing gum, and Dairy Milk chocolate.

We embarked on more explorations of the old city, climbing with my parents to the lofty heights of holidaymakers, which came easier than we expected after many months of living on the road. We even joined them for a couple of nights in a spa hotel further along the coast, at the most stylish outfit that we had the good fortune to encounter on the entire continent.

With some reluctance, a couple of days later we left them by the sea and resumed our ride south towards Medellin, where we planned to meet them again with Vanessa to celebrate Christmas.

We left the city that had become so familiar to us and hit the open road, where more would-be Formula One drivers kept us on our toes. Countless mountain villages and rural townships paved the way, before we stopped for the day in Caucasia. The ride had been long and hot, and large sections of tarmac had been compressed and distorted into deep furrows that were a challenge to navigate without losing control of the front wheel. We checked into the cheapest hotel room we could find which, in great contrast to the previous couple of nights in a spa, boasted the world's smallest double bed and little else.

A knock on the door at three o'clock in the morning woke us from a hot and cramped sleep. It was the night watchman and he urgently beckoned Byron downstairs. Half asleep, but anxious to know what was wrong, Byron followed him in some confusion and was led to the car park, where we had left the bike. It was raining heavily, and the guard pointed to the bag attached to the front windshield with concern. It turned out that he had woken us up in the middle of the night to let us know that the soft pannier army surplus bag, which was screwed onto the windscreen of the bike and had long been exposed to almost every type of weather condition, was getting wet.

We couldn't get back to sleep in the humid room afterwards, so waited out the rest of the night before joining an early rush-hour commute to continue our southerly bearing.

During a similar mountain ride to the day before, we stayed alert for risky overtakes and colossal tankers at blind corners, but the racetrack driving began to lessen as we made progress.

Spectacular rolling knolls, jagged peaks, and jungle rivers adorned the route, which led us into high altitude mist and cold fog before dropping through small villages that were nestled deep in the hillsides or sprawled across mountain crests. Scavenging buzzards circled above us as we weaved past no end of lone donkeys, horses and carts, and small motorcycles carrying entire families.

An impressive view of the Aburrá Valley eventually came into sight, and we descended towards Medellin on a flawlessly smooth open highway. We had pinpointed the location of a hostel on our map, but it was soon clear that we had misread the numbers in the address. As we rode aimlessly around the outer reaches of the huge city, a group of guys spotted us studying our map.

Like the apple pastry gang outside Cartagena the week before, they were enjoying a few Saturday afternoon beers but were eager to help when we asked them for directions. After deliberating where the correct location of the hostel actually was, one of them promptly jumped into a car and motioned for us to follow him. We tailed him to the other side of the city before he gestured towards the area we were looking for and, with a wave goodbye, he disappeared into the heavy traffic. It would be a rare day in London when anyone asked a lost tourist if they could help them, let alone drive through city traffic for almost an hour to direct them.

We parked the Flying Aga next to a Christmas tree in the hostel garage. Our room was in the same lockup and consisted of a bed that had been partitioned off from the rest of the garage with thin chipboard. Car alarms reverberated off its metal door throughout the night, and, at two o'clock in the morning, a couple of people parked directly on the other side of it and proceeded to play a repertoire of terrible, cheesy music. They eventually had us wide awake, and, when we could stand it no more, Byron opened the door. His half dressed, bald, and feral-bearded state was enough to see them scarper, but the damage was done, and we couldn't get back to sleep.

Although we had stayed in much worse places, for the most part they had always been clean. However, after the sleepless night, the stale bed sheets and the discovery of excessive pubic hair in the communal shower had us packed up and checked out first thing the next morning.

At some point on our ride down through the mountains, we had hit a high speed bump, where a bolt on the sump of the bike had come loose, and we had been leaving small puddles of oil wherever we parked. We had arrived a couple of days before the Christmas gathering to work on the bike, anyway, and, on our way to find a new room, we stopped to buy a new bolt and some more oil.

Byron went into a shop, while I stayed with our full load, and, within minutes, about seven guys, who had been washing cars, promptly surrounded us.

They were captivated by the bike and showed few inhibitions about touching it. Colombia was a country with an even greater passion for motorcycles than the rest of Latin America, and they inundated me with questions. Our Spanish was improving, and I did my best to answer them, while they seemingly forgot all about their work. Their enthusiasm couldn't be tamed, and, even by the time Byron had returned, they showed little sign of leaving. We had to squeeze through them to climb back on and ease the bike away.

Bryce had reached Medellin after leaving Cartagena and was still in town when we found a new hostel. We soon met up again, and he took us on a tour of the area, where he had already tracked down the best of the motorcycle shops. We put in an order for parts and a new tyre at Motoshop, before setting off on our collective favourite pastime of finding food. Bryce stayed true to his roots in a local restaurant and ordered two main dishes, which he promptly polished off, while Byron looked on wistfully, wishing he had thought of doing the same.

Having unearthed a motorcycle-friendly hostel, Bryce had stayed much longer in Medellin than he had planned. On Christmas Eve the next morning, we met up with him and Al, his hostel's Scottish owner, and over empanadas and strong coffee, Al offered to lead us all on a ride out of the city to the Peñón de Guatapé, a two hundred meter vertical rock that had once been an ancient indigenous site of worship.

It was a beautiful day, and, equipped with three sturdy sunflowers that I had bought to mark what would have been

my brother Edward's birthday, we ventured out on a perfect
ride that twisted and turned through the Colombian hills. A
vertical zigzag of steps led up the exterior of the enormous
rock, and, after Al declared that one climb in a lifetime was
enough for him, he watched over our gear, while we took on
the challenge.

Scores of Colombian families were also scaling the seven
hundred steps, severely testing their lungpower and leg muscles
in order to witness a stunning view of a hydroelectric dam
reservoir and its islands that sprawled across the landscape
below. A Christmas pizza with more strong coffee toasted the
day back at the bottom, before we parted ways with Al and
Bryce. They went back to the city, while we set off to join the
family Christmas gathering.

Vanessa's friends lived on a finca in the hills outside Medellin,
where the festivities were getting started. In characteristically
generous Colombian style, Paola, who owned the rural estate,
had given our British contingent her recently built guesthouse
to stay in, and, once we had offloaded our luggage inside, we
joined the party.

Spontaneous dancing was accompanied by rum and
champagne. Distributions of masks and party horns soon

did the rounds, while wine was poured and declarations of international love were declared. Beer flowed, and fireworks were fearlessly lit and launched by hand. More rum toasted a Secret Santa, before whisky complemented further dancing and impulsive cat-calls. Six hours after it all began, an enormous dish of paella was served up before the dancing resumed.

The following day was spent in recovery on the finca with a hair of the dog and leftover paella for breakfast. Later, in the hot afternoon sunshine of the Colombian hills, a barbecue of mouth-watering steak was served up for Christmas dinner.

The following day, Vanessa's family took us to explore Medellin, and we reconvened with the rest of the party later that night. They had hired a minibus to take a tour of the spectacular city Christmas lights, and we climbed onboard, equipped with bottles of the strong national liquor, aguardiente, accurately translated as firewater, and set off to recreate the merrymaking of Christmas Eve. The revelry concluded some hours later on our way home, where a stretch of highway had been commandeered by local kids and bikers who were performing death defying stunts to the cheers of a huge crowd, and the mischievous encouragement of Byron.

After breakfast the following morning, the festive period came to an abrupt end when Vanessa and her family set off back to Bogota and took my parents with them to catch their flight home. An emotional goodbye left us downhearted. Over the previous three weeks, we had unwittingly dropped our guard in the company of so many different friends and family. However, as my parents drove out of sight, a false sense of homeliness and familiarity suddenly diffused, and the prospect of once again tackling the great unknown felt a bit hollow.

Plantations and Petrol Plundering

227 Days on the Road | 21,404 Miles on the Clock

We arrived back in the city just in time to say a final goodbye to Bryce before he continued south, and we moved into his room at the hostel. We stayed there for a couple more nights, while Byron carried out the Flying Aga's fifth full service. We'd ridden over 21,000 miles through the continent and, although the old bike was still going strong, we had tested it enormously.

Rico, the owner of Motoshop, had ordered our spare parts and given us free rein over his forecourt to get to work. Byron fitted our very first new front tyre and fixed the loose bolt on the sump. He changed the gearbox, engine, and drive shaft oils and replaced the engine oil filter, spark plugs, and gearbox shift link seal.

The next day, Byron changed the fork oil and fitted new fork seals and gaiters. He adjusted the valves and ignition timings and balanced the carburettors. By the time the work was done, we had recovered our taste for adventure.

The surrounding mountains offered a peaceful backdrop to the ride out of Medellin. We had another hot spring resort in our sights and soon pulled off the main road to meander through the hilly backwoods. The weather had taken a turn for the worse by the time we reached the end of the rough route, and, after taking a look inside a solitary spa hotel where the hot spring was hidden, we elected to blow the day's budget on an all inclusive stay, rather than backtrack down the dirt trail in the rain.

The outdoor hot pools were filled by a plume of thermal water that fell from an enormous height through the vines and foliage of the adjoining mountain. We wasted no time in warming our cold bones in them before plucking up the courage to brave the cold air and race inside for the inclusive dinner.

The hotel was furnished like an alpine chalet and smelled of gas heating and winter stews. It was like nothing we had come across on the continent so far and was the first place that actually suited the festive snowy decorations and frosty baubles. Luckily for our budget, it was fully booked the following day for New Year's Eve, so, after the inclusive breakfast and the inclusive lunch, we set off again under a miserable cloak of mist and drizzle.

The short mountain ride was relatively deserted, aside from some particularly eerie New Year effigies of people that lined the roads and stood outside houses. They would be set on fire that night to mark the end of the old year and were filled with explosives to see in the New Year with a literal bang.

Early that afternoon we arrived at an old coffee plantation house in the small mountain town of Salento. It had been converted into a hostel and, through glassless windows, it offered exquisite views of the region's rich vegetation that the recent rains had lit up to an electric shade of green. We celebrated the New Year in the main square that night with cold beers and a delicious local dish of trout and flattened plantain.

The next day we took a ride into the nearby Cocora valley to witness some of the tallest trees we had ever seen. They were fifty-meter high, wax palms that swayed serenely in the wind across the knolls and mounds of the green mountains. They were an unusual spectacle in a landscape that was roughly 2,000 meters above the sea and would normally be associated with mighty oaks or bristling pines. After soaking up the surreal scene, we raced back through the stunning national park to Salento, where we scrambled on foot through the hills to a small coffee farm.

Unlike the larger plantations in the region, the farm was an independent setup that, as well as coffee beans, grew the side products of bananas, pineapples, oranges, and bamboo. It stretched across a deep valley and took a lot of lungpower to explore. After the trek, a lone guide led us up to its small plantation house, where he showed us the start to finish process of making coffee. Using a manual husker, an arm breaking grinder, a small pan, and a single hob he produced the most alluring aroma and tastiest brew we had ever drunk.

We had shared the tour with Leandro and Valentina, an Argentinean couple who we met up with again the next morning when we were packing the bike to leave. They helped us to mark our Argentinean roadmap with places that they implored us not to miss when we eventually reached their country and, before we set off, they also gave us their contact details and insisted that we look them up when we arrived in Buenos Aires.

After knocking back the last of the plantation coffee, we set off into the hills and made our way towards Ecuador. Some of the most outstanding views paved the route and sent our camera into overdrive. Rolling hills were sprinkled with vibrant colours, and broad mountain peaks were swathed in thick blankets of green velvet. We cut through the luminosity for miles until we coasted around the base of one incline and rode into a complete contrast.

The temperature rose, and all signs of vegetation were replaced by dry, jagged rocks. The air lay heavy across the arid terrain, and we began to dread the prospect of a day in draining heat. However, another rise in elevation soon brought back a refreshing nip to the air, as well as a return to the green veneer. As we weaved higher into the enormous peaks, the road narrowed, and the most inferior of barriers lay between us and a terrifying sheer drop.

We spent the night in a small colonial town before setting off early the next morning. It was just two hundred miles to the Ipiales border town, but the ride was by no means a quick one. At altitudes of over 2,000 meters [6,561 ft], more twists and turns led high into the peaks, before the road dropped through river valleys then climbed again into cloud banks. It was spectacular and on a par with the ride we had taken one Sunday along the Mexican Federal Highway 182. We skimmed the peak summits for many hours and were pressed precariously close to dizzying drops every time a hasty car overtook us or a trucker overshot a sharp turn.

Groups of pedestrians emerged along the route and congregated around hazardous blind corners, where they signalled to passing vehicles if the road was clear of oncoming traffic. Others stood beside huge craters with shovels and outstretched hands, catching coins that were flung to them, either as a deterrent to stop digging up the road or as encouragement to continue filling it in.

Another potentially lethal scheme was carried out by elderly women, who sat on the grass verge clutching the end of ropes. The ropes were attached to tree stumps on the opposite verge and were made vaguely visible by burst balloons that had been tied at random along their length. At the sight of an approaching vehicle, the ladies raised their end of the rope to create an instant roadblock. Presumably, they asked the stopped vehicle for money before lowering the line, but we never found out because, although a few of them began to lift their barriers, none ever followed through by keeping them raised on our approach.

The flow of traffic had slowed down in a small mountain village, where a mass of people were gathered in the road. As we drew closer, we could see that a truck had toppled over and was lying wrecked on its side. There was no sign of it being an emergency, though, and, instead, a buzz of excitement came from the nearby crowd. As we drew closer to them, we noticed that they had formed a loose queue and were carrying buckets and bottles.

It was only then that we realised the truck had been carrying fuel, and that the local villagers had assembled ranks to plunder its load. Once we realised what was going on and then noticed a few lit cigarettes hanging from the mouths of some waiting pillagers, we sped up, before their favourable situation took a turn for the worse. For miles afterwards, we passed small motorbikes transporting at least three people each, who were all happily laden with bottles and jerry cans of free fuel.

The rural backdrop continued to turn our heads, while we dipped and weaved around tight corners and over undulating crests. The skies had remained blue throughout, but we eventually hit a cloud bank, where cold rain set in and caused the Flying Aga to gasp and choke as it usually did in wet, high altitude conditions. We never fully lost power, though, so persevered at a frustratingly slow pace that did nothing to help our plunging body temperatures.

After two hours in the clouds we were drenched and freezing cold, when we eventually pulled into the border town of Ipiales. We shivered uncontrollably in our inadequate attire as we toured the streets, hoping to find a place to defrost for the night.

We lucked out at a hotel, where the staff immediately took pity on us when they saw that we could barely grip our bags. They had soon poured fresh coffee and swathed us in blankets, and, when we stepped inside our room, we dived for the hot shower and stood under it until the water ran cold. A full hour was spent shivering in bed under an enormous pile of blankets until we eventually thawed out.

An ancestral celebration at the town stadium was being aired on the local television, and we sat in a café with a crowd of proud locals to watch the footage for the rest of the evening.

Our clothes were still damp the next morning when we wrenched them back on before leaving early in the hope of avoiding more rain, but also to make headway and reach Quito that afternoon.

A week earlier, Bryce had professed to have experienced the end of the chaotic border crossings when he had passed into Ecuador within thirty minutes, and we were hopeful that it hadn't been a fluke.

We pulled up at the border crossing full of expectation, but an ominous queue of people encircled the very first building we saw, and the sight dashed all of our hopes in one fell swoop. As the queue continued to grow, I left Byron with the bike and raced to get a place, before it began a second circuit of the building. Byron stood with the bike, while it took me three hours to receive the Colombian exit stamps in our passports.

We wasted no time in dashing to the Ecuadorian side, where it took another hour to receive entry stamps. All that was left to sort out was the temporary importation of the bike, and Byron joined a short queue to complete the paperwork. Although the queues had been long, the crossing had still been relatively hassle-free, and we guessed that we would be back on the road within thirty minutes.

Our estimation was quickly proved to be optimistic when the officials disregarded any concept of staggered breaks and locked the office for lunch. They sauntered back an hour later, when a further thirty minutes passed before Byron finally got his turn.

By the time we had conquered the queues and were ready to leave, we were told that road insurance could only be purchased in Tulcan, the nearby border town. Time was ticking on, and we only had an hour to find the insurance office before it shut for the day.

The first office was closing just as we arrived, but the clerks directed us to an alternative place, which completely eluded us in the hectic town. Eventually, we came across a couple of Colombian lads who had also been queuing at the border and were searching for the same office. Between the four of us, we managed to track it down just in time.

While we waited in another queue, the two lads explained that the holiday season was drawing to a close, and, after both Colombia and Ecuador had hosted concluding festivals, everybody was returning home that weekend. Our lack of planning had got us caught right in the middle of the transfer, and we had spent a record eight hours covering a grand total of two miles. We stayed in Tulcan that night and hoped that we had experienced the last gruelling border crossing of the trip.

CHEEKY MONKEYS AND
BRIDGE JUMPS

234 DAYS ON THE ROAD | 22,023 MILES ON THE CLOCK

The elevation continued to rise the next day as we made our way to Quito. Although the route was not as dramatic as southern Colombia, its craggy mountains were still striking.

We passed no end of distinctly dressed Andean inhabitants, who were shepherding llamas and alpacas. The men wore fedora hats and colourfully woven ponchos, while the women had all manner of different size and shaped bowler hats balanced on top of their heads. They wore heavy skirts and slung bright blankets across their backs to carry fresh produce or young children.

That afternoon, we crossed the Equator and entered the Southern Hemisphere, where we stopped to explore Quito for a couple of days. We trekked the hilly cobbled streets of its historic quarter and soon discovered that it was possible to climb to the top of the national cathedral.

Upon reaching its roof, the steps continued upwards, and we followed them to the very tip of one of the church's stone spires. The view of the sprawling valley below was an incredible sight, but it didn't take long for vertigo to set in on the precariously lofty spot, and we soon inched our way back down to stable ground.

An array of beautifully conserved plazas were patrolled by immaculately dressed policemen in polished riding boots, white helmets, and gold trimmed hats. Others were dressed in riot gear and lined the buildings of one plaza, where a politician stood on a traditional soapbox and riled up a group of fist-waving men.

During the stay, we rode out of the city to visit an equatorial monument, only to later discover that the spot had been miscalculated and that the actual zero degree latitudinal line lay some two hundred meters south of where the marker had been built.

We spent each night in the city on a gradual progression through the hostel's rooms before we eventually pitched our tent on its roof. After staying a couple of nights longer than we expected, the hostel was fully booked, but when the owner found out we had a tent, he offered us the use of his small flat roof for the handsome sum of five dollars. So, two weeks after using it to camp on a tranquil Caribbean beach where electricity was scarce, we spent a night buried under blankets listening to the racket of a city whose lights never went out.

We crammed the camping gear back into the panniers early the next morning and set off east towards the Amazon jungle. Banks of mist cut our visibility to almost nothing on the ride, exposing only brief glimpses of wild moorlands and gloomy crags.

As the route rose higher, the bike began to sputter again, a result of the troublesome combination of thin altitude air and poor grade fuel. We shivered and hunched against the cold that ate away at the sensation in our fingers and toes, until, suddenly, the road took a dive into the jungle.

The temperature hit a swift rise, and the bike enjoyed a return to uninterrupted power. Eventually the cloud cover disappeared completely and unveiled a transformation in the landscape, where the bleak moors and jagged rocks had been replaced by snaking rivers and tropical foliage.

Humidity had engulfed us by the time we arrived in the small village of Misahualli and we checked into a hostel, where the door to the only spare room hung off its hinges and the middle of the bed had caved in.

Monkeys ran amok across the village square and were shameless in their pilfering of local produce and fearless in their outright theft of possessions from passersby. While we ate breakfast the next morning, we witnessed them raid a fruit stall and divvy up the spoils on its roof, before swinging back through the village trees to begin another day of mischief in the square.

We had arranged to visit the neighbouring jungle that day and met up with three guides and a couple of other tourists in the hut next door to the hostel. We all pulled on rubber boots before climbing into the back of a pickup truck that drove us out of the village. A few miles away, the driver dropped us at a nondescript section of road, where we followed the guides to clamber through a gap in the hedgerow. Like the wardrobe into Narnia, it led straight into another world of primary Amazon rainforest.

The three guides had grown up in the jungle before advances in technology and industry had seen its boundary slowly encroached upon. They had all left the area to study before returning to undertake field research and lead environmental tours. We followed them up steep, mud and clay hills, high into the forest, where the foliage was so dense and the canopy so high that only thick and humid air hung in the shade below.

They led us along a faint path that had been trampled over the years, and, although it often disappeared beneath fallen debris, the guides betrayed little sign of ever having needed it.

The two other tourists talked loudly throughout the day, running a commentary on how hungry, tired, and hot they were. Their inane chat was easy to block out, until the main guide explained with irritation that they were reducing any chance we had of spotting wildlife. Whether it was their incessant dialogue or simply bad luck, we saw nothing but butterflies, spiders, and insects the whole day. However, we did stumble upon discarded banana leaf baskets designed to carry dead monkeys, 600-year old trees, and no end of tropical flora.

We stuck close to the guides, especially after they told us about a tribe in the vicinity that would still kill any trespasser who strayed into their territory. We followed them up muddy hills, scrambling over the enormous carcasses of fallen trees, before using the thick, exposed roots of other trees as makeshift steps to scale steep banks. Once we succeeded in reaching high ground, it was never long before we were slipping and sliding down treacherous verges, rolling on ankles, and falling hard on wrists to enter flat terrain again.

The eight-hour trek ended with a long clamber down to the banks of the Napo River, where two of the guides took the noisy boys off for more days of exploration. The third guide set about hacking at some wood with his machete to create a rudimentary ledge, on which he balanced his bag in a long, tree trunk canoe. We perched on small planks of wood at intervals inside the narrow vessel before setting off to paddle down the tranquil Amazonian river, back towards the village.

Hemmed in by a soaring tangle of foliage, the calm water carved a peaceful channel through the dense forest. We passed three separate duos of men dredging the riverbed for gold and two savage dogs that threatened to rip us apart, but otherwise we coasted through the wilderness for two hours without seeing another soul.

The guide left the canoe at a small hamlet, before we flagged down a bus that dropped us at the road where we had climbed through the hedgerow ten hours earlier. Shortly after commencing a long walk back to the village, a passing pickup truck pulled over ahead of us. Taking the guide's lead, we jumped into the back, where we perched between massive bunches of bananas and held on tight, as the driver sped towards the village. When the road ended, the driver stopped to let us jump out, before making off without exchanging a word.

We ended the incredible day back in the square, where a monkey feigned friendship with Byron before biting him on the arm, luckily drawing no blood. The locals were out in force, watching a Spanish league football game, while the rest of the monkeys competed with a chicken to wreak havoc on the same fruit stall that they had raided that morning.

Another picturesque ride led us away from the jungle the next day and back into the rolling green mountains, where we stopped in a beautiful town that was nestled in the valley of an active volcano. Although it was the second week of January, the festive season was still in full swing, and a school nativity procession marched through the town.

After the cold mountain passes and the humid rainforest, the valley was unexpectedly pleasant. With white water rapids, towering waterfalls, and steep canyons nearby, all manner of extreme sports were on offer, and it wasn't long before we decided to extend our visit.

After the nativity parade passed us by, with its real donkey and miniature holy family, we came to a bridge that led out of town across an enormous canyon. An excited buzz of activity was coming from a gathered crowd, and, as we walked closer, we spotted glimpses of people flinging themselves from its terrifying height. It wasn't a bungee jump, as they weren't bouncing back up, and we raced to see what was going on.

The jumpers wore harnesses attached to climbing ropes and, once they had launched themselves from the bridge, they swung back and forth underneath it like a pendulum, until someone lowered them onto the bank of the deep ravine below. We watched them for a while, declaring to one another that nothing in the world could get us to do something so daft. As more and more people flew into the massive gorge, screaming with delight, we saw them all reappear in one piece and began to wonder if wasn't as frightening as it had first looked. Before the afternoon was over, we had paid to do it the next day.

To kick off another unusual Sunday, we met up with a local man in the morning and followed him as he rode the father of a small horse family towards the active volcano. We rode the mother and son of the family and ambled through the cobbled streets of town to join a dirt track that wound its way into the hills, high above the valley. We crossed through a stream and continued until the trail was cut short by a deep rift in the ground that had been caused by a volcanic eruption less than a month earlier.

Unfortunately, the volcano was concealed by thick cloud, and the damage left by its last eruption was the only indication of its presence. The wide fracture in the ground meant that we could go no further, so, after filling our bottles from a natural, fizzy water spring, we set off on a peaceful mosey back towards town.

If Byron had been nervous about the bridge jump, he gave nothing away, whereas I had been unable to sleep the night before and was petrified all morning. Jumping a few meters into the Mexican sinkholes had taken a fair bit of self-convincing, and, even then, my stomach had jumped to my throat.

Although not afraid of heights, it was the prospect of jumping from one that terrified me, and, in an attempt to build up my courage, we spent a while watching more people dive head-first from the bridge. I knew I would eventually cop out of the challenge if I didn't join them quickly, so I approached the organiser, who strapped me into the harness and secured me with karabiners to two climbing ropes, all the while telling me to embrace the fear.

As I mounted a tiny mesh platform on the outer side of the bridge, my adrenalin was pumping at a heart stopping rate. Byron kept our camera filming, while I proceeded to stand for ten more minutes, willing my frozen legs to move.

My brain had evidently intervened on the madness with a more rational line of defence, and it was refusing to communicate with my legs. I bent my knees and wiggled my toes, but they were locked fast, and, the longer I stood on the platform looking down at the ravine hundreds of meters below, the more fearsome it became.

Still eager to experience a taste of what everyone else had been enjoying, and in a determined effort not to chicken out, I asked the guide to push me. He refused and told me to look into my soul, which was not helpful, since my soul was making it perfectly clear that it was in a situation that it didn't appreciate. Nothing could get me to budge. However, at some point, when I bent my knees, I went flying.

Before I could process another thought, I jerked violently forward and was suddenly swinging high above the water, letting out a howl of exhilaration. A later look at the film footage showed a hand lightly push the base of my back, before I let out a blood-curdling scream and kicked and punched my way through the sharp drop from the bridge, in possibly the most ungraceful jump of the day.

Byron followed me off the platform in considerably swifter and braver style, but with what turned out to be equal trepidation, as his dive became more of a belly flop, before he swung exuberantly through mid air. We made a swift exit from the site, and both confessed that we would be in no hurry to repeat any sort of jump, from any sort of height, tied to any sort of rope, any time soon.

We packed up and set off early the next day to ride southwest towards the Pacific coast. Although the urgency to meet people and catch boats had fallen away, we wanted to maintain momentum and reach southern Argentina before the region grew too cold and the winds that whipped across the flat landscape became too fierce.

The ride took us high across more mountains and into the clouds again, where poor visibility kept us on our toes and the Flying Aga chugged through the thin, damp air. The journey was tense and exhausting, as we only caught brief glimpses of other vehicles and pedestrians just seconds before we passed them on the road.

It took seven hours to cover two hundred miles, before we knocked on the door of an unassuming hostel in the mountain city of Cuenca. In Latino style, we wheeled the bike through its front door and parked in the hallway, where two tall atriums hosted a collection of beautifully furnished rooms that were all completely empty. Apart from the owner, who let us in, we didn't see another soul there and spent most of the night wondering if other people knew something that we didn't.

Memories of the most recent eight-hour border crossing had us packed and on the road early the next morning. We resumed our route through the cold mountains, still unable to see more than five meters ahead, when we began to run low on fuel.

After pushing an empty motorcycle a few miles along a French hard shoulder a couple of years earlier, we had done well so far not to run out of fuel at all on the journey.

It was possible that we had missed a garage somewhere in the low visibility of the mountain roads, but we assumed that there had to be more than one refuelling point on the route.

The mist had lessened by the time we passed into a small village and spotted a mechanic shop. We stopped to ask a group of men there if they had any spare petrol, and, although they told us that they didn't, they assured us that the next town forty miles away would have. Knowing our reserve supply would not take us that far, we persevered in the village. After riding around aimlessly and asking a few other locals, the mechanic group took pity on us and gave us directions to a house back along the road that we had just travelled from.

We pulled into a muddy yard, where a cheerful lady in an apron and wellington boots came out to greet us. She pulled back the awning on a rudimentary wooden structure to reveal dozens of barrels. After asking how much we wanted, she filled up a bucket from the tap of one of the barrels, placed a plastic funnel in the top of our tank, poured in the fuel, and saved our skin.

We rode back through the town and continued along the wet mountain route until we gradually descended towards the coast, where miles of banana crops encased the road. With vivid memories of the hungry hours spent queuing to enter the country, we decided to stop a short distance from the border and eat a good lunch in preparation for whatever lay ahead. The return to sea level had sent the temperature spiralling, so we stripped off our bike kit and got comfortable outside a café, where the owner proceeded to warn us against pickpockets that operated on the border.

After a hearty menú del día, we set off towards the crossing with our usual degree of caution. This particular border had even come with its own warning in the travel guide that had been given to us in Cartagena. However, we were soon wondering if we had made a wrong turn when we rode along one of the newest paved surfaces we had seen in months.

We pulled into a modern complex that was well signposted, and any indications of the chaos and queues that had become synonymous with borders were nowhere in sight. Had it not been for a coach that pulled in ahead of us, we would probably have been stamped out of Ecuador and into Peru, bike and all, within thirty minutes.

We still managed it in the record time of one hour, and, with nowhere to exchange the few dollars we had left over, we marked the occasion by spending them on a second lunch at another rarity of a border café.

Desert Winds and Coca Leaves

145 Days on the Road | 22,815 Miles on the Clock

Heavy duty winds battered shanty towns as we rode through the coastal desert of northern Peru. We stopped early for the day in Mancora, where the streets were buzzing with tourists and hard-sell merchants, but managed to escape their attention by ducking through a large hostel door where we parked next to another Canadian plated motorcycle. It turned out that the bike belonged to the hostel manager, who was actually British and hailed from Nottingham, a city very close to where Byron had grown up. They launched into some motorcycle adoration chat together, before we ventured up to our third storey room.

The hostel was the closest we had come to staying in a holiday resort, and we didn't quite fit in with the predominantly Argentinean gap year clientele. Regardless, we used the next day to do some crucial laundry and wash the Flying Aga before lazing about in hammocks, grateful that our Spanish was still not quite good enough to completely understand the Argentinean students.

After setting off early the next morning, we continued our bearing south along the west coast, where the landscape smouldered. An immense blanket of dry, rocky mounds paved the way for a couple of hours before eventually levelling out onto a swathe of white sand that was speckled with patches of scorched scrub. Primitive wooden shacks and stone shelters lay exposed to the brutal winds that whipped in from the nearby Pacific coast. Dried palm leaves and reeds had been fashioned into protective shelters, but most had been twisted and bent to such an extent that they were rendered ineffective.

Refuse and a nasty stench greeted our entry and exit through most of the desert towns, where brightly coloured trees and vibrant paintwork offered a respite from the monotonous landscape. Patches of cultivated land would occasionally emerge in the miles of sand and dust, but the rice paddies and crops were always bordered by the grim sight and smell of rotting waste.

We passed more than one car that had pulled over to shamelessly dump rubbish sacks at the roadside and also got caught in the crossfire of flying litter from many minibus and coach windows in what appeared to be the adopted national strategy for rubbish disposal.

Halfway through the desert, we stopped at the only café we had seen in some time and peeled off our helmets and jackets, eager to replenish our dwindling energy levels. A young girl served up the menú del día of rice and bistek, and, with no water in stock, we washed it down with Inca Kola, the Peruvian equivalent of Irn-Bru [a popular Scottish softdrink]. Flies buzzed lazily in the clammy air of the stone hut, and we ate fast, desperate to get back to the relief of the drag that the moving bike generated.

The girl pointed out towards the desert when we asked to use the toilet. It was not an unusual gesture and normally signalled a visit to a small hut that offered privacy, but little hygiene. We went to investigate and came upon three brick walls surrounding a hole in the ground. The desert itself would have been preferable, had it not been for the wide expanse of flat nothingness, where nothing and nobody could hide from the countless truckers just a few meters away in the café.

Whether through poor aim or intention, excrement splattered the concrete floor and breached the walls of the simple structure. The steaming hum of baking waste rose unceremoniously from its vicinity, but, despite its gruesomeness, for some reason privacy still triumphed. The shelter proved to be a good test in holding our breath, and we took it in turns to rush in and rush out, losing a small ounce of self-respect in the process.

In a bid to ward off the worst of the heat, we ploughed on through the sparse desolation for the rest of the day and stopped only once more to refuel. Although the sand prevailed, the landscape continued to change in form, ranging from level plains, with no signs of life at all, to scrub covered yellow dunes and gnarled trees. Dry rocky peaks occasionally appeared in the distance, before they fell away to reveal an endless horizon.

Regardless of where the road led us, the sun was unforgiving throughout and the wind thrashed us remorselessly. Byron fought to hold the bike at a forty-five-degree angle for most of the day, while we both leaned against the onslaught. Our necks strained painfully as we battled to resist the powerful current, which made a chill of the continuous sweat that formed beneath our heavy kit. Our music normally offered a good distraction from tough conditions, but it was drowned out by the deafening force.

Finally after ten exhausting hours, we pulled into the small coastal town of Huanchaco. It was dark, but we found a cheap room at the back of a hotel where, after squashing a few cockroaches, we showered away layers of sweat and sand.

A cold draught through an open window woke us early the next morning with sticky throats and sore heads. Our muscles ached from the day before, too, but we hoped a day beside the sunny coast might return us to better health.

A hustler near the beach immediately singled us out from a crowd and began a familiar dialogue that we knew would lead to a sales pitch of some kind. Being too polite and exhausted to brush him off, we jumped onto a conveniently passing bus instead. It was travelling via the ancient city of Chan Chan, where we had planned to go at some point anyway, and the guy looked on in surprise as his catch drove away.

The enormous 1,100-year-old site had been constructed entirely from an adobe mixture of sand, clay, and straw. It covered a vast patch of coastal desert and had been built by the Chimu Kingdom which, following an impressive eleven-year siege, had eventually fallen to the Inca Empire. After wandering for hours through its ancient walls and vast arenas, the combination of the day's heat and the weakness that we had woken up to finally caught up with us. We trekked back across a vacant mile of desert and flagged down a bus to town.

Byron fell into bed almost immediately with the very first sickness of our entire trip. We couldn't work out whether the draining ride from the day before, the chill from the draughty window in the night, or the foul desert toilet had caused it, but it kept him up all night and in bed all of the next day. With some disbelief that it had taken so long for us to fall ill, it soon caught up with me, and we suffered together throughout the following day.

In between dashes to the toilet, we executed a couple of raids on a local pharmacy, where we discovered that just about anything could be purchased over the counter, so we stocked up on no end of remedies.

In our weakened state, for the very first time on the journey, we began to yearn for a break from the uncertainty of life on the road. While we lay feeling sorry for ourselves, we dreamed of our own bed, which was waiting in storage for us back home. We longed for a kitchen with a fridge that we could fill and for an oven in which we could cook more than one small pot of food at a time. The few clothes that we were carrying had long worn ragged, and we wished for the variety of a proper wardrobe and the ease of doing our own laundry.

By the next morning, the small dispensary of pharmaceuticals that we had ingested seemed to have kicked in, so we set off into the desert once again. The relentless wind battered us as we journeyed through long stretches of sandy plains and rubbish strewn roads, passing through shanty towns and sporadic splashes of crops and plants, before we turned off onto an unpaved track.

Before we had left Medellin, Al had marked our map with a few essential routes to ride on the continent, and this particular turnoff took us directly through Cañón del Pato. The spectacular canyon marked the meeting of the rocky Cordillera Negra and the snow capped Cordillera Blanca ranges of the Andes.

The magnificent gorge offered a merciful relief from the gruelling wind. Its unpaved road ran parallel to a deep ravine, and we made our way inland, riding against the current of the River Santa for seventy miles. We traced the foot of parched cliffs and craggy peaks, bouncing and bumping along the coarse stony track. The wild dogs that terrorised the roads of Latin America proved to be the one enduring sign of existence as they emerged from behind rocks to race down precipices and chase us from their territory. Occasionally, residents from one of the valley's tiny hamlets led small herds of cattle along the road, but, otherwise, there were few signs of life in the vast canyon.

It was quickly apparent that the route had not been designed for modern travel. The road tapered dangerously close to high overhangs, where terrifying games of chance played out with fearless oncoming or overtaking vehicles.

As if to intensify the ride, the uneven road passed through thirty-five single-lane tunnels that had been blasted through the solid rock. They lay ahead in the road as ominous, tiny black holes, where signs instructing drivers to beep on the approach to them were the only measure that helped to discern if anything was coming through from the other side.

We met at least two huge cargo trucks and many cars head on in the tunnels and we hadn't seen any of them coming until we were deep inside the dark, narrow passages. Luckily, our small size helped us squeeze against the walls as they edged past, but a precarious retreat would have been in the cards had we been tackling the trail in a larger vehicle.

We jiggled and rattled intrepidly over the gravel tracks and across rustic wooden bridges on a ride that was as close as we were going to get to an off-road adventure with our old road bike.

After ploughing through the gorge for four hours, we were beginning to wonder if there would be an end to the route, when it took an abrupt ascent out of the canyon. Large trucks stopped traffic while they reversed in the middle of the road to squeeze around sharp turns in the steep, narrow track, and we fell in behind a van that was transporting kids, who were balanced on its roof, in what must have been a fearsome ride as it swung around the tight corners.

Eventually, the steep climb ended, and the trucks motored off into the distance. We stopped for a break in the first small town, where we had missed the last serving of lunch in its only café. No shops were open, so we copied a couple of truckers and bought tins of tuna, dry crackers, and ice cream from the café's shelves to form the strangest meal of the trip. We knew the mix would do nothing for our delicate stomachs, but we were famished and decided to deal with the consequences later.

Having roasted alive in our heavy bike kit through the desert and the canyon, we set off from the pit stop on a long climb back into the chilly mountains.

Later that day, we arrived in the heart of Huarez, 3,000 meters above sea level, and we snapped another makeshift ramp as we rode up a steep pavement into the garage of a hostel. The city was a sprawling metropolis in comparison to the places we had visited over the previous couple of weeks, and, with its illuminated shops and the carcass of a dead dog lying ignored on the steps to the main plaza, it was not the most elegant of locations.

During the previous century, floods, avalanches, and earthquakes had destroyed much of its original infrastructure, but the dramatic, snow covered mountains which framed it and the rapids that roared through it gave the city a unique edge.

We had arrived in an exhausted state, once again. The thin, high altitude air sapped our energy and made a struggle out of the simplest of tasks or shortest of walks. Having sweated through the first half of the day, then shivered through the rest of it, we realised we had been hasty in our departure that morning and should have given ourselves more time to recover. The bug returned with a vengeance, and Byron spent a sleepless night running in and out of the bathroom.

The next morning we decided to take another day off, and I went on more raiding missions to pharmacies, as the illness weakened Byron. Although I had escaped the worst of it, an agonising toothache struck me down. Despite the misfortune, we knew we were lucky to be able to sleep off our ailments in the comfort of a bed and with a roof over our heads, instead of inside a tent or in a damp cabin on a choppy ocean crossing.

Another twenty-four-hour rest eventually returned Byron to full health, but my toothache raged on, sending excruciating pain through the left side of my face. It had been building up over the past week and originated in a spot where the same agony had struck me down six years earlier in Croatia. Since then, after having the culpable molar pulled out, a second one had grown in its place, and it was the new tooth that was repeating the grief that its predecessor had inflicted. I bought whatever the nearby pharmacy had in stock for the pain, and we waited out another night, hoping that our recent complaints would fade away by the morning.

We woke up to a freezing wet day after a night of broken sleep. Although Byron had made a full recovery, I was still popping painkillers to keep the toothache at bay, but we were eager to get back on the road so, after layering up to the point of near immovability, we lowered the bike down the steep pavement.

The sun eventually shone on the mountain ride and lit up precious scenes of rural Andean life, which we had missed in the thick mists that had plagued our last days in Ecuador.

Men and women wore fedora hats or high topped bowlers and were dressed traditionally in brightly patterned ponchos and woven blankets. They tended to herds of sheep and llamas or carried huge loads of produce in improvised slings that were fashioned from colourful blankets and tied around their backs.

Some villages were made up of brick and stone houses, each with a separate outhouse, while others were more primitive, with flat roofed huts built from a mixture of mud and clay.

The high terrain was rich in rugged hills, mossy cliffs, and streams that had forged channels through the dense moorland. Unruly stray dogs continued to pursue their vendetta against us, often ending up annihilated across the road, as they paid no heed to other passing traffic. With a bravery reinforced by the protection of thick trousers and boots, we tested their determination to catch us and watched as their previously blind resolve faltered each time we slowed down.

Eventually, we began another descent, thawing out as we plummeted into territory where the only vegetation in the area grew within the banks of a dried river bed. The wide corridor of crops and trees formed a winding green passageway through otherwise parched land. As we followed it to the coast, we gave a wide berth to small, modified motorcycles, whose improbable quantities of refuse at the front and rear concealed any sign of a rider. Equal distance was given to similarly stacked carts drawn by horses and guided by riders who sat balanced at least five meters above the road, on top of dried leaf and straw loads.

As the gradual plunge in elevation saw the mountainous terrain fall away entirely, discarded refuse returned to blight the landscape, and we lost our defence against the brutal winds.

The density of buildings and cars had increased tenfold by the time we reached the outskirts of Lima, and the resulting mass of traffic spawned nerve-racking disorder. Most drivers failed to look before pulling out at junctions, cutting up everyone and everything in their way. Incorrect indicating took us by surprise, as cars turning right invariably signalled left and vice versa, while others gave nothing away by driving permanently with hazard lights flashing. Beeping horns were used by most vehicles as warnings for every conceivable manoeuvre, creating confusion, as well as adding a cacophonous element to the chaos.

Somehow, we reached the city centre without incident and tracked down a hostel that had been recommended to us by a fellow biker further up the coast. We rode through two enormous wooden doors to park the Flying Aga in the atrium of a hostel that was like none we had come across before. Chandeliers hung from the ceilings, while replica Roman busts, ornate furnishings, and extravagant artwork decorated its three storeys. After checking into a room with no less than four beds, we explored the building and made our way up to the roof, where a merry band of animals, made up of two tortoises, one macaw, and one vain peacock, were joined by a collection of dreadlocked travellers. We all gathered to witness a fantastic, panoramic view of the city that was lit to perfection by the setting sun.

That night we got an insight as to why the hostel was so cheap when flying bugs plagued us in the hot and airless room. By that point in the journey, we had lost all desire to explore cities, anyway, and were eager to return to scenes that did not exist in Europe, so we set off early the next morning. After surviving Lima's city roads again, we continued south along the desert coast and arrived at the small oasis setting of Huacachina later that day.

A murky lake was surrounded by magnificent towering dunes and palm trees. We were lying in the shade of one of the trees the next day, when a few young local boys clocked us. After a brief exchange, they came to the conclusion that Byron must have been a teacher, on account of the fact that he was reading a book that had no connection to either Jesus Christ or God, and they promptly asked us for money. Once we had shaken off the cheeky gang, we joined ten other people in the back of a dune buggy to drive into the enormous playground of the colossal desert.

Encouraged by a group of female Argentineans, the driver of the buggy proceeded to launch an assault across the desert. He drove directly up the face of the tallest and steepest mounds before descending down the other side at full speed. He would turn sharply along the narrow ridge of another dune and drop straight down its slope, much to the screaming delight of his passengers. The clapped out cage of a buggy groaned and strained every time we crash landed, while its radiator had to be cooled with a squirt of water whenever we paused to take in the incredible view.

After exhausting his repertoire of tricks, the driver took us to the top of some particularly mountainous dunes, where he handed us wooden boards that were spitting out splinters and nails. After using broken candle sticks to wax the underside of them, we added sand boarding to the growing list of non-motorcycling activities undertaken on the journey.

A final, death defying ride in the buggy finished the desert venture, and we bailed out just above the oasis. We ended the day with a lung-stretching trek to the top of the highest dune that loomed above the little village, where we watched a stunning sunset fall across the desert.

The next day took us through the vast plateau of the Nazca desert, where ancient lineal depictions of animals and plants marked the desert floor. They were thought to have been created more than 1,000 years earlier and were formed by the simple process of removing the top layer of red desert rock to reveal the white minerals below. Unable to afford a flight to see them from above, we settled, instead, for an isolated, metal viewing tower at the side of the desert road. For a few Peruvian soles, we got a glimpse of the large tree and hand lines that had been totally invisible at eye level.

After leaving the viewing tower, we carved a route inland and rode high over crumpled ridges and crests of sand that spread for as far as we could see. No other signs of life were visible until the road began to rise and delivered us back into the lush green mountains, which invariably seemed to come hand in hand with cloud cover and icy temperatures.

Somewhere between the desert and the green landscape, we had stopped in a tiny mountain community, where a lady and her young daughter served us up rice and bistek for lunch. We washed it down with coca leaf tea, an Andean drink that had firmly replaced our devotion to coffee.

After quizzing us on where we were from, the lady searched for an English speaking channel on her television. In the heart of the Peruvian Andes, inside a small concrete home that didn't even have plumbing, she tuned into footage of the BAFTA awards and was fascinated when we confirmed that we could understand every word. When it came to leaving, we asked her where we could go to the toilet, and, with a chuckle, she pointed out to the surrounding mountains and told us to go anywhere we wanted.

The road climbed higher and higher into the weather beaten landscape, where herds of llama and vicuña grazed among the rugged rocks and on the desolate plains. Traditionally dressed locals in thick skirts, fedora hats, and colourful woollen ponchos shepherded the animals, while the day progressed fast. When we eventually came upon a town, we decided to stop for the night and woke up a receptionist from her camp bed behind the counter of a half-built hotel.

A few doors down, we ate a dinner of fresh trout in a tiny restaurant that was run by a woman, who was assisted by her four children. In between watching a local talent show that was being aired on television, the kids took it in turns to stand outside and tout for business at passing vehicles.

We had checked if they would be open to serve breakfast the next day, and, when we turned up in the morning, the mother pointed to the same menu from the night before. We knew that breakfast wasn't always distinguished from the other meals of the day, but at seven o'clock in the morning we couldn't stomach chicken and rice. Instead, the lady rustled us up some eggs and was clearly annoyed that we had woken her so early to perform such a menial task.

That morning, our route out of the town led us over 4,000 meters above sea level. Although the sun beat down from a clear sky, the momentum on the bike at such a high altitude made the ride feel glacial. To fight the biting cold, we stopped a couple of times to squeeze into more layers of clothes and to brew cups of coca leaf tea on the moss covered, rocky ground.

It was a typical Sunday, and we encountered hardly any traffic on what became another fascinating ride. The bike struggled with the thin air and low grade fuel, but it remained steadfast and never conked out once.

As we passed the outskirts of a mountain village, we struck our first casualty of the journey. Having seen a chicken in the middle of the road ahead, Byron slowed down and beeped the horn. It was usually all that was needed to send animals scampering out of the way, but this one was playing a literal game of chicken and didn't budge. At the very last second Byron swerved to avoid it, but, in the same instant, it decided to move and ran straight into the front wheel. A small bump and flutter of feathers told us of its demise, and we turned back to see a small boy run out to retrieve its remains, hopefully to prepare a Sunday roast and not because it was a family pet.

After a near head on collision with a car on a sharp corner, we battled through a final hour of potholed, weatherworn road to arrive in Cusco eleven hours after we had set off that morning. A long ride in circles around the old city burnt some clutch on many a steep, cobbled, back street, before we tracked down a cheap hostel and parked the bike inside another reception lobby.

There was a paved road that covered a large section of the route to Machu Picchu, however, it turned into a twenty-mile dirt track, where river crossings and boulder obstacles led to a tiny mountain town. From there, a train service or a long walk was the only way to reach the valley of the ancient Incan city.

We realised that we had risked the welfare of the Flying Aga a little too often along rough tracks and dirt roads for the time being, so we looked into alternative ways to reach Machu Picchu.

There was no end of organised, four-day treks that followed the Inca trail from Cusco to Machu Picchu, but we couldn't justify the cost from our budget and we didn't have the kit to hike.

The final option was to take the pricey train service from Cusco all the way to the valley town that lay below the ancient site, so we bought tickets to leave the next day.

The ruins of the city dated back to the fifteenth century, although it had remained unknown to the outside world until the early twentieth century. It sat high above the sacred Urubama Valley and was so remote that it is thought the city was simply used as a retreat for ruling Incas.

The site was still sleeping beneath heavy clouds when we entered its gate at six o'clock in the morning. Small glimpses appeared through the mist of huge stone boulders and rocks that had been so precisely carved and interlinked to form the city's original, enduring walls and footpaths. A family of llamas grazed on one of the agricultural terraces close to a narrow track that led away from the main city towards its sun gate.

The clouds continued to hang around us, and we passed very few people on the trail that wound through thick tropical foliage. An hour after setting off, we reached the original Inca entrance to the city, oblivious to the sites we had passed along the way and exhausted by the rising altitude. Climbers with walking sticks and solid boots emerged from the sun gate, having just completed the arduous four-day trek to get there, and we joined a few of them to wait patiently for the clouds to lift.

The bank of mist had begun to break apart once we set off back towards the city, and we walked in awe of the spectacular setting that was gradually unveiled. Towering, rounded pinnacles were swathed in thick jungle and soared majestically from the ground far below. As we ducked and dodged the flourishing undergrowth on the trail, more and more of the magnificent scene became visible. The snaking Urubamba River was eventually revealed at the foot of the peaks, just as the stone temples and walls of the Inca city came into view.

The city and its famed agricultural terraces were nestled in an awe-inspiring spectacle beneath the towering Huayna Picchu summit, but, as we drew closer, a colourful array of plastic ponchos, backpacks, and anoraks began to materialise and deplete some of its mystery. However, we found a peaceful spot high up on a terrace where we sat away from the crowds for some time, absorbing the unique site and its tremendous backdrop.

Another trail traced the perimeter of a peak to a different Inca entrance, and we ventured back into the undergrowth, along another slippery stone path to see it. It led to a terrifying precipice that loomed a hundred meters above us and dropped to at least a hundred meters below. A barricade blocked the path just before it reached an ancient bridge that rested on a thin cliff outcropping. The narrow lip supported a skeletal wood and stone platform, which led across the cliff face and into the abyss.

We returned to the main site and settled on the eastern terraces to soak up the scene of the sacred valley below. Eventually, hunger began to dominate our every thought, and, many hours after arriving under a shroud of mist, we withdrew from Machu Picchu under bright sunshine, utterly content that we had broken our ride and shelled out the small fortune to visit the incredible site.

The next morning, we refuelled and added air to the tyres before leaving Cusco and venturing into the rugged highlands and vast plains of the Andean plateau. The landscape was dominated by herds of grazing alpacas and llamas, while indigenous populations farmed the terrain and shepherded the animals against a backdrop of weather-beaten rocks and distant frosty mountains. We passed through scores of modest hamlets and rural small holdings before larger, grimy towns occasionally emerged that were plagued by reckless drivers and careless pedestrians.

An aggressive storm broke out in the afternoon and launched an assault of painful hailstones and heavy rain, which drenched us for the final two hours of the day. We arrived in Puno frozen to the bone and undertook a wild goose chase in the rain to find a hostel with parking. Eventually, we came across a small guesthouse in the waterlogged city, where the manager was a motorcycle enthusiast and soon took my place on the back of the Flying Aga to direct Byron to a nearby parking garage.

We spent the rest of the evening in a familiar state of attempting to thaw out beneath piles of blankets. As we shivered and our teeth chattered, a local brass band decided to rehearse a song on repeat beneath the draughty window of our room, until a surprise snowstorm mercifully sent them packing.

In spite of the icy night, the sun melted the remaining dusting of snow the next morning, and we ventured to the shoreline of Lake Titicaca. After wandering through Puno's busy streets, passing a cathedral and one of Latin America's many Catholic parades, we roamed through a local market. A colourful array of produce was on sale, and a multitude of locals wearing high bowler hats and patterned blankets moseyed through the cluttered lanes, while bicycle rickshaws and tiny tuk-tuks weaved in and out of the tarpaulin covered stalls to carry people to and from town.

Beyond the city streets and the market stalls, ladies in thick, long skirts sat along the verge of a railway line selling every imaginable shade of potato that had been grown in the surrounding mountains. Not too far from the railway and a lamp post to which three pigs had been tied up like dogs on leads, we sampled some cactus fruit before finally reaching the seemingly infinite lake.

Lake Titicaca lay 3,500 meters above sea level, and, as soon as we were in sight of its stagnant water, we were accosted and sold a ticket to visit its floating Uros islands. The collection of man-made, reed platforms lay about three miles offshore and had originally been constructed in response to hostile invaders on the mainland. Over forty of the islands were still maintained and inhabited by pre-Incan, Uru people, who mostly survived on the proceeds of tourist visits.

The floating islands were extensions of natural, underwater plant beds, and their sturdy platforms were constantly replenished with bundles of drying reeds that were cut from the lake's native vegetation. As well as the platforms of the islands, the same reeds were used to construct houses, watchtowers, and boats by the few hundred Uru people that still lived on the lake.

Like the Kuna inhabitants of the San Blas, near Panama, the Uru were business savvy, and we were soon sold crafts and trinkets before being ushered onto one of their reed boats, for which another fare was collected. It dropped us at another island, where a café was serving fresh fish, and, conveniently for its owners, no boats were scheduled to leave for at least another hour. Their commercial acumen was faultless, and the fish was delicious.

My tooth had continued to pound away every day since we had caught the stomach bug, and a daily dose of painkillers had been delaying an inevitable visit to a dentist. We stocked up on more pills in town before marking our final evening in Peru by eating the national delicacy of guinea pig and alpaca, accompanied by coca leaf tea to fight off another cold night.

The next morning, we traced the western shoreline of the lake to the border with Bolivia. Low levels of traffic indicated that another Sunday had arrived, and, with minimal crowds and fatigued officials, we left Peru and crossed into Bolivia in the record time of forty-five minutes.

On the way across, a lady sitting at an old wooden desk gave us one of the most favourable exchange rates to date and filled us with optimism about the new country ahead.

TOOTH PULLING AND
MARDI GRAS

A Bolivian law had been instated, which ruled that foreign plated vehicles were required to pay three times more than national motors for petrol in the country. The ruling was in response to residents from neighbouring countries, who had been taking advantage of Bolivia's subsidised fuel. Even at three times the price, it still cost considerably less than the tax-inflated UK prices back home, however, problems arose with the resulting paperwork that accompanied the measure. Some petrol stations lacked the right documents or the literate staff to complete the necessary forms for foreign sales, and we had been warned that quite a few found it easier to simply refuse to serve foreign vehicles.

Although the law was fair enough, the directive from the government did us no favours with its general connotation that foreign nationals could afford to pay higher prices for goods. Although we were used to being charged a gringo rate for most non-marked goods, anyway, it didn't bode well that a government had indicated that it was OK to do so.

After navigating the rippled tarmac on the highway towards La Paz, we were soon ducking and diving along a congested network of dusty suburban roads. Passing unpredictably driven old bangers and buses that pumped out thick, black smoke, we weaved a path into the city centre.

Unusually, we were looking for a specific hostel and had missed an exit so began to make a U-turn, when one of the many police officers that lined the city roads pulled us over. He pointed down the busy thoroughfare and seemed to suggest that we could make the manoeuvre at a traffic light further along. We rode through the crawling mass of vehicles and reached the point where we thought he had indicated to make the turn.

After successfully doubling back on ourselves, another officer waved us over. Confident that the U-turn had been executed with the approval of his colleague, we pulled over without concern. Being fresh from the border, our documents were still to hand, and, when he asked to see them, we forgot all about the security of photocopies and gave him the genuine articles. Within seconds he had walked off with Byron's passport, and, in a panic, Byron followed him into what turned out to be the conveniently located police headquarters.

The building was directly opposite the spot where we had been waved over, and, after handing the passport to a clerk, the officer hastily headed back out onto the street. I saw him exit the building alone and watched as he resumed a methodical practice of pulling over almost every other driver that had the misfortune to be passing through the area. He took their papers and systematically sent them inside, presumably to pay fines for whatever offence he had conjured up, while groups of his colleagues idled in the doorways, content to watch him single-handedly fill up the coffers on their behalf.

Back inside, Byron haggled the fee that the clerk had placed for the return of the passport but, with little choice, he eventually paid up. When Byron tested the authenticity of the apparent fine by requesting a receipt, the clerk picked up about six small sheets of torn scrap paper, stapled them together, and scrawled something illegible on the top. With a smile, he exchanged the scrap paper bundle and the passport for our money in the first crooked incident in over eight months on the road.

It was a lesson learnt to never part with an official document outside of a border, and we left the vicinity annoyed with ourselves at having done so. We rode with extra care to the hostel that we had been looking for and stopped traffic, once again, while Byron rode the bike up another improvised wooden ramp, into another foyer.

The building was a vast backpacker hostel, where Adam and Mackenzie's two Kawasaki bikes were already stationed beneath the stairway. After meeting in Leon for the first time, we had last seen them in Cusco and had arranged to meet for a final time in La Paz, before going our separate ways once again.

Over a free pancake breakfast, we caught up with them the next morning and learnt that, although they had so far avoided any troubles with the police, they had encountered the work-shy petrol pump attendants.

Bolivia would be the last inexpensive country of our journey before the cost of living was due to take a sharp rise. The previous few months of sleeping in hostels and cheap hotels would draw to a close when we left it behind, and our camping gear would, once again, be liberated from the depths of the panniers. During the heady heat wave back in the US, we had cleared space on the bike by exchanging our sleeping bags for small blankets, but we were edging closer to the South Pole and needed to find decent sleeping insulation, once again.

After hearing that cheap camping gear and outdoor clothing was readily available in La Paz, we made a beeline for the shops and arranged to rendezvous with Adam and Mackenzie later that day.

Balaclava-clad shoe shiners sat in groups on the pavements near our hostel, as traffic beeped and honked its way through the busy streets. Like most Latin American cities, ornate cathedrals and colonial plazas were juxtaposed against high rise financial districts and outer breeze block boroughs.

The disparity in fortune had never been so stark as when we watched some suited businessmen ride by in a taxi just as an impoverished young woman knelt from a pavement and scooped water from the gutter into her mouth.

We headed towards the ramshackle network of market streets and roamed through a maze of bazaars, outdoor stalls, and indoor labyrinths, where just about any product or trade was on offer. After noticing an abundance of shrivelled llama foetuses hanging outside shops, we soon learnt that the disturbing talisman was used on building sites, where construction only began once a llama foetus had been buried in the foundations.

We kept searching and eventually stumbled on the camping shops, where, after a hard fought haggle, we became the proud owners of two down-filled sleeping bags.

Upon regrouping with Adam and Mackenzie later that evening, our prized purchase was trumped by their own ultimate find of a slim, five-litre jerry can that would fit perfectly into one of our panniers. Considering the petrol difficulties we were likely to encounter in the country, we ventured back into the chaos early the next morning to find one of our own before filling it, and the Flying Aga's tank, to the brim with city fuel.

Somehow, we squeezed the new purchases onto our already burdened bike before saying goodbye over another free pancake breakfast to Adam and Mackenzie for the final time.

We hit the full brunt of rush hour traffic on our way out of the city and dodged back to back minibuses that swerved across lanes without warning to pick up passengers. By the time we reached the highway, the backlog had subsided, but the rain had increased, and it wasn't long before we felt the heart-sinking wobble of the back wheel.

The stretch of road was undergoing construction, and the hard shoulder that we pulled onto was quickly transformed into a muddy quagmire. Following the tried and tested techniques of the previous three flat tyres, we set about unloading the luggage and digging out the tools. Byron got straight into removing the front wheel before tipping the bike forward onto the front forks and securing the centre stand with our luggage straps. After removing the exhaust, he finally took off the rear wheel.

While he was busy sorting the bike, I stood waving away the speeding trucks, cars, and tankers from our increasingly camouflaged position in the mud. Our trusty, if a little holey, red tartan picnic blanket soon came in handy, and, although it offered a vaguely stable surface to carry out the repair on the wet ground, it soon blended with the sludge and did nothing to help our visibility.

Just as we had pinpointed an inch-long nail that had made a clean slice through the inner-tube, Deb pulled over on her yellow F650GS to check if we needed a hand. She had been travelling with a group who were struck down with illnesses and mechanical problems in La Paz, so was riding ahead alone.

Luckily, by then we had a complete puncture repair kit that eliminated the need to flag down help and take wheels to workshops, so we thanked Deb, and she continued on her route south. Despite our collections of tools and gadgets, the repair still took three hours, and, by the time we were ready to move again, the rain had passed and the emerging sunshine crusted over our muddy clothes and bike.

An hour later, we found ourselves stuck behind a huge truck, when a policeman jumped out of nowhere and flagged us down. We pulled over ahead of him and had a couple of seconds to formulate a plan that amounted to an agreement not to fall for the same trick that the La Paz policeman had pulled.

He ran towards us waving a speedometer, and, with half-forced and half-genuine smiles, we shook his hand, hoping we could resist whatever he was about to throw at us. He tried to tell us that we had been riding at ninety kilometres per hour, but, when we asked why hadn't pulled pull over the truck that was in front of us, his response was to drop the accused speed to eighty kilometres per hour.

We were determined not to cave in to the swindle, partly because he would think nothing of fleecing the next tourist that came his way, but also in indignation that we were already paying over the odds for everything else in the country.

We persisted with our usual defence that the Flying Aga was too old and in poor condition to speed, a fib made easy by its current, mud-caked state. We tried to exploit our own dishevelled appearance, too, claiming that we needed to get to the next town quickly after just narrowly escaping a crash. We nearly had him on side, when two of his colleagues joined us. They were having none of it and took him away to formulate a plan of their own in what became a battle of wills.

The other two kept chiming in, while we tried to make casual conversation with the first guy, sticking to a combination of particularly poor Spanish and dramatic hand gestures. When our confusion at the speeding charge eventually began to work, we were well-positioned to feign further misunderstanding when they asked outright for petrol and beer money, instead.

After a long struggle, their resistance began to crack and, eventually, they pulled the papers move on us. We counteracted with photocopies, and they soon grew tired of the fight, all the while missing no end of potential speeders that passed by.

They soon begrudgingly waved us away, making a cheap dig at Byron for having no hair, which probably would have made them feel better if Byron hadn't proudly thanked them for the compliment. We were aware that we had pushed our luck by resisting their authority so, with a degree of fear at having become too cocky, we didn't delight in our triumph until we were at least a mile away.

We kept an eye out for police officers from there on, dropping to twenty miles per hour whenever we passed them, hoping that an accusation of excessive speed was the only weapon in their arsenal.

A welcoming party of uniformed officials surrounded the entrance gate to Oruro later that day. Already jaded by the country's law enforcers, we vowed to turn around and head straight for the border if any of them asked us for money.

We were prepared for another battle of resistance as a couple of them advanced to meet us, but they began to make friendly conversation and explained that there was a carnival in town and they were stationed there to prevent troublemakers from ruining it. They checked our photocopied papers and waved us through without another word, as an attack of guilt set in at having tarnished the whole country with mistrust, following a couple of run-ins with traffic police. We soon found a hotel in the city, where a hot shower did the world of good, before we sampled the best steak of the trip so far.

The next morning we joined a queue at a petrol station on the outskirts of town. We hadn't filled up since leaving La Paz and didn't want to leave the city without a full tank. After twenty minutes of waiting, we reached the pump, and the attendant took one look at us, before shaking his head. He told us he couldn't serve us, and, although we had half anticipated that response, it would have been helpful not to have queued for so long to hear it. We decided to deploy the tactic that had worked on the police the day before and tried to wait out his resolve.

We explained that we had nothing left in the tank and desperately needed fuel, but he stood his ground and told us they didn't have the correct receipts for a foreign sale. We told him we didn't need a receipt and had no fuel to go elsewhere, when he callously threw in a curveball and told us to get a room in the hotel behind the station.

He was more skilled in the game than we had given him credit for, and our only advantage was that we were blocking the pump from a long queue of his waiting customers. He grew increasingly irate, until a policeman came over and, to our annoyance, took his side. Eventually, we got the message across that we genuinely needed to fill up, and he pointed us towards the manager's office.

We had no idea where the next petrol station would be and, with a long ride through the mountains ahead, we couldn't afford to chance leaving the town without a full tank. The new jerry can only held five litres and was strictly for emergencies, so we tried our luck with the manager.

After knocking on his small wooden door for ten minutes, he eventually answered and, once we explained that we didn't care about a receipt, he became incredibly accommodating. Within minutes, the pump attendant, who we had been bickering with, filled up the tank before taking our inflated payment, of which the difference between local and foreign price was presumably pocketed by the manager.

We set off into the desolate Andean altiplano with our hard won, full tank, braced to encounter more opportunistic police officers and time consuming punctures. Instead, we were met by rain and little else. We barely saw another vehicle along one of the straightest and well paved roads we had ridden since entering Medellin, back in Colombia.

The unbroken tarmac cut straight through the vast plateau of dry shrub and pasture that nourished more grazing herds of llamas and alpacas. Enchanting, and almost medieval, hamlets made up of earthen walled dwellings, with thatched roofs and stone animal enclosures, dotted the route.

Banks of grey clouds unleashed heavy rain, while a bitter wind whipped across the elevated table land. Despite the weather, the resilient locals, dressed in heavy skirts, smart hats, and thick ponchos, continued with their outdoor work.

During the ride, my long suffering tooth began to ache with an entirely new level of agony that could not be tamed by the painkillers. An intense throbbing reverberated through the left side of my head and dominated every thought. The sight of so many locals with metal rimmed false teeth, or no teeth at all, had kept me from braving a dentist so far, but, as the pain worsened, I was ready to rip it out myself.

Hail and rain accompanied the last hour of the journey into the city of Potosi, where we edged through narrow cobbled backstreets and parked in the foyer of another hostel.

After racing to find the nearest clinic, a dentist agreed to see me straight away in an unexpectedly pristine surgery. She had poked around and drilled the tooth before explaining something that we couldn't understand. It sounded complicated, though, and, when she mentioned something about it taking three days, I asked her to just pull it out there and then. I had done without a tooth in its place before and, since the same problem had returned, I had little affection for the spot. Luckily, the extraction was done under local anaesthetic, and the service cost less than a tenth of the price back home.

Together with the 4,000-meter altitude and the weeks of popping pain killers, the drilling and the pulling had made the left side of my face swell up like a hamster's cheek. Although the relief was immeasurable, I was wiped out, so we stayed in Potosi for a couple more days to recuperate.

One thing we had learnt over the previous few months was that Latin Americans loved a religious festival, and the biggest of them all was unfolding that weekend. It was Mardi Gras, and, unlike the low key observance back home when pancake eating marked the start of forty days before chocolate eating, four days of complete carnage had already begun.

The festival consisted of drinking, throwing water bombs, squirting foam, setting off bangers, dancing to brass bands, and marching in parades. Our stopover in the town was mostly spent ducking and diving from the path of water bombs that were launched from balconies, around corners, and over walls, and foam spray that was dispensed from the windows of passing cars.

After the weekend passed, and my swollen cheek had deflated, we said goodbye to the hostel owners, who were rarely seen without wads of coca leaves in their own bulging cheeks. They had affectionately nicknamed Byron "Rasputin" during our stay, due to his increasingly rampant, rusty coloured beard that he flatly refused to trim or shave.

At another petrol station on the edge of town a solitary attendant explained that their pumps were empty, because the delivery drivers were still celebrating the festival. It was Shrove Tuesday, and the grand finale of the long, carnival weekend, when apparently nobody worked if they didn't have to.

We were heading back into the desolate altiplano, and it was essential to fill up before we left town. After trying our hardest to request just a litre or two, it was clear that the pumps were well and truly drained, as no end of other vehicles were turned away. The same story greeted us at the next station, and, with nothing but open road ahead, we made the bold decision to see how far the remains in our tank would take us before we resorted to the jerry can.

Just as we reached the edge of the city, we caught sight of a container of petrol, hanging from the handlebars of a parked moped. We stopped beside it before seeking out its owner among the revellers nearby. After a brief haggle, we purchased the contents of the bottle for more than it would have cost the owner and less than it would have cost us at the pumps, in a deal that left everybody satisfied.

Typically, just twenty miles later, we came across a petrol station in the middle of nowhere. We filled the rest of the tank at the tourist price, for which we received no receipt, and it was a relief to spend the rest of the day at ease to take in the fantastically remote plateau.

Daunting stretches of bleak mountains encircled the flat terrain, where lakes, streams, and waterlogged grass reflected an unusually clear sky. We eased down from the cold mountains later that day, dropping a few hundred meters into an arid landscape, where heath and pasture were replaced by cacti and rocky red peaks.

A sign told us that the end of the road in Tierra del Fuego was just 3,182 miles away, an, as we pulled into the border town of Villazon, a sense of near accomplishment began to sink in.

Within a record breaking thirty minutes, our passports were stamped out of Bolivia and into Argentina. We were geared up to enter the fifteenth country of our trip, when an Argentinean official refused to stamp the Flying Aga's temporary importation paperwork until we bought insurance.

Road insurance had been a standard requirement in South America, and there was usually an agent selling it at the border or in the nearest town, so we asked the official to point us in the right direction. He explained that everything was closed because of the festival, but that an office would be open the next day. He still wouldn't stamp the papers, so, with no other option, we rode back into Bolivia to spend another night in the country that we had just officially left.

After hiding the bike in a hotel lockup, we explored the town that was in the full throes of its festival. Most of the evening involved taking cover behind trees and inside cafés, as more water bombs and foam were launched indiscriminately from passing trucks.

Early the next morning we returned to the border, assuming a quick trip to buy insurance would send us on our way. It was crucial that the temporary importation papers were approved on entry into each country, or we risked getting the bike confiscated once inside. I waited with our luggage and the bike on the Bolivian side of the border, while Byron flagged down a taxi to take him into La Quiaca, on the Argentinean side.

We had not yet picked up any Argentinean currency, so Byron asked the driver to drop him at a cash point, where a queue of roughly fifty people was wrapped around the block. Understandably, the driver wasn't happy to wait and, in irritation, he left Byron there without taking a fare.

Two hopeless hours saw Byron trek around the hot, dusty town in thick bike trousers and heavy boots. He visited six different shops before queuing in a bank, where he had been assured that insurance could be purchased. After another two-hour wait, a bank clerk explained that, although it was possible to buy national vehicle insurance, nowhere in the town sold foreign vehicle insurance.

While Byron was on the fool's errand, I had settled down on a pavement to write the next entry for our blog while the sun burnt through the morning haze. A stream of people passed through the border unchecked, as they pushed wheelbarrows that were piled high with grains and produce from Argentina into Bolivia. Meanwhile, every vehicle and bag passing the other way was inspected by sniffer dogs and x-ray machines, with a level of precaution that we had not witnessed since North America.

Other than a few other vehicles facing the same insurance predicament as us, the traffic flowed, and the hours passed by slowly. We had met a Romanian couple the night before, who were also travelling by motorcycle. Ana and Sol were riding the opposite way to us, from Argentina into Bolivia, but had also been refused passage without road insurance. Consequently, we had all returned to spend the night on opposite sides of the border the evening before, and we met them again just as Byron arrived back from his four hour mission.

Considering there was nowhere in the vicinity to buy insurance for Argentina, and nowhere that seemed to sell it in Bolivia at all, we weren't too sure what the officials expected us to do. The new clerk on duty gave us the same response that his colleague had given the day before, but he, too, had no suggestions as to where the elusive cover could be obtained.

During this time, the Romanians had worked some charm on the Bolivian officials and had succeeded in getting their bike papers stamped. With their own victory in the bag, they joined our cause and did their best to try the same method on the Argentinean officials, but they were tougher nuts to crack and refused to budge on the matter.

As time ticked away, we were joined by a trio of Ecuadorian guys who were facing the same insurance problem with their car, and it was clear that the deadlock would only be broken when we all found a way to get hold of a broker.

One of the Argentinean officials eventually approached our growing posse and explained that a friend of his was on the way to help us out. A woman turned up shortly afterwards and told us she could arrange to get us insurance. Her offer was our only hope, so Byron and two of the Ecuadorian guys followed her back into the Bolivian border town. Assuming the matter would now be resolved quickly, Ana and Sol also set off into Bolivia, leaving me to await the outcome with the Flying Aga, while the other Ecuadorian went back to their car with their pet dog in tow.

A company of stray dogs joined me while I finished off the blog entry and exhausted the battery on the iPod. The hours ticked away slowly, and, later that afternoon, a bank of ominous clouds filled the sky. I covered the bike seat with our helmets and waterproofs before moving under the shelter of the Argentinean immigration building to watch another daily downpour fall across the land.

At some point during what eventually became a six-hour wait, Francisco and Sebastian pulled up. They were curious about the Flying Aga and, after hearing of our insurance predicament, they generously donated a supply of cookies and a tin of olives to my wait before wishing me luck and making their way home to Ecuador.

My conversation with them had drawn the attention of a guard who had been patrolling nearby, and it wasn't long before he handed me a cup of coffee and began asking why I had been there so long. After hearing the story, he explained it to a few other guards who had all been keeping an eye on me during the long period that the Flying Aga had been parked on their patch.

By the time darkness eventually fell, the heavens were letting rip and I had no clue where Byron was. We were still only travelling with one emergency mobile telephone and had no way to contact one another.

By the time it reached nine o'clock, all the border guards began to show real concern. I had relayed the details about the insurance problem and the lady who had led the boys back into Villazon, and none of them could understand where anyone could buy insurance for Argentina in Bolivia. I went to find the third Ecuadorian guy, who had stayed with their car, but he hadn't heard from his friends, either, and it was then that all manner of scenarios began to run through my mind.

Upon learning that I wasn't carrying any money or a phone, one of the guards leant me some coins to go and check the Internet in town, in case Byron had emailed. I left them to watch the bike and set off to traipse through the dark, wet streets. It wasn't long before I realised that I had no idea where an Internet café was and, as I wandered aimlessly through the shadows, I came across the entrance to the hotel where we had slept the night before.

We had told the Romanians that it was a decent place to stay, and I went inside, knowing the chances that they might actually be there were incredibly slim. However, I remembered that they had seen the woman who led the boys away, and I was sure they might remember something crucial.

By a huge stroke of luck they had checked into a room, and they greeted me with surprise, before they, too, became worried. They couldn't remember anything about the woman, but it had been over six hours since the guys had followed her from the border, and they suggested that I might need to call the police.

Convinced that the three lads would more than likely be OK if they were together, I decided to check the Internet first, in case Byron had sent me a message. After tracking down the only Internet café in town, we were waiting for the slow connection to kick in when I noticed the two Ecuadorian guys sitting at a computer. Then, as if on cue, Byron walked through the door.

It turned out that the woman who had met us at the border was a lawyer and had a colleague in Argentina, who was purchasing the two insurance policies. The procurement was being done over the phone, though, and in any other country it would have been a two-hour job, at most. However, it wasn't any other country, and the three lads had spent the majority of the day chasing down shops with fax machines that hadn't been knocked out by the storm and photocopiers that were actually stocked with paper and ink. Phone lines had been affected by the weather, too, so all the calls had to be made elsewhere in town. In the intervening time, the boys had been waiting and eating.

My relief was quickly replaced by anger. For the entire six hours, they had only been ten minutes away, and Byron had not thought to come and let me know what was going on or, more importantly, bring me any food. When it had finally occurred to him to find me, he had arrived at the border just as I had set off to check the Internet.

Eventually, the lawyer came through with the documents, and the Ecuadorians went off to resume their two-day drive to Buenos Aires. We went back to retrieve the Flying Aga, where the guards were relieved that we had found one another and berated Byron for leaving me for so long. They wished us a good night, and we ended the day back at the hotel with the Romanians and a much needed beer.

The same guards met us early the next morning, and, after greeting us like old friends, we received our stamp on the bike paperwork a whole forty-three hours after first arriving at the border.

Infuriatingly, the new official that placed the stamp didn't even ask for evidence of our hard earned insurance cover.

TENT FLOODS AND PAMPAS

275 DAYS ON THE ROAD | 25,550 MILES ON THE CLOCK

We were sweltering by the time we wound our way out of La Quiaca, where Byron had spent the morning the day before. A police checkpoint greeted us on the highway almost immediately, and our hearts sank with dismay as the all too recent diligence of Argentinean red tape still smouldered. We weren't carrying anything that could have got us in trouble but, after the border experience and our perpetual state of alert through Bolivia, we were cautious of any more encounters with uniforms. We were also conscious of riding the bike with its particularly prominent Union Jack and Great Britain stickers into a country where the government had recently exhumed its age-old issue over the Falkland Islands.

We rolled up to the officer who had flagged us down, while sniffer dogs were sent onto the trucks and coaches that were lined up along the side of the road. With a smile, he asked us to turn on our front headlight that was positioned just above the biggest of the Union Jack stickers. After bracing ourselves for a request to dismount, it was a surprise to be waved on our way, and all tension drained away in an instant, as our frame of mind was turned on its head, and we rode away past groups of truckers and tourists who hadn't been so lucky.

The sun blazed across multicoloured, sedimentary layers that rippled in waves through the mountains in a scene that was like nothing we had ever witnessed. The piles of litter and burning refuse that had cropped up along the roads during the previous five months were nowhere to be seen, while impressive volcanoes rose in the distance and huge, bulbous cacti were scattered across the immediate landscape. Everything seemed to be going our way until another frustrating wobble of the rear wheel brought us to an abrupt stop.

We pulled onto a patch of gravel beside the road and, as the sun beat down mercilessly, we got to work on fixing our fifth puncture. The luggage was unloaded, the front wheel was removed, and the bike was tilted forward onto its front forks, before the exhaust was disconnected and the rear wheel finally came off. Although it was the most breathtaking of breakdown locations to date, it was also one of the hottest, and our water supply soon ran out. Predictably, the repair did not come without its complications, either.

The flat tyre was the result of a burst puncture patch on the inner tube, and we set about replacing it with our only spare rear tube. The spare had been repaired following the previous puncture outside La Paz, in Bolivia, but it hissed ominously when we began to inflate it. We soon identified an undetected grazed section of rubber next to the fresh patch but, annoyingly, we had no puncture patches to seal it. Our only option was to chance using the spare nineteen-inch front tube on the eighteen-inch rear tyre and hope that it would get us to the nearest tyre shack where we could patch the two damaged rear tubes.

Two hours passed before we set off again, and we were in desperate need of water. A careful ride along the roasting tarmac eventually led us to a long line of buildings set back from the road. A modest gomeria, the latest name for the workshops that dealt solely in wheel repairs, was set up under a corrugated canopy. Stacks of defunct tyres littered the small forecourt where nothing else but the end of a compressor and a trough of dirty water hinted at the nature of the business.

A quick dunk in the trough pinpointed the scrapes and holes in the damaged inner tubes. The elderly man who ran the place explained that the location of the graze meant one tube would be near impossible to seal, but he agreed to have a go at re-patching them both.

While the old man went to find glue and patches, Byron borrowed his pump to increase the pressure in the rear wheel. The solution with the larger inner tube seemed to be working a treat, so we decided to take a gamble and leave it in the tyre until we could purchase a completely new tube. However, seconds after attaching the compressor to the valve, a resounding bang followed by a hiss put another spanner in the works.

We got started on the process of removing the now third flat inner tube, when a highway patrolman pulled up in a pickup truck. He soon concerned himself with our problem and took control, while a stream of clapped out cars and trucks also pulled in for repairs and air. It was clear that we would be there for a while and, as well as being desperate for water and food, we had still not withdrawn any currency.

When Luis, the highway patrolman, offered to drop me in the local town, the offer was too good to refuse. We had got used to gauging the intentions of strangers over the past nine months, and, although I clutched a canister of pepper spray in my pocket just in case, our instincts about Luis proved to be sound, and he dropped me five minutes around the corner in the cobbled streets of a beautiful colonial town that was in the midst of yet another festival.

While I queued to withdraw some pesos, jesters and masked revellers threw flour and water at each other as they danced through the narrow streets and sang in the main plaza. I picked up water, puncture repair glue, and no end of patches before trekking back to the main road, where the bike had been bolted back together and was ready to leave.

The burst patch on the first inner tube had taken a second patch and was now snug inside the rear wheel, but the graze on our only rear spare wouldn't seal, and we had to scrap it. It transpired that the nineteen-inch spare tube, whose valve had burst under the compressor, had passed the trough test and no other problems could be identified with it, so it took its place back in the pannier as the only spare for both wheels.

Sunset was closing in, so we rode the short distance to stay the night in the picturesque town of Humahuaca behind the gomeria. After tracking down a hostel that wasn't overflowing with flour-bombed, drunken revellers, we ventured out for a first taste of legendary, Argentinean meat. We soon discovered that the days of affordable meals had conclusively come to an end, but we savoured a llama stew as a final treat.

While we ate, the heat of the day literally ruptured the sky, and a deluge was unleashed across the town. It didn't let up all evening, and eventually we braved a mad dash back to the hostel. The narrow cobbled streets and pavements had disappeared under raging rivers of rainfall, and we were soaked to the bone within seconds of stepping outside. Upon our return to the hostel, we realised we had forgotten to stock up on more drinking water. The irony of the oversight and the weather was not lost on us, and we ventured back into the downpour to hold up our empty bottles and catch the plummeting rain.

We were soaked, sunburnt, and exhausted from the day and we fell asleep with relief that we had not made a return to camping on that particular night.

The air had cleared the next morning, and we woke up full of hope that the new country might bring an end to the white bread and butter hostel breakfasts that had filled the past month. Sadly, it was not to be, and, after a nutrition-free start to the day, we continued south through the vast country

Unsure if riding with just one spare inner tube would prove to be a jinx, we called in at the same shop where I had picked up the puncture repair materials the day before and bought a new eighteen-inch tube of dubious strength and construction. It was very unlikely to hold the weight of the Flying Aga but it was the only option on offer in the town and was so cheap that if it didn't work it wouldn't be a big loss. Every part of us clung to the hope that we would never have to test its durability anyway.

We crossed the Tropic of Capricorn later that morning before embarking on a westerly detour to visit a salt desert. The largest salt flat in the world had been flooded back in Bolivia, and, for fear of losing the front wheel down a concealed crater or rusting the bike's bodywork, we had forfeited riding there. Instead, we elected to visit the much smaller and dryer Salinas Grandes that lay one hundred miles from Humahuaca.

Petrol troubles had struck the region, and we had been unable to fill the tank before we reached the closest village to the desert. Everywhere was clean out, including a small hardware shop where we had been told that fuel could usually be bought for double the price of the regulated pumps.

The salt flat lay fifty miles away, across a steep, cloud-skimming mountain, and we needed petrol to get there so, for the first time on the trip, we resorted to our reserve supply and poured five litres of low octane, Bolivian fuel from the jerry can into the tank.

The geology through the mountains was breathtaking. Rocks and rising mountain peaks were embellished with more mesmerising patterns and colours of ancient sediment that varied with every twist and turn. The bike chugged into the high altitude, and we froze through a thick blanket of cloud before descending towards the distant expanse of glassy white desert.

A paved road had been laid directly above its centre, and we pulled into a lay-by, where a man stood guard over the salty dip that led down onto the desert from the tarmac. Local communities extracted the salt as a means of income, and, to prevent contamination, they blocked vehicles from driving on the surface, so we went for a walk instead.

Although from a distance, the vast layer of salt gave the impression that a snowstorm had hit the mountains, the crusty, crystallised surface proved otherwise. In some sections it had cracked into large, tortoise shell patches that were shaped by a network of shallow streams and crooked lines of salt deposits. In other areas, it was indiscriminately broken by tiny deep holes or wide, superficial craters. The vacant miles of pure minerals confused all sense of perspective, and we set about exploiting the setting by taking photos that made us look tiny against actual tiny objects.

Salt residue quickly covered us from head to toe and mixed with our mud encrusted bike kit to form a brittle blend of grime. We were desperate to include the Flying Aga in the photo antics and persuaded the local sentry to let us roll the bike down onto the periphery of the salt, without turning on the engine. Frustratingly, though, our camera ran out of battery just as we set the centre stand down on the white surface.

We took it as a signal to get back on the road so, caked in a concoction of mud, salt, and sweat, we rode back across the majestic mountain pass. The petrol stations were still empty on our return, but fortunately our reserve supply stretched to the city of Jujuy.

We filled up in the first of many petrol stations where we would spend an unanticipated amount of time during our final month on the road, then, after tracking down the auto district of the city, we checked into a hotel with a car park, where we could change the oil and clean the bike the next day.

Although the city buzzed with the usual hustle and bustle of South America, the diversity of its population soon put an end to our previously unavoidable distinction by local residents of being gringos. We found the first supermarket that we had come across in weeks and excitedly stocked up on toiletries and groceries before fashioning a feast of a lunch back in the hotel.

On a full stomach, Byron set off to join an hour-long queue to top up on more of the region's short supply of fuel, while I took advantage of the hot water and set about scouring the encrusted grime out of our bike gear.

Our budget was officially tight again, so we ate dinner in a nearby petrol station that night before cooking some oats for breakfast in the car park the following morning.

The bike was clean once again, and the oil had been changed, but we still needed new inner tubes and a new rear tyre. The mammoth final leg to the end of the road was fast approaching, and we needed to find replacement tubes and tyres before civilisation was replaced by miles of southern Argentina's sparsely populated nothingness.

Some hours later, we were just shy of a wine region, when a wearisome rear wobble interrupted our ride for the sixth time in 26,000 miles. The heat from the sun was ruthless, and there was nothing in sight to offer shade. However, unlike previous puncture scenarios, we had just stocked up on groceries, water, and sun block.

With an acceptance that only experience could breed, we spread our trusty tartan picnic blanket across the overgrown verge, peeled off our heavy bike kit, and had a picnic before we did anything else.

Following the usual process of unburdening luggage, removing wheels, and disconnecting exhausts, we discovered that the puncture was caused by another burst patch on the inner tube. We were in desperate need of strong new tubes and fresh wheels but, until we found some, we had to make do with the unconvincing spare that we had bought two days earlier in Humahuaca.

The tube was inserted into the tyre, and water and soap were applied in preparation to ease the bead back over the rim. The water dried up within seconds, and the metal of the tyre irons heated up to such an extent that, when one of them brushed against the new inner tube, it sliced a hole right through the cheap rubber. Alas, our hopes for a simple puncture repair were yet to be fulfilled.

Wondering why we had bothered buying it in the first place, we scrapped the shoddy tube and dug out the front nineteen-inch spare. We fitted it back inside the smaller rear tyre and bolted the bike back together, praying that whatever had made the valve burst last time would hold out until we found new supplies.

After the long delay, we set off again and approached the Calchaqui Valley, where wide rivers and fascinating rock formations lined the stretch between Salta and Cafayate. The red cliffs of the region had been sculpted and weather-eroded with all manner of huge cracks and crevices, while towering, fortress-like buttes and huge cacti paved the way.

The extraordinary landscape altered again after leaving Cafayate, where stunning vineyards grew in neat lines for thousands of acres.

The route soon took another dramatic turn when we ventured into the surrounding mountainous terrain. After experiencing the heat of the valley, freezing cold winds took us by surprise, and thick fog rendered us blind. We tailed the rear lights of another vehicle for miles, until the mist eventually cleared and revealed rocky fields, where tall cacti burgeoned across the elevated landscape.

Just as a full rainbow appeared to our left, the road took a descent out of the cloud line. It accompanied us all the way into Tafi del Valle, where grassland replaced the dry highlands and we looked for a guesthouse to shelter from the rain.

We got lucky with a hostel, where the owners were hosting a homemade pizza party. Up to that evening, little had been said to us about the Falkland Islands, despite the latest bout of international airtime being afforded to the country's government on the matter. No end of questionably necessary road signs had lined the route from the north, simply stating Las Malvinas son Argentinas (the Falkland Islands are Argentina's), but whenever we had told anyone that we were British, they rarely raised an eyebrow.

That night we joined a group of students at the pizza party and asked where public opinion stood on the issue. The topic rose as quickly as it sank. One of the girls began to tell us how there were more important matters that their president should be concerned with, when her friend abruptly cut her off and declared that politics and food should never be mixed. No more was said on the matter, and we went to bed none the wiser, albeit truly shattered by another eventful day on the road.

We passed out of the Andes for the final time the next morning and ventured into almost 300,000 square miles of flat, grassy plains, known as the pampas. Aside from the low-lying vegetation, the monotonous landscape was not too dissimilar to a desert, and the same fierce wind that had battered us through Nevada and along the coastal roads of Peru left our necks aching as we leaned against its force, while Byron wrestled to keep the Flying Aga on course.

After hours of riding through the desolate plains, we spotted the familiar outline of two heavily loaded bikes on the hard shoulder ahead and pulled over to see if they needed help. A Canadian couple from Québec were on two R1200GS bikes and had stopped to pile on layers of insulation against the miserable weather. Following a quick chat, we rode on to a petrol station, where we all warmed up over hot coffee in a scene that was reminiscent of similar pit stops many months before in Alaska and Canada.

Chantal and Jean had been riding a similar route to us and were also in need of new tyres. The next day they planned to take a diversion via Buenos Aires to collect a specific brand that, unlike us, they had already sourced.

For the first time since the hostel rooftop in Quito, we camped that night on the outskirts of Cordoba and spent the evening taking refuge from the rain under a shelter with the Canadians and a campground dog, while we ate cheese, crackers, and some burgers that we had been carrying for two days.

Our hard-bargained-for Bolivian sleeping bags proved their worth, and we slept soundly through the cold and the rain. After another breakfast of oats the next morning, we parted ways with the Canadians to embark on separate quests for new tyres.

Our dislike of cities was soon reaffirmed as we trawled the long roads and one-way streets of Cordoba in search of a garage. Just before lunchtime, we stumbled on the first BMW dealership we had seen since Costa Rica and couldn't believe our luck. After learning that they stocked the correct size rear tyre that we needed, the workshop closed for a long lunch break.

Following the success of our new sleeping bags the night before and the fast deterioration of our budget, we had committed to camping for the rest of the trip. To pass the time, while we waited for the workshop to reopen, we decided to undertake a serious restock of sustenance for the journey ahead.

We executed a mammoth grocery shop at the nearest supermarket but struggled to carry the load back to the workshop, where we realised that we had inadequate space to transport the stash. Somehow, though, we managed to squeeze every last packet of pasta and bag of oats into the top box and a foldaway rucksack that we had used for the same purpose throughout most of the US.

It wasn't until the workshop reopened that we learnt the tyre they had in stock was not of the durability we had hoped for. Although it would have carried our heavy weight all the way to Tierra del Fuego, it was still a long way back up to Buenos Aires, from where we would head home. We really didn't want to use two tyres to complete the distance, and, as we deliberated what to do, one of the mechanics gestured for us to follow him.

He led us to a neighbouring warehouse and picked up a hard-wearing tyre and two of the most heavy duty inner tubes we had ever seen. Had we known about the warehouse in the first place, we could have saved ourselves the time and money that the dealership ended up costing.

Not only had we waited around for their lunch break to pass, but the other mechanics had begun prepping the Flying Aga on a workbench while we were at the warehouse. After giving the bodywork a clean with chemicals that had suspiciously scrubbed off half of one Union Jack sticker, they had attempted to balance the carburettors without warming the engine first. We got back just in time to explain about removing the exhaust before they wrenched off the rear wheel.

We were kicking ourselves when it came to clearing the substantial bill. After buying the tyre and inner tubes elsewhere, although the guys had been incredibly friendly, we had paid to watch them do the simplest of jobs on a bike that Byron knew like the back of his hand.

By the time we reached a campground on the western outskirts of the city, the sun was setting, and we had a short window to set up camp before darkness fell. Byron set about rectifying the job on the carburettors while the bike was still warm, and I began to unload our camping kit. At some point during the frantic rush, we gained a companion in the form of a German man, who told us he was living on the site. While Byron tried to concentrate, and I attempted to create some order out of our heap of possessions, the man judged his audience terribly.

He launched into a one-way dialogue that mostly consisted of advice on the best way to undertake the trip that, by then, we were more than nine months into. He explained that he had completed a much more exciting motorcycle journey, for a much longer period of time, visiting many more countries on what had generally been a much better trip to ours. Byron did his best to ignore the strange approach to making friends, but, conscious that we were about to sleep in the open air with just a thin sheet of fabric as protection, I deemed it worthwhile to humour the man.

He continued to spout criticism of our setup and belittle our Spanish, until we both tuned his voice out and got on with the tasks at hand. He continued to hang around our pitch, staring at us in eerie silence while we frantically worked against the clock to beat the encroaching darkness. It was a relief to see him eventually wander off in silence, but the experience was unnerving. As a result, we slept restlessly, anxious that he might return in the night to exact some sort of vengeance for our disinterest in what he had to say.

We capitalised on the broken sleep and the resulting early morning the next day and set off back into the flat, lowlands of the pampas. With literally nothing else to see for the next 1,000 straight miles, a coffee break in every petrol station became the most anticipated activity over the following few days.

We huddled against driving rain and powerful winds for what felt like infinite hours, straining to hear anything over the deafening weather. The bike faltered towards the end of the first day and eventually bought us to a standstill on the side of the road. After checking the spark plugs, the rain soon subsided, and the ignition leapt back into life.

We pulled into a nearby campground, where trucks, caravans, and other travelling circus vehicles were the only other visitors on the site. Hoping for a better night of sleep, we pitched our tent at the opposite end to them and set about fashioning a bespoke [made to order] seal for the ignition cables using a plastic drinking bottle and some cable ties. As darkness fell outside, an overdue wash of our entire wardrobe was carried out in the site's cold, cockroach-infested showers.

Despite the travelling circus, we slept soundly in the heart of the country and woke the next morning to a welcome break of sunshine. The resulting warmth had arrived too late to dry out our laundry, though, and, when we set off to spend another monotonous day on the road, our damp clothes added a few extra pounds of weight to our bags.

The deadly combination of warm rays and repetitive terrain sent me drifting in and out of sleep on the back of the bike. Other than abrupt recoveries each time my nodding head bashed my helmet against the back of Byron's, there was nothing I could do in my restricted pillion position to shake the drowsiness. Luckily, Byron avoided the affliction, but, after two hours, we pulled over anyway to load up on the strongest possible coffee.

Our return to camping meant we rarely had access to mains electricity, so we were using a device that Jeff had given us back in Albuquerque in the US. It ran off the bike's power outlet and charged our smaller electronics while we rode.

Shortly after reviving on caffeine, I noticed that the device had fallen out of the outlet, and we had just pulled over to look for it when a pickup truck pulled in behind us. The couple driving it had spotted the black plug flying from the bike and had picked it up for us. The incident was by far the most interesting thing that happened for the rest of the tedious day.

The following day, we passed into the region of Patagonia where the price of fuel dropped by almost forty percent and, to our delight, remained that way for the rest of the 1,300 miles south.

The sight of similarly overloaded, heavily clad, adventure motorcyclists on the route had increased tenfold. We met many fellow riders from Argentina or neighbouring Brazil at petrol stations, as well as exhausted international riders, who were either on the last push south or fresh on a bearing north.

A miserable return of strong winds and dismal rain accompanied the next day. Although we began to spot wildlife roaming in the previously vacant plains, the ride had become an arduously cold and tiresome slog, and, for the first time on the whole journey, our dedication to reaching the end of the road was genuinely tested.

After riding through the remote lowlands for three solid days, the coastal city of Comodoro Rivadavia was a welcome interruption to the otherwise mind numbing route. We refuelled and bought groceries before leaving the city roads behind to continue further along the coast.

A provincial border roadblock stopped us half an hour later, and the guards estimated that the next campground was at least fifty miles away. Darkness had already begun to fall, and we decided to camp in a lay-by, close to the checkpoint.

Trucks and eighteen-wheelers were also pulling in for the night, so we selected a spot out of their way, in a far corner among some wild bushes of rocket and herbs. Considering there were so many empty miles between each inhabited area, rough camping in the country was par for the course.

We pitched the tent in a cleared space of scrubland that was bordered by the plants. The wind was strong, and we weren't sure how secure the frame would be on the relatively soft ground, so we positioned the Flying Aga near the entrance and secured a few guy ropes to its frame for good measure. After cooking a stew, we made use of the natural facilities, before a light rain filled the air. With little else to do, we fell asleep to the sound of the Atlantic Ocean raging below the cliff on the other side of the road.

We woke early, after a sleep that had been broken by a continuous rumble of trucks. The drizzle that had continued since the previous evening soon transformed into a heavy deluge, and we dozed in the morning dawn, hoping to wait out the downpour. However, an encroaching puddle in the porch swelled, and, within minutes, the entire tent was floating on inches of fast rising water.

We threw on our already partially soaked clothes and loaded anything of value into the waterproof roll-bags. A few uncomfortable nights would have been in the cards if we hadn't salvaged the bedding fast, so we raced to squeeze the sleeping bags and mattresses into the panniers. By the time we were done, everything else in the tent was submerged under a pond of murky rainwater.

Although it wasn't low ground, the whole area was so uneven that small lakes were multiplying across the entire lay-by and the nearby road. Nothing was safe, and all we could do was load the bike up as fast as possible and evacuate.

The truckers were still sleeping in their high cabins and had no idea what kind of palaver was playing out just a few meters below them. We fished out the sheepskin seat cover, the tartan blanket, our helmets, gloves, and everything else that had swelled to five times its usual weight in the flood.

The only positive thought we could extract from the entire catastrophe was that it had not happened during the night, while we were asleep.

As we fumbled through the debris, the tent frame wrenched forward and then promptly slackened, as we heard a splash outside. The bike had fallen from its stand, and the guy ropes that we had secured to it had just been ripped clean off.

The Flying Aga was half submerged in a separate lake of its own, and we clambered over to heave it upright, while the rain surged remorselessly. We wheeled the bike onto the only patch of non-flooded ground beside one of the trucks, before returning to salvage the rest of our kit.

Somehow, we succeeded in rescuing every last peg from the carnage, before we wrung everything out as best we could in the continuous rain. Half an hour after the weather had turned on us, we had wedged on our saturated helmets and were riding away from the disaster zone.

Believing the worst of our troubles to be over, we concentrated on getting to the nearest petrol station, dreaming of the hot coffee and croissants that would soften the blow. The rain continued to pummel the region, freezing us to the core in our damp clothes, while the wind blew viciously from the coast and thrust the bike all over the road. Waves from the nearby sea slammed up against the cliffs and sent water crashing across the route, where it mixed with the rain to flood stretches of uneven tarmac.

An hour passed before we eventually spotted the redeeming sight of a petrol station. As we slowed down to its approach, the front wheel of the bike struck a hidden obstacle beneath the flooded road and launched us directly into the path of an oncoming car. With astonishing fortune, the car swerved perilously close to the edge of the cliff on its right and avoided hitting us by mere inches. The move gave Byron just enough leeway to regain control of the steering and get us back onto our side of the road, seconds before we would have collided with the cars that were still approaching through the heavy rain.

We skidded and slid to a halt on the hard shoulder. Shaken up and dejected, it was the closest shave we had encountered in almost ten solid months on the road, and all we wanted to do was go home.

Our clothes quickly formed large puddles around the table in the petrol station café, where we gulped down hot coffee which failed miserably to lessen the cold and the shock. It was only nine o'clock in the morning, but there was no question that we were done for the day.

With little care for the budget, we checked into a hotel in the nearby town of Caleta Olivia. The entire area was flooded, and we moored the Flying Aga under inches of water in the car park, before wading into the hotel with as much luggage as we could carry. Two flights of stairs led us to the dry sanctuary of an expensive room, which we promptly decorated with drenched clothes and soaked belongings.

We wasted no time in running the first hot bath we'd had in months and were soon soaking the warmth back into our blood stream as we bathed away the blues.

Later that day, it was a relief to find the rain had subsided and the wind had dropped. A quick reconnaissance of the building revealed a substantial boiler room, and, with the sanction of the maintenance man, our kit was soon hanging up to dry. Our tent, picnic blanket, seat cover, sleeping bags, mattresses, gloves, helmets, and boots were either hanging from the pipes, propped against the cylinders, or resting below the tanks.

Our entire kit had successfully dried to a crisp overnight, and, after another breakfast of oats cooked in the fully drained car park, we psyched ourselves up for another day on the road.

An abundance of wildlife kept our minds occupied as we pushed south along the windy but dry route. Herds of guanaco and vicuña, relatives of the llamas and alpacas we had passed on higher ground, grazed on the grass verges and across the plains of Patagonia. Some bolted at the sound of the bike, while others simply stared as we passed them by, in much the same way that the bears had done in Canada.

Flightless packs of greater rhea birds with ostrich-like, long necks and plump bodies bounded away on powerful legs whenever we drew close. Distant glimpses of pink flamingos, sneaky foxes, and scavenging buzzards joined them all to keep me occupied with the camera for the first time in days.

Later that morning, the Flying Aga began to lose power once again, and we inched our way to the refuge of another petrol station. We were soon discussing the issue with Carmen and Murray, who were making their way north.

Byron and Murray set about changing the points, spark plugs, and HT leads, while Carmen and I exchanged crosses on our respective roadmaps of places to stop at along the way. With little idea of how far we would get that day, we parted ways once the bike had regained full power, and we rode a further one hundred miles before it began to stammer again.

After months of riding on low grade petrol, it was possible that the fuel filters were clogged and could have been the cause of the latest spate of hiccups. A quick change of them at another petrol station followed another cup of coffee, before we rode a further one hundred miles without incident.

That evening, we pitched the tent in a naval campground beside a river, just as a beautiful sunset filled an unusually clear sky. Although the sun had blazed all day, we were closing in on Antarctica, and the air was turning increasingly frosty. Biting cold took root during the night, and, when we woke up, the tent was so saturated with condensation that we thought there had been another flood. The Bolivian sleeping bags prevailed, though, and, despite being able to see our breath inside the tent, they remained toasty.

The rising sun soon burnt off the remnants of the cold night, and we set off under a glorious morning sky that brought out more birds and camelids to liven up the monotony. By lunchtime, we had arrived in the final mainland city of Rio Gallegos, where we stocked up on fuel and groceries to keep us going until we reached our long awaited, final destination. Just an hour later, our pre-planning hit a hurdle at the border with Chile.

BEADS IN THE HEADLIGHT

286 DAYS ON THE ROAD | 28,940 MILES ON THE CLOCK

An array of natural produce that was prohibited from being transported across borders had featured on posters at all the international crossings we had ridden through. At first we had paid attention to them, until a gradual lack of enforcement left us assuming that the restrictions were no longer relevant, and, as we ventured further south, we had stopped registering them altogether. However, when we arrived at the border with Chile, the signs were prominent and looked like they had been recently hung.

Having overlooked the fact that we had rarely experienced a trouble-free crossing in five months, we assumed it would be a breeze to pass through the remote border post. After sorting our passports and temporary importation documents without any hassle, we were handed a form to declare that we were not carrying any illicit fresh produce. We assumed the form was a hollow strip of red tape and began to sign it, when the official who had given it to us pointed at the guards outside. They were sending sniffer dogs into every single vehicle, and he warned us about a heavy fine if it was found that we had lied. With far too many groceries to hide, we confessed to our haul.

At his request, we wrote a list of the extensive shopping we had carried out just an hour earlier. Inevitably, he told us that all of the fresh produce would have to be discarded before we could enter the country. The sacrifice was too great to contemplate on our tight budget, and, after some deliberation, we asked the guard if we could camp at the border for the night, instead. If we couldn't take the goods with us, we decided to eat as much of them as possible that evening.

The guards were indifferent and agreed that we could set up camp in a small field where their sniffer dogs were taken for exercise. So we rode down a steep, overgrown bank and pitched the tent in the clumps of grass around a neglected football goalpost.

We cooked four meals worth of rations, while a few rogue foxes prowled close by, hoping for a slice of the action. It took three separate pans to cook the food, and, while it simmered away, we forced down the fruit we had bought to last for three breakfasts.

We were close to incapacitation by the time we flew a white flag on the huge stew and stored the remains of it in one of the pans. The three saucepans packed down into one another, and, unless the dogs went to town on us in the morning, there was a good chance we might be able to smuggle the leftovers through for a cold lunch. After all, we had cooked away whatever had once been fresh about them.

We slept soundly on heavy stomachs before waking up to another sunny morning. After a breakfast of more fruit, only two apples and a banana were sacrificed to the food-police compost from our entire, three-day stash. The guards made a point of ransacking every bag we were carrying before annoyingly confiscating a woven vine that I had been given back in Guatemala on my birthday. In a minor triumph, though, they overlooked the saucepan of cold stew before waving us into their territory.

We eagerly searched for whales and dolphins during a twenty-minute ferry crossing over the Strait of Magellan before arriving on the archipelago of Tierra del Fuego, where our target destination of Ushuaia lay just 280 miles away.

We stopped in a pretty town, where a refuel of the bike and a cash withdrawal from inside an actual bank turned out to be the most expensive petrol and currency purchases of the whole trip.

A seventy-mile stretch of unpaved, ripio road lay a few miles out of the town and offered the only route back into Argentinean territory, where Ushuaia lay. The Flying Aga bounced and rattled across the bumpy surface for three hours, while we crossed our fingers and toes in hope that the recent new rear tyre would hold out against any tiny rocks or pieces of rogue metal. A newly laid concrete path lay enticingly to our left for most of the way, but it was interspersed with trenches and bordered by a steep mud verge that prevented any temptation to test it out.

The Flying Aga did hold out against the track, and we reached the end of the route caked in layers of grime and dust, but without incident. Having devoured the cold leftovers from our cookout the night before, we crossed back into Argentina with nothing to declare in an unexpected matter of minutes.

A powerful aroma of the sea greeted us fifty miles later when we passed through the coastal city of Rio Grande. Following an onerous week of riding through repetitive flat grassland, the closing leg to Ushuaia delivered an incredible conclusion to the journey.

After traversing the South Atlantic coast, we rode through huge areas of blackened, fire-damaged tree stumps before cutting through the periphery of a rugged mountain range and skirting the edge of magnificent lakes. The route steered us down to the north coast of the Beagle Channel, where we crossed the finish line on our epic ride and arrived at the end of the road just as the sun began to fall.

Although more Chilean territory lay further south in the archipelago, there was no road to reach it, and Ushuaia was as far as the Flying Aga could go. Despite earmarking the small coastal city as our southernmost finishing point before we had even set off on the trip, we hadn't actually planned our arrival there.

In keeping with the rest of the adventure, a stranger with a liking for motorcycles helped us out as we rode aimlessly up and down its busy streets in the hope of finding somewhere to stay. He shouted from his minibus and motioned for us to follow him, so we tailed the van back through the busy streets and pulled up behind it at a hostel owned by the driver's friend. Unfortunately, it was fully booked, but the minibus driver was undeterred and called some other friends to see if they could accommodate us.

It wasn't long before we were parked in the garden of a guesthouse and had unpacked our bags into a well-heated room, with a hot shower next door and a fully equipped kitchen downstairs. A Michael Caine lookalike, who enjoyed the sound of his own voice, ran the place and made us grateful that our command of Spanish was still a little sketchy.

During the long slog down from Cordoba, we had been looking into methods of getting home that avoided a lengthy 2,500-mile ride north to Buenos Aires. We had failed to find a feasible alternative, though, so we intended to savour the comfort of a gas fire and solid roof over our heads for a couple of days, before we embarked on the mammoth backtrack to the capital city.

We stocked up on food and Argentinean wine to prepare a celebratory feast that night, before devouring a pleasingly oat-free breakfast the following morning.

Later that day, we took our entire wardrobe to a nearby laundrette for its first machine wash in weeks. By then, we were conscious that our dwindling budget might not extend to a flight home, so, as part of an effort to save pennies, we spent some time trying to persuade the woman in charge to do the load in two washes, rather than three.

The pent up strain of the previous week soon came to a head when, having nearly convinced the woman, Byron gave up on our efforts and told her that it didn't matter, either way.

The move kicked off a quarrel between us that left us stewing in silence by the time we returned to the hostel, and we went our separate ways to carry out a few chores.

A while later, Byron claimed to have located the cause of the bike's long running power problems and asked me to help him outside. Distracted by an effort to keep up the earlier squabble, when he asked me to unscrew the headlight I did so without registering that the task didn't actually require any assistance. Even when he pulled a paper bag from the light's interior and feigned surprise, I hadn't clocked what was going on. It was only after he handed me the paper bag from the Native American shop back in South Dakota that I saw the intricately beaded bracelet that I had wanted to buy inside.

Down on our knees beside the Flying Aga, with the beautiful beads in hand, Byron asked me to marry him.

The bracelet had been almost everywhere with us on the journey after he had hidden it in the headlight eight months earlier. During that time, children and marriage had cropped up in conversations, and, although we both wanted to build a family of mini adventurers, Byron had been most vocal about not getting married. He had done a good job, too, because I had to ask a few times if he was serious...before saying, "Yes!"

It turned out that he had already asked my Dad before we had even left home, and just about everyone he knew had been expecting to read about an engagement in our blog for months. It was a terrific surprise that killed off laundry-gate in an instant.

We celebrated reaching the end of one journey and beginning another with an extravagant meal in the sunlit town. We were broke, homeless, and jobless, but we were together, and everything felt golden.

The following day was not so glorious, and, after another happily oat-free breakfast, we strolled around the small city and soaked up its wintry mood. The air was frosty, without the warm glow of sunlight, and, when a descending fog was joined by rainfall, we decided to begin the long slog north the next day.

We ruled out riding up the west side of Argentina and into Chile, where a final blast through the Andes, via glaciers and national parks, would have topped off the journey perfectly. Regrettably, we had grown weary of riding in a perpetual state of alert, wondering when the drive splines that had been in a precarious state since Costa Rica, might completely deteriorate. The spate of punctures over the past few months was still fresh in our minds, too, as were all the electrical shorts that kept stopping us in our tracks. We had no surplus funds left to cover a part replacement or a tow off a mountain, so we resigned ourselves to returning back along the least problematic east coast that we were already familiar with.

The next morning we psyched ourselves up for more days of tedious, straight rides and fierce winds before setting off, back towards the mainland. We crossed into Chile later that afternoon and camped at the sister border to the one where we had cooked the enormous stew of illegal produce on the way down. After tackling an unforgiving wind to peg the tent firmly into the grass, we tucked into a dry sandwich for dinner before going to sleep when darkness fell at nine o'clock.

The seventy-mile ripio road lay ahead in the morning, and, somewhere along the rough route, the speedometer and tachometer broke free of their screws and began dancing wildly on the dashboard. It was the least of our concerns, though, as the powerful southern winds whipped up dust and grime all around us. Despite the road, we reached the Strait of Magellan without any further damage to the bike and had soon parked on the loading deck of an empty ferry.

When we went to pay for our passage, with a quick wink the cashier closed the shutter to his booth and granted us a free ride. We spent the twenty-minute crossing back on the top deck, desperate to catch a glimpse of an unseasonal whale, but we reached the mainland in disappointment.

That night in Rio Gallegos, we discovered that five of the eight bolts, which held the speedometer and tachometer in place, had snapped off, and a cog had jammed in the debris.

Byron fixed them up, while we had a good look at the
roadmaps and decided on our next move.

Having witnessed almost every variety of landscape that
the American continent had to offer, like the elusive whale,
we were yet to observe one major aspect. Although we had
ruled out riding up the west side of the country, we decided
to pay it a fleeting visit the following morning and went in
search of a substantial glacier.

Another Sunday was marked by quiet roads and warm
sunshine, and we crossed the narrow breadth of the country
with a restored taste for adventure. We stopped two hundred
miles later for a picnic on a high ridge, where a breathtaking,
panoramic view of the surrounding plains stretched before us.
The scene was bordered by a jagged ribbon of white and pale
blue peaks, where the glacial Andes rose in the distance. As we
tucked into a salami and cracker lunch, three Brazilian guys,
who we had bumped into twice already in the region, rode up
on their R1200GS bikes and joined us.

It was late in the afternoon, when we passed two more
heavily loaded, adventure motorcyclists. We pulled over to
talk to the riders and found that Deb, who had stopped to see
if we needed help with a puncture outside La Paz in Bolivia,

was one of the duo, and Alison, who had ridden with our friend, Bryce, further north, was the other. They were on their way back from the Perito Moreno National Park and gave us their entry tickets on the off-chance that we might be able to use them. After a brief chat, they left us with a gem of a tip for a wild camping patch, just outside the park.

The tickets worked a treat and got us though the park gates with two hours to spare before they closed. We heard the glacier before we saw it, as enormous blocks of ice, bigger than the size of cars, broke away from the colossal main bulk and crashed into the lake below. Reverberations bounced off the surrounding mountains with the rumble of thunder, while small islands of broken ice bobbed peacefully on the resulting ripples. We followed a lengthy walkway around the shore of the lake, while the resounding booms of tumbling ice grew louder, as we caught glimpses of the glacier through the trees.

We had never encountered anything remotely comparable. A three-mile wall of jagged white ice loomed between soaring mountain peaks in front of the pale blue, glacial lake. More miles of solid ice extended behind the natural dam for as far as the eye could see.

Even at close proximity, the sheer scale of it was lost on us, until we caught sight of what had been a sizeable ferry back near the park entrance. It was navigating through the ice-strewn water and was diminished to the size of a small speck against the towering seventy-meter white wall.

Time slipped away unnoticed as we watched the remarkable spectacle, and, before we knew it, the park was ready to close, so we trekked back around the lake to retrieve the bike.

After leaving the park, we followed the directions that the girls had given us to the wild camping spot. We veered off the main road and crossed through a dry field to a small mound that played host to the only cluster of gnarled trees in the area. The site was framed by distant mountain peaks and offered a prime view across a vast, yellowing plain that reached to the edge of the glacial lake. We watched all manner of wildlife graze in the grassland and lit a campfire with the dead wood that had dropped from the old trees.

The night was the darkest and most peaceful of the entire trip, and we woke up to a serene morning, where little else stirred. After packing up and stopping for petrol and a customary strong coffee in the nearby town, we returned to Rio Gallegos on the country's east coast.

We had prepared for the long slog north by washing clothes and stocking up on food, just before a power cut wiped out the area and gave us an excuse to get an early night.

Although the rain held off over the following two days, grey skies shrouded the landscape in gloom and the wind was a force to be reckoned with. Guanacos and greater rheas kept our minds occupied as we tried to capture the perfect photograph, while petrol stations continued to offer the only reprieve from the monotony of the ride and the treachery of the weather.

At some point during the second day, the rear wheel began to wobble with a different motion to that of a puncture. Byron checked it out and tightened a few bolts that we assumed had suffered the same fate as the speedometer on the ripio road. For good measure, he also changed the brake pads before we set off again.

We winced at the memory of the lay-by flooding when we passed the scene of the debacle a couple of hours later. Then, on the approach to Comodoro Rivadavia, the rear wheel began to feel unsteady again. Having learnt many a lesson about breakdowns, we kept riding slowly, until we reached a more accommodating area to stop.

There was definitely no puncture in the tyre, and all screws had been tightened less than an hour earlier, so, with little optimism, we pulled onto the porch of a small motorbike parts shop.

Our worst fear was that the drive splines had finally given in, and, with some trepidation, we unloaded the luggage, detached the front wheel and exhaust, before finding that the rear axle wouldn't budge. We spoke to the owner of the bike part shop, just before he locked up for lunch, but he didn't have anything in stock that would help to loosen it. It was a new predicament to add to our repertoire, and Byron had a pretty good hunch that the bearings had somehow welded to the axle.

The shaft simply wouldn't budge, and, after trying to help, the owner went off to lunch. We still had over 1,000 miles to ride to Buenos Aires, and our revived taste for adventure had just taken a serious hit. We sat jaded on the side of another road, surrounded by our scattered belongings, wondering how we were going to resolve the latest dilemma.

Byron wrenched, twisted, hammered, and kicked the axle, but it just wouldn't budge. When a drizzle began to fall, and it was clear that we wouldn't be leaving the area anytime soon, we checked into the conveniently placed hotel next door. After offloading our surplus luggage into a room, we returned to bash away at the axle in the rain.

Two hours had passed when the shop owner reopened for business, and a customer called in. True to form, and in common with every scrape on our journey, Mario was a motorcycle enthusiast who was eager to help. Before long, he had called his friend, who owned a trailer and a workshop.

Danny turned up an hour later, and the guys got the Flying Aga strapped to the back of his trailer. While Byron went off with them to his garage, I decided to make use of the time and research how we were going to get home in a couple of weeks' time.

Friends and clients came and went in Danny's workshop, while a mate gourd was passed around. Mate tea was an incredibly popular national drink and, as well as excessive amounts of coffee, it had replaced our taste for the Andean coca leaf brew. It was made from the dried leaves of the yerba plant and was brewed in a gourd, then drunk through a flared metal straw that had a sieve base.

Every trick in the book was applied to shift the wedged axle, while the gourd did the rounds and bikers came and went. Eventually, the extensive group effort did loosen it and confirmed Byron's earlier prognosis. The bearings had, evidently, been pounded into such submission that they had melted into a messy bulk, which had to be sawn in half in order to release the axle.

By absolute chance, Danny had a spare set of the correct size bearings to replace our mashed up ones in a save that, once again, reinforced our indebtedness to the kindness of total strangers.

The wind returned the next morning and whipped us violently back and forth every time a truck or lorry passed us on the road. We edged farther north through the sparse landscape and eventually reached the bulge of Peninsula Valdes, which jutted out of the mainland, halfway up the east coast.

Whales were the only mammal on our wish list that we were yet to catch a glimpse of, and, although the season was wrong for spotting most species, orcas were known to hunt all year round off the peninsula. It was also a hotbed for penguins and sea lions, so we veered off on a minor detour and descended down to the coast.

We checked into our very last backpacking hostel, where, for the first time in almost ten months, we spent a night apart in gender-separated dormitories.

We met Evan the next morning over a nutrition-free white bread and black coffee breakfast. He was undertaking a similar trip around the continent on a Honda XR400. After discussing the route with him, we set off to explore the northern loop of the road that circumnavigated the balloon of land, where a sea lion colony provided a choice hunting ground to orcas.

Despite the short cut, the track still covered a hundred miles of bearing-melting, wheel-beating, suspension-collapsing gravel that became the final gamble we took with our tired bike.

We chugged across the uneven surface, while Evan left us in a cloud of his dust, before spontaneously appearing around corners, where he would snap a few photos then race off again on his nippier bike. Thankfully, the sun burned through a clear sky and highlighted every groove and pebble on the coarse road.

We pulled into a lay-by at the top of a small cliff, where a penguin colony was basking along the length of a long beach below. As the sun glistened exquisitely off the turquoise sea, we could have watched them for hours while they shot through the water like torpedoes and waddled on the beach. They were a fascinating sight, but, when two busloads of other tourists pulled up, we took our cue to leave and rode to the base of an elephant seal colony.

The seals had ventured far out from the land to a large sand bank where, although we could hear them, they were barely visible, so we hopped back on the bikes and rode to the northernmost point of the peninsula. High tide was due, and we were full of optimism that it would bring in a few orcas.

We had taken shelter from the unusual heat of the day to sit in the shade on a bench a few meters away from our two bikes. While we watched the world pass by, an overweight guy climbed onto the sheepskin covered seat of the Flying Aga. His friend began to take a photo of him in a deed that would have been far from acceptable had it been a car, and their cheek riled us no end. We had become so attached to the bike that, when it was manhandled by a stranger who had no idea of its tendency to fall from its centre stand, it felt like a personal affront. We shouted towards him, and he quickly climbed off, while gesturing that he was just taking a photo, as if that wasn't clear to us already and should not in fact have been a problem.

The bike had received an unforeseen amount of attention since we set off from Alaska, and the man's actions left us contemplating just how many photos might be in circulation of it after ten months on the road.

At the northernmost point on the peninsula, colonies of sea lions were dotted along the beach in a smelly, grunting, chaos of prime hunting fodder. We settled in with other avid spectators to wait patiently for the tide to rise, while the antics of the blubbery beasts and the armadillos that scuttled through the sand around us kept us entertained.

Two uneventful hours passed by, until we were forced to weigh up the benefit of waiting longer in the hope of an orca sighting then navigating fifty miles of gravel in the dark, or leaving our wildlife search incomplete.

Riding back in daylight triumphed just as we noticed a hub of activity near the path where we had parked. All manner of long lens cameras and binoculars were focussed down the coast, as excited chatter circulated of a sighting. The well-equipped tourists gave running commentaries of a hunt that was underway on a stretch of coast where the adjacent land was off limits.

Private properties were rented out to passionate wildlife photographers at thousands of pesos per day, for weeks at a time. We met one of them later that evening, after he had just flown in from Hong Kong. He was planning to stay as long as necessary in order to capture images of an orca, mid-hunt, with his $6,000, camera.

Unable to venture onto the restricted land, we stood on the very edge of it, willing the creatures to bring their hunt closer. Our whale watch peaked during a five minute window on a coin-slot telescope, when we caught glimpses of a couple of black fins moving among some seemingly oblivious sea lions, before a breach of black and white preceded an explosive exhale from a blowhole.

The sun was setting fast, and we reluctantly gave up the telescope and raced to the bike, eager not to get caught out in the dark on the rough track. Our headlight was still unreliable and had never recovered after supporting the weight of an army surplus bag for ten months, not to mention concealing an engagement gift among its wires for eight months.

The ride back proved to be the battle we had hoped to avoid. The grooves in the ripio road disappeared from sight in the waning daylight and took hold of the front wheel more than a few times. We lost our bearings when darkness fell completely and were only saved by Evan, who rescued us from ploughing through another circuit of the trail, by waiting for us at the turning back onto the paved road.

Gruelling wind and blistering sunshine accompanied us the following day, while expensive petrol and predominantly dry pumps returned when we left Patagonia behind.

Red ribbons had hung from the registration plates and bumpers of vehicles throughout the country, but as we entered the province of Buenos Aires later that day, small red shrines and flags frequently appeared at the roadside. They had been placed in honour of Gauchito Gil, the Argentinean equivalent to Robin Hood, who, among other things, is revered by road travellers in Argentina.

We rode relentlessly until dusk fell that day and, after failing to spot a hostel or a campground, we pulled into a small wooded area beside the road to set up the tent for the final time. We picked a spot inside the miniature forest that appeared to be well sheltered from both the weather and the road and, after cooking up a simple dinner, we crawled inside the tent to sleep.

As the trip had progressed, we had been sewing up tears, taping up holes, and gluing split seams together in the tent. However, since the bike had ripped out the front guy ropes during the lay-by flooding episode, the problems had escalated beyond our capabilities. The zips to the front doors refused to fasten, toggles that secured the ground sheet had been lost, and the repair job on the guy ropes blocked up the ventilation mesh, leaving the interior claustrophobic and airless.

Our assumptions about being well sheltered in the trees were quickly disproved, when the wind ripped through the door that no longer zipped up, sending it into a constant and irritating flap all night. The slack guy ropes joined the racket, too, while the headlights of trucks and cars that thundered past on the road cast all manner of creepy shadows onto the inside of the tent. After drifting in and out of consciousness for most of the night, in the morning we discovered that the wind had worked most of the pegs out of the ground, and the tent had partially collapsed around us.

With some relief, we packed it away for the final time before blasting along the final four hundred miles of windy autopista to reach the city of Buenos Aires. Although we later discovered one snapped rear wheel spoke and a hairline fracture in the rear brake disc, we arrived in the capital with utter exhilaration at having avoided any further mechanical troubles.

After a customary two-hour search, we unloaded our luggage into the very last hotel room that we stayed in on the continent before setting off to roam the city's scenic boulevards. We devoured a slap up meal in a restaurant and toasted our achievement with mixed emotions of pure relief and immediate nostalgia.

The next morning, we found the warehouse of Dakar Motos, a family venture that specialised in the transportation of motorcycles around the world. We spent the next three days sleeping on a couple of bunk beds in the back of their workshop, while we organised the shipment of the Flying Aga back to the UK.

An extensive operation played out as we scaled down our luggage, sought out shipping offices, arranged paperwork, and handed over thick bundles of the last of our cash to total strangers.

The process ended with a final international ride to the airport, where we secured the Flying Aga to a palette with enormous quantities of cling film, ahead of its long journey home.

It had faithfully carried us 31,254 miles since we broke it free from a crate in an Alaskan car park, and, suddenly, the whole journey was over.

We had met no end of incredible people and witnessed more amazing landscapes and wildlife than we could have hoped for. We had eaten copious amounts of delicious food and drunk a different beer in each of the sixteen countries along the way. The entire experience was like nothing we could possibly have imagined before we decided to leave a perfectly decent life back in London.

After leaving the bike at the warehouse and booking our own flights home for the next day, we spent the very final evening of our entire trip with Valentina and Leandro, the couple that we had met at New Year on the Colombian coffee plantation.

They cooked us the most delicious asado barbecue on the roof of their home during an evening that encapsulated every single unexpected friendship and experience that our bike had instigated.

We returned to the Argentinean workshop late that night and reflected with pure joy on the very best 302 days of our lives. Sleep came easily as we envisaged the next step that we would take together, knowing that the Flying Aga would be close by.

EPILOGUE

Since their return home, Byron and Isabel reluctantly settled into life off the road. They exchanged their waterproof roll-bags for suitcases, which they continued to live out of for many more months, while Isabel undertook the challenge of writing this book and Byron set up his own business.

They began saving again, with no idea how long it might take to pay for the onward adventure of their wedding or, perhaps, another road trip!

The Flying Aga received a new side panel to replace the one lost outside Kamloops, in Canada, as well as a new final drive unit, two new wheels, new brake discs, and a thorough service. Byron continues to ride it to work every day.

If you enjoyed this tale, there are photos and more accounts of the adventure at the following destinations:

Travel blog
https://www.travelblog.org/Bloggers/Adventures-on-the-flying-aga/

Facebook page

https://www.facebook.com/BeadsInTheHeadlight

Twitter

https://twitter.com/BeadsHeadlight

Trip Kit

The Bike
BMW R100RS 1979
Two WorldBeater panniers
One top box
One army surplus soft pannier bag
One sheepskin seat cover (purchased in Alaska, USA)
One Starcom intercom system
One first aid kit
One Camelback hydration system (purchased in Las Vegas, USA)
One five-litre fuel jerry can (purchased in La Paz, Bolivia)

Spare Parts
One set of spark plugs
One set of HT leads
One set of points
One condenser

Two carburettor diaphragms
One rotor
One diode board
Small length of fuel line
Two spare inner tubes
Crush washers (gifted to us by Chris at Boxer Metal)

Tools

One standard BMW tool roll containing spanners, Allen keys, screw drivers, and feeler gauges
One 3/8" Teng Tools Mecca Rosso socket set
One set of mole grips
One Leatherman multi-tool
Two tyre levers
One hand axe
JB Weld resin/hardener
Cable ties
Gaffer tape
Homemade buzz box (for testing continuity and static timing of points)
C-clamp (purchased in Durango, Mexico)
Compressor pump (purchased in San Jose, Costa Rica)

Motorcycle Kit

One leather armoured jacket (Isabel)
One wax cotton armoured jacket (Byron)
Two pairs of all-weather armoured motorcycle trousers
Two pairs of leather padded gloves
Two flip front [modular] helmets
Two pairs of motorcycle boots
Two waterproof jackets
One pair of waterproof trousers (sent home in Cody, USA)
One pair of motorcycle handlebar muffs (sent home in San Diego, USA, in the box that never arrived)

Camping Gear

    One miniature lantern

    One head torch

    One three-man tent

    Two down-filled inflatable mattresses

    Two sleeping bags (swapped for two aeroplane blankets)

    Two down-filled sleeping bags (purchased in Bolivia)

    One cotton duvet cover and two pillow cases (to sleep inside and save washing sleeping bags)

    Two camping pillows

    One mattress coupling kit

    One enormous tartan picnic blanket with polythene backing

    Bear spray (purchased in Whitehorse, Canada)

    Two water bottles

Electronics

    One iPad

    One iPod Nano

    One handheld camera

    One DSLR compact camera and two SD cards

    One netbook computer (purchased in USA)

    Two universal USB and charging adapters

    One motorcycle USB charger (given to us by Jeff in Albuquerque, USA)

Cooking Kit

    One petrol-fuelled camping stove

    One three-piece saucepan cookset

    Two titanium knives and sporks

    Two camping stowaway meal-kits

    One wooden spoon

    One sharp knife

    One foldaway water carrier

    One small flask (later discarded)

    One camping mug (later discarded)

    Matches and cigarette lighter

Personal Luggage

Two waterproof roll-bags
One foldaway backpack
One microfibre travel towel (each)
One pair of running/walking shoes (each)
One pair of flip flops (each)
One pair of trainers (Byron)
One pair of flat shoes (Isabel)
One pair of jeans (Byron)
Two pairs of jeans (Isabel)
Various T-shirts (each)
One fleece (each)
Two pairs of shorts (each)
Swimming shorts and bikini
One pair of tiny hair straighteners (not Byron)
Pack of playing cards
Diary
Roadmaps and waterproof map case
Travel chess set (sent home in San Diego, USA, in the box
    that never arrived)

Trip Maintenance
and Repairs

Maintenance

Services: 6 (Langley, Canada; Connecticut, USA; San Francisco, USA; Mexico City, Mexico; Medellin, Colombia; Jujuy, Argentina)

Rear tyre changes: 3 (Wisconsin, USA; San Jose, Costa Rica; Cordoba, Argentina)

Front tyre changes: 1 (Medellin, Colombia)

Repairs

Ignition barrel (Surrey, Canada)

Exhaust mounting bolts (Chutes Provincial Park, Canada)

Connection of power cable to battery (Connecticut, USA)

Overhaul of final drive, including replacement of all bearings and re-shimming (Pennsylvania, USA)

Replace drive shaft (Pennsylvania, USA)

Exposed battery cable (Baja California Norte, Mexico)

Rear puncture #1 (a nail, Baja California Sur, Mexico)

Rear puncture #2 (a metal shard, Baja California Sur, Mexico)

Rear puncture #3 (a glass shard, Puntarenas, Costa Rica)

Rear puncture #4 (a nail, La Paz, Bolivia)

Rear puncture #5 (a burst puncture patch, on route to Humahuaca, Argentina)

Rear puncture #6 (a burst puncture patch, en route to Tafi del Valle, Argentina)

New battery (Durango, Mexico)

New front wheel (Managua, Nicaragua)

New rear suspension (Managua, Nicaragua)

New front fork seals and gaiters (Medellin, Colombia)

Connection of brake to brake light (Puntarenas, Costa Rica

Right-hand helicoil cylinder head spark plug threads (San Jose, Costa Rica)

Ignition coils (en route to Uvita, Costa Rica)

Rear wheel fracture weld (Puerto Lindo, Panama)

Loose bolt on sump (Medellin, Colombia)

Re-wire intercom system (Quito, Ecuador)

Fabrication from a plastic bottle of two covers to deflect rain from ignition coils (Eduardo Castex, Argentina)

Points and new fuel filters (Fitz Roy, Argentina)

Release welded axle and new rear bearings (Comodoro Rivadavia, Argentina)

Snapped rear spoke and two fractured brake discs, (discovered in Buenos Aires, Argentina—fixed back home!)

Trip Destinations

IN ORDER

United States
   Anchorage, Alaska
   Denali National Park, Alaska
   Chena Hot Springs, Alaska
   Tok, Alaska

Canada
   Whitehorse, Yukon Territory
   Liard Hot Springs Provincial Park, Yukon Territory
   Fort Nelson, British Columbia
   Dawson Creek, British Columbia
   Grande Cache, Alberta
   Jasper National Park, Alberta
   Banff National Park, Alberta
   Kamloops, British Columbia
   Surrey, British Columbia

Vancouver, British Columbia
Langley, British Columbia

United States

Odessa, Washington
Beavertail Hill State Park, Montana
Yellowstone National Park, Wyoming
Cody, Wyoming
Gillette, Wyoming
Mobridge, South Dakota
Savage, Minnesota
Iron Mountain, Michigan
Sault Ste. Marie, Michigan

Canada

Chutes Provincial Park, Ontario
Petawawa, Ontario
Bourget, Ontario
Berthier-sur-mer, Québec
Québec City, Québec
Saint-Luc-de-Bellechasse, Québec

United States

Gorham, Maine
Monadnock State Park, New Hampshire
Stamford, Connecticut
New York City, New York
Hammonasset Beach State Park, Connecticut
Melrose, Massachusetts
Boston, Massachusetts
Yardley, Pennsylvania
Mt. Pocono, Pennsylvania
Roulette, Pennsylvania
Geneva State Park, Ohio
Kendallville, Indiana
Mukwonago, Wisconsin

Milwaukee, Wisconsin
Chicago, Illinois
Pontiac, Illinois
St Louis, Missouri
Lebanon, Missouri
Tulsa, Oklahoma
Amarillo, Texas
Albuquerque, New Mexico
Cortez, Colorado
Mesa Verde National Park, Colorado
Monument Valley, Utah
Grand Canyon National Park, Arizona
Las Vegas, Nevada
Tonopah, Nevada
Yosemite National Park, California
San Anselmo, California
Napa, California
San Francisco, California
Santa Clara, California
San Luis Obispo, California
Santa Paula, California
Ojai, California
Pomona, California
Los Angeles, California
San Diego, California

México

La Fonda, Baja California Norte
San Quintín, Baja California Norte
Guerro Negro, Baja California Sur
Mulegé, Baja California Sur
La Paz, Baja California Sur
Cabo San Lucas, Baja California Sur
Mazatlán, Sinaloa
Durango, Durango
Zacatecas, Zacatecas

Querétaro, Querétaro
Toluca, México
Mexico City, México
Tuxtepec, Oaxaca
Villahermosa, Tabasco
Campeche, Campeche
Merida, Yucatán
Tulum, Quintana Roo
Chetumal, Quintana Roo

Belize
San Ignacio, Cayo

Guatemala
El Remate, Petén
Tikal National Park, Petén
Cobán, Alta Verapaz

El Salvador
Metapan, Santa Ana
Lago de Coatepeque, Santa Ana
La Unión, La Unión

Honduras
Enter at El Amatillo, La Unión
Exit at Guasaule, Choluteca

Nicaragua
Somotillo, Chinandega
León, León
Managua, Managua

Costa Rica
La Cruz, Guanacaste
Puntarenas, Puntarenas
San José, San José

Uvita, Puntarenas

Panama
Santiago, Veraguas
Panama Canal Locks, Panama
Puerto Lindo, Colón
San Blas Islands, San Blas

Colombia
Cartagena, Bolivar
Taganga, Magdalena
Palomino, La Guajira
Caucasia, Antioquia
Medellin, Antioquia
Guatapé, Antioquia
Llanogrande, Antioquia
Santa Rosa de Cabal, Risaralda
Salento, Quindio
Valle del Cocora, Quindio
Popayan, Cauca
Ipiales-Narino

Ecuador
Tulcan, Carchi
Quito, Pichincha
Misahuallí, Napo
Banos, Tungurahua
Cuenca, Azuay

Peru
Máncora, Piura
Huanchaco, La Libertad
Huaraz, Ancash
Lima, Lima
Huacachina, Ica
Puquio, Ayacucho

Cusco, Cusco
Aguas Caliantes, Cusco
Machu Picchu, Cusco
Puno, Puno

Bolivia
La Paz, La Paz
Oruro, Oruro
Potosí, Potosí
Villazon, Potosí

Argentina
Humahuaca, Jujuy
Salines Grandes, Salta
Jujuy, Jujuy
Tafí del Valle, Tucuman
Jesús María, Córdoba
Córdoba, Córdoba
Villa Carlos Paz, Córdoba
Eduardo Castex, La Pampa
Las Grutas, Río Negro
Rada Tilly, Chubut
Caleta Olivia, Santa Cruz
Comandante Luis Piedrabuena, Santa Cruz

Chile
Border route 3 and 255 near Pali-Aike National Park, Magallanes y de la Antártica Chilena

Argentina
Ushuaia, Tierra del Fuego

Chile
Border route 1 and 255 near San Sebastian, Magallanes y de la Antártica Chilena

Argentina
    Rio Gallegos, Santa Cruz
    El Calafate, Santa Cruz
    Perito Moreno, Santa Cruz
    Fitz Roy, Santa Cruz
    Comodoro Rivadavia, Chubut
    Puerto Pirámides, Chubut
    Bahía Blanca, Buenos Aires
    Buenos Aires, Buenos Aires

Acknowledgements

A great number of people contributed to this book just by helping us on our journey. The generosity shown to us by this long list of people, as well as a few organisations that probably don't know how useful they were to us, was invaluable, and I hope they enjoy reading about the adventure of which they became a part.

Vern, Project VND, UK; Giles, James Cargo, UK; Jean and Bruce, Two Pegs to Patagonia, UK; ADVRider forum; Horizons Unlimited HUBB; BMW MOA forum; Alaska's Northern Riders BMW Club, USA; Stephanie and Brandon, Wasilla, USA; Debbi and Dario, Langley, Canada; Carol and Jerry, Sunny Breeze Campground, Iron Mountain, USA; Genevieve and Jean-Francois, Berthier-sur-Mer, Canada; Rita anhd Rolf, Stamford, USA; Becky and Rich, Boston, USA; Paula and Tom, Rubber Chicken Racing Garage, Yardley, USA; Sonia and Jeff, Albuquerque, USA; Bryce, Colorado, USA; Thor, San Francisco, USA; Lucas, San Diego, USA;

Marty, Mulege, Mexico; Carmen and Mario, Cabo San Lucas, Mexico; Jorge, Durango, Mexico; Ivonne and Garry, Mexico City, México; Aaron of Conde & Cohen, Miami, USA; Chris at Boxer Metal, California, USA; Connie and Aaron, Managua, Nicaragua; Tony, Lucas' friend; USA; Steven, Puntarenas, Costa Rica; Jose, San Jose, Costa Rica; Johnny and Adolfo, BMW, San Jose, Costa Rica; Rosemary and Owen, Kent, UK; Vanessa and Henry, London, UK; Ruben, Carmen, Valentina, and Ruben, Bogota, Colombia; Paola, Juan David & Orlanda and Carlos, Llanogrande, Colombia; Al, Shamrock Pub, Medellin, Colombia; Rico, Motoshop, Medellin, Colombia; Deb and Alison, El Calafate, Argentina; Mario and Danny, Comodoro Rivadavia, Argentina; Sandra and Javier, Dakar Motos, Buenos Aires, Argentina; Valentina and Leandro, Buenos Aires, Argentina.

Thanks are also due to the rich variety of people who became great friends along the way, most of whom I hope I have managed to capture in the story.

There were many more people whose names we never knew but who still helped us to succeed in our mission in some way, particularly the guys who gave up their mice-infested room for us at the border in Nicaragua, the man on the Mountain of Death who called the garage in San Jose for us, and the couple who left us their guide book and maps in Cartagena.

My deep gratitude goes to my parents, Rosemary and Owen, for allowing me to commandeer various corners of their home to write for endless hours, weeks, and months on our return, and to Allington Manor, in Lincolnshire, and the Vincent family, for the use of a room to finish off the challenge.

My thanks also go to Rosemary, Owen, and Henry for reading through various drafts of the book and for being as honest in their feedback as I made them promise to be. Their everlasting support has always been treasured, as was Edward's, who I am certain helped during a few close calls on the trip.

I cannot thank Owen enough for the time he took to meticulously proofread the final draft, as well as his unparalleled teaching that bred a great passion for writing in the first place.

Lastly, there are no words that can express my thanks to my best friend, Byron, whose ceaseless support has helped me to lock our adventure in the realms of time. Without him, the tale in this book would never have been quite as exciting as it turned out to be.

Thank you.

GLOSSARY

adobe.................... *a traditional Spanish-Mexican construction material made of sun-baked clay and straw*

airhead .... *an old school, air-cooled, BMW flat-twin engine*

altiplano .... *a high mountain plateau/tableland*

archipelago .... *an extensive group of scattered islands*

arepa .... *a flatbread made of ground maize dough or cooked flour, often filled with cheese*

asado..................... *a barbecue or a technique for cooking meat on a grill or an open fire*

autopista .... *a motorway (in Spanish)*

bearings................. *a machine element that constrains relative motion between moving parts*

bistek..................... *salted and peppered sirloin steak, usually flattened and sometimes fried in breadcrumbs*

blog........................ *an online web log or website that records a personal journal or individual opinions, on a regular basis*

breaking the bead. *to release or detach the steel ring inside the edge of a tyre (the bead) that creates an airtight seal with the rim of the wheel, making it possible to remove the tyre from the wheel*

burrito.................. *a flour tortilla that encloses a filling of beef, beans, or cheese*

callejoneadas .... *a spontaneous Mexican street party*

camelid.................. *a family of two-toed mammals with a three-chambered stomach, including the camel, llama, and vicuña*

carburettor..............*[Am: carburetor] a device in an internal combustion engine that mixes air with a fine spray of fuel*

drive shaft .... *a rotating shaft which transmits torque (a force that causes rotation) in an engine*

drive splines.......... *metal ridges or teeth that mesh with grooves (splines) and transmit the rotational force from the drive shaft to the rear wheel*

empanada.............. *baked or fried folded dough that is stuffed with meat, potatoes, cheese, and vegetables, much like a Cornish pasty*

enchilada............... *a corn tortilla rolled around a filling of meat or cheese and covered with a chili-pepper sauce*

final drive .... *the last part of the transmission system in a motor vehicle that transmits power from the engine shaft to the rear axle*

finca....................... *a country estate or a ranch (in Spanish)*

frijoles .... *stewed and mashed kidney beans*

gomeria .... *a roadside workshop dealing solely in puncture repairs, air pressure, and tyre changes (South America)*

gringo.................... *a slang word to reference mostly English-speaking foreigners in Latin and Hispanic countries*

llantera.................. *a roadside workshop dealing solely in puncture repairs, air pressure, and tyre changes (México, Central America)*

menú del día......... *a very cheap, set lunch menu, usually made up of soup, chicken or beef, rice or potatoes, vegetables, and a dessert*

palapa..................... *a wooden framed structure with a thatched roof made from dried palm leaves*

pannier.................. *a pair of bags or secure boxes that are hung or secured either side of the back wheel on a bicycle or motorcycle*

pupusa................... *a thick corn tortilla filled with cheese or meat then squashed flat and fried*

ripio....................... *a gravel and rubble surface, laid in place of tarmac or paving*

sump...................... *the base of an internal combustion engine that acts as a reservoir of oil for the lubrication system/the oil pan of an engine*

taco........................ *a folded, fried tortilla filled with seasoned chopped meat, beans, and salad or salsa*

top box.................. *a solid, lockable storage compartment fitted to the rear luggage rack*

tramitador .... *a fixer, dispatcher, or middleman (encountered at Central American border crossings)*

eighteen-wheeler.. *a big rig truck with eighteen wheels*